*"**Moving Out** provides insight into residential options and how they work, and practical tips for planning and structuring choices. It also looks at roles and responsibilities families might play during this complex and often intimidating process. The authors approach the subject with sensitivity, understanding, and respect for families. I wish I'd had this comprehensive guide when making the decisions associated with planning my daughter's move."*
—Sharman Davis Barrett, Co-Director,
National Parent Technical Assistance Center, PACER Center

*"Parents and family members face many complex practical and emotional issues in locating appropriate housing and needed personal supports for an adult child with an intellectual disability. With many years of experience creating, managing, and explaining services for adults and families, the authors of **Moving Out** provide thorough, thoughtful step-by-step guidance (including checklists, forms, and resources) about housing options, financial planning, government benefits, other sources of funding, and much more. "*
—Stanley D. Klein, Ph.D., co-founder and former editor-in-chief,
Exceptional Parent magazine

MOVING OUT

A Family Guide to Residential Planning for Adults with Disabilities

Dafna Krouk-Gordon & Barbara D. Jackins

Woodbine House ▪ 2013

First edition

All rights reserved. Published in the United State of America by Woodbine House, Inc., 6510 Bells Mill Road, Bethesda, MD 20817. 800-843-7323. www.woodbinehouse.com

Library of Congress Cataloging-in-Publication Data

Krouk-Gordon, Dafna.
 Moving out : a family guide to residential planning for adults with disabilities / by Dafna Krouk-Gordon and Barbara D. Jackins. -- First edition.
     pages cm
 Includes index.
 ISBN 978-1-60613-021-6
 1. People with disabilities--Housing. 2. People with disabilities--Care. 3. Adult care facilities. I. Jackins, Barbara D. II. Title.
 HV1569.K76 2013
 363.5'97--dc23
                                                                                      2013011738

Manufactured in the United States of America

10   9   8   7   6   5   4   3   2   1

Table of Contents

APPENDICES / 165

Acknowledgments

*M*oving Out would not have been possible without the help of a great many people. We appreciate everyone who offered their support, encouragement, and expertise.

Barbara especially thanks her friends, clients, and others who shared their stories and generously allowed her to tell them.

Dafna is most appreciative of the many families who have served as an inspiration to TILL, Inc., as it developed its varied residential alternatives. Without their vision and tenacity, the many new and exciting program models would not have been possible.

Many housing professionals gave their time and expertise: Catherine Boyle, Autism Housing Pathways, Winchester, MA; Timothy Gray (housing consultant); Trisha Kenyon Guditz, City of Newton, MA; Pat Pakos and Evelyn Hausslein from Support Brokers, Waltham, MA; Emily Starr (attorney), Fitchburg, MA; Margot Wizansky, Specialized Housing, Inc., Brookline, MA; and Amy Yuhasz, Planning and Development Department, City of Newton, MA.

A special thanks to Barbara's very patient husband, John L. Mason, Jr., who supported her throughout the process. He read her drafts and offered many helpful suggestions that improved the tone and substance of the book.

Thank you to Les Gordon, Dafna's husband, and her daughters, Lani and Lexi, who have been an essential part of TILL's history, which provided the inspiration for her to co-author the book and share her experiences with its readers.

We are both grateful to Linda Norton, Communication Specialist with TILL, Inc., who capably organized our materials and got them to the editor on time.

We both thank Woodbine House, Inc.—the acquisitions editor, Nancy Gray Paul, for accepting our proposal—and our hard working editor, Susan Stokes, who challenged us to expand our thinking and improved the book in many ways.

Foreword

By Susan Senator

One of the worst questions anyone has ever asked me about my son Nat, who has autism, is: "Where is he going to live as an adult?" I'd say, "Umm, I don't know. I hope to have him live in a group home, but—not sure how that will happen." Then I'd roll my eyes, sigh, and shake my head. Not really funny, and not a good plan at all. But truly how can anyone answer this question satisfactorily? You work so hard, and your child works even harder, towards his independence, but the world is impatient and demanding—and so complicated.

This became painfully clear as Nat approached 22, when public education for a disabled student must end, and the sticky spider web of adulthood threatened to trap me. I forced myself to confront it. I swung into action, attending overwhelming workshops, reading jargony websites from the state agencies, and talking to other panicked moms and dads. I figured out on my own the best way for me to digest all that information: do a little at a time, then take time off to rest my brain, process, and cry.

Only a few years ago, this is what parents in my situation did: we made it up as we went along. There were few books that were at all readable, the school system was almost as ignorant as I was, and I depended almost entirely on my state department of developmental services liaison—who retired soon after I realized how great she was. There was really no path for me to follow, so I had to piece together information and hope to God I was getting it all—and understanding it accurately. I figured out somehow that I had to visit group homes, get to know some service providers, develop some kind of modus operandi for learning what I had to know for Nat's sake.

After a few false starts, disappointments, and crises, eventually a few parents and I pulled together a group home—with a lot of help from our service provider. I drew up list after list of what I needed to do, what our mission was, and what to expect, but it was all guesswork and intuition. Even now I sometimes get the feeling that I missed something.

Then I learned about Barbara and Dafna's book, *Moving Out: A Family Guide to Residential Planning for Adults with Disabilities.* Incredible. How was it that this book had not been around until now? I had been out there reinventing the wheel for Nat! But here is a book that even the most bleary-eyed, overtaxed parent can easily use. You can dive in and plow through it, or you can leaf through it picking out the chapters you need at a given time. In the back, there are exercises and checklists, templates for things like resident behavioral rules, and residential models to follow. And I was surprised to learn that the book is not just for Massachusetts residents; there are suggestions, resources, and paths to follow for families nationwide.

But what moves me about this book is that for all their expertise, the authors do not dictate or speak to you from On High. The tone is authoritative yet warm, creating the space for individual residents, caregivers, and families to come up with their own solution of what works for them. With all of the common sense advice in the book, the overall feel is still very much rule-of-thumb, not didactic or lecturing. I particularly love the Ten Commandments to Follow When Planning Residential Services; this sort of dialog box is an effective device for delivering a message. In this case "Ten Commandments" is a clever subtitle and yet is not actually written in stone at all. The section is mostly about validating what the reader already suspects is true. This kind of affirmation comes throughout the book, giving the reader confidence that he or she really *can* do this.

Even though the only way to get through your child's transition into adulthood is to get through it, this process need not be depressing or debilitating. Rather, with this book at your side, you will find yourself empowered and sometimes even excited about planning for your child's future. You'll realize that dread need not be a part of it, as long as you have a vision and the accurate information to put it into place. I wish I had had this book when I first started down that road with Nat, but at least now I have something to recommend to the next generation of panicked parents. So much wisdom and strategy to gather up. Read it—and reap.

Introduction

This book was written for families who have a member with special needs. It is designed to help you navigate the complicated emotional, financial, and practical aspects of planning and implementing residential services. In addition to assisting families, the book should also be useful for policy makers, funding sources, and professionals who work with families, such as financial planners, attorneys, and educators.

We—the authors—bring over sixty years of experience in developing residential services and assisting families to turn their dreams into reality. Dafna Krouk-Gordon, as the founder and President of Toward Independent Living and Learning, Inc. (TILL), has assisted hundreds of families to find the most appropriate living arrangement for their family member. TILL is a widely recognized leader in developing creative living options for people with disabilities. In addition to working with individual clients, Dafna has also served on many residential funding working groups and planning committees. Barbara Jackins is an attorney with extensive experience in special needs planning, public benefits, and real estate. She has served on many boards and committees of agencies that provide residential services to adults with disabilities. Barbara is also the parent of a young adult with developmental disabilities who lives in a TILL residence.

In working with individuals and families over the years, we both noticed that they were confronting many common dilemmas. Many families were stuck and didn't know where to begin. Some were paralyzed by the self-imposed pressure to find the "perfect" arrangement. Many families were overwhelmed by the number of options, and most didn't know where to turn for funding. We wrote this book in order to share our knowledge with as many people as possible beyond those we could reach directly through conversations, meetings, and workshops.

A theme of this book is that everyone's situation is unique. There is no "one size fits all" when it comes to residential planning. The options are as diverse as the people who need residential services. Still, families have much in common with others in their situation. Everyone wants a satisfying arrangement that takes into account their child's needs, preferences, and desires. Above all, you want your child to be happy in his home—whether he lives by himself with support, with another family, or with a group of other people with disabilities.

This book guides you through the process of getting yourself and other family members ready and then identifying the best residential arrangement. If the arrangement doesn't already exist, we show you how to create it and perhaps even run it yourself.

Chapter 1 explains how to find out if your child is ready to live apart from your family, and if he is not, how to get him ready. We describe things parents can do to prepare their child to live outside their home. We also describe some common obstacles that families confront and how to overcome them.

Chapter 2 describes three common living arrangements: independent living with supports, shared living, and group living. We give several examples of each.

Chapter 3 shows you how to narrow the possibilities to find the best living arrangement for your child. You can get a residential assessment that will help you focus on what would work best. We also help you decide whether you should manage your child's residential program yourself or use an agency.

Chapter 4 explains the financial factors in residential living. We tell you about public programs that can help you purchase a residence or pay for staff costs. We also show you how to pay for residential services by combining public benefits with family resources. There are nine sample budgets that cover different living arrangements.

Chapter 5 discusses the different options for legal ownership for people who choose to own the property where their child will live. We cover many choices, including condominiums, housing cooperatives, trusts, and limited liability companies.

Chapter 6 covers the pros and cons of hiring an agency that provides residential services versus employing the staff yourself. If you choose to become the employer, we explain your basic responsibilities. We also explain how to protect yourself from liability by having adequate insurance and doing background checks. Agency-family conflicts are also addressed.

Chapter 7 shows how you can help your child transition from your home to his or her new residence. After your child has settled in, you must decide what your new role will be. How much do you want to be involved in his life and—most importantly—how involved does your child want you to be? We give some suggestions about how you can be helpful without being intrusive.

Chapter 8 discusses the day-to-day running of the household (house rules, chores, etc.). We give you some ideas about how to anticipate and avoid problems that can come up in group living, such as lack of individuality, reduced privacy, and conflicts with housemates. We also cover sexuality, relationships, and abuse prevention.

Chapter 9 explains some strategies to keep the residential arrangement going after you are gone by using wills, trusts, and life insurance. Financial planning and asset protection are also discussed.

We hope this book will be useful to you. We are grateful to the families who have shared their experiences with us over the years. We hope you will benefit from those experiences and will add to them as you turn your own vision into reality.

Chapter 1
Getting Ready & Letting Go

"Letting go was the hardest thing I ever did," parents have repeatedly told us when describing the time that they were making plans for their child to live outside of their family home. They have recounted many common worries: Who will take care of my adult child? Who will know what makes him happy or sad? Who will watch out for him? Who will make sure he cuts his nails, changes his clothes from one season to the next, and ensures that the foods he likes are available? For parents of adult children with disabilities, concerns typically range from the details that make up daily life to the larger issues of safety and growth and relationships.

There are no simple answers, only questions that will guide you toward making the best decision and plan possible for your particular situation. Because there are no right answers, guilt and worry seem to follow parents of a child with disabilities no matter what choices they have made. This book is intended to provide you with many of the questions that will help you to find answers that best fit your situation as you embark upon the journey of transitioning to adult, independent residential services. We have included successes and experiences of many families and private and public agencies who have blazed the trail to create the exciting opportunities that exist today as well as set the stage for ones that have not yet been created.

Each family's situation is unique. However, there are similarities for everyone as they begin the planning process for residential services. Five decades ago people who were different were locked behind brick walls in institutional settings with only custodial care provided to them. Now those same individuals are our neighbors and part of our communities. They appear on TV shows and are characters in books and movies.

We have come a very long way in the past fifty years, but we have much further to go. Families who insisted that their children have opportunities to live and work in varied settings in the community have helped to expand society's tolerance and desire to accept differences. In the same way that society has come to understand that cultural differences are valuable when integrated within communities, we need to continue to advocate for the integration of intellectual differences, which will strengthen our communities. There are many laws that protect against discrimination in housing and employment for people with disabilities, but we need to continue to create new models as people live longer and are capable of handling responsibilities that we would not have imagined even two decades ago.

The emotions that accompany the developmental stages of a child with a disability vary over time. When you first learn that your child has a disability, there is fear of the unknown, questions about what to expect about growth and development, confusion, and grief, as well as many positive emotions that accompany the birth of any child. The impact the disability has on your family life, routines, and emotions, especially in the early stages of life, will depend on the type, severity, and complexity of the disability, as well as on the constellation of your family and your religious beliefs. Initially you are concerned about how to inform friends, relatives, and other siblings. How much information do you share, when, with whom, and how soon are realistic and common questions. As you get to know your child and grow with him, you also enjoy the many developments of which you are a vital part.

As your child passes through each developmental stage of life, graduates from the educational system to adult services, and passes through different social milestones, the questions change and the emotions that accompany them change. Over time, you gather information and resources and create friendships and supports that allow you to deal with the next stages of life.

When Is the "Right" Time to Start Planning?

When we began considering writing this book, we were struck by the one question parents repeatedly asked; namely, "When should I begin planning for my son's (daughter's, sibling's) adult residential arrangements?" Parents are faced with making decisions for their child with a disability throughout their lifetime. The difference with their other children is that typically at some point the parent stops being the principal person who makes the important life decisions and becomes more of an observer and advisor. In the case of a child with a disability, the family continues to play an active role well into the adult years and probably indefinitely. Families who realize that their goal of parenting has been to prepare their children for independence also see the transition to adult residential services for their child with a disability as a way to prepare him to leave the nest while being there to participate in and enjoy the process of making it happen.

There is no one "perfect time" to begin planning, as each situation is different. However, generally, when your child enters the transition years (around age fourteen in most states) in school is a good time to begin seriously researching options and models and making connections with other families. Even if residential living outside of the family home is not something that seems realistic for your child while he is still in school, remember that it may take several years before something becomes available or before you can establish something—if that is the route you choose to take. Therefore, you can start early without worrying that if you do so, your child will be living elsewhere before you are ready for him to do so. Planning allows you to be in control of the ultimate setting. In contrast, if you make the decision when there is a crisis, you may have to accept something that is totally inappropriate. Too often, families make the mistake of waiting until they feel it is time for the move to occur, which then limits their options.

As with all important decisions, parents take their cues from experiences as they occur throughout life, from their friends and other daily support sources, and from the child himself. How you think about residential settings will change as your child grows up. Initially it may be impossible to think of your child surviving, let alone thriving, in any setting other than in your home and with you. As he begins school, your views change as you see him having some independent experiences. As you begin to see other friends' children consider external residential arrangements, you begin to think more realistically about such possibilities.

Letting Go Was the Hardest Thing I Ever Did

Placing my daughter Marian in a residential program was definitely the hardest thing I have ever done. My husband died in April and I had just turned eighty-one. I knew I couldn't live forever, but I definitely did not want her to move out. We were comfortable and used to each other. However, I knew I wouldn't live forever.

Unfortunately, there were not as many options as there are today and the first alternative was a large group home. Marian was not used to dealing with so many people and was extremely unhappy. My other daughter was pushing me to look at an apartment complex where several other individuals lived. We were shown a large two-bedroom apartment with a comfortable living room and dining area. Though it was near a main highway, there were lots of trees and even a swimming pool.

I was told she would have a roommate and that staff generally float from one apartment to another so there is always someone nearby. I asked if there would be sleepover staff, and they said that Marian would not need it. She could easily use the phone if there was an emergency.

Coincidentally, Marian knew her roommate, Kim, when they were children. They seem to get along well. Marian has her own bedroom and comes home often.

I can't believe how independent she is. She showers without any supervision, gets up on her own, and lives a very active life. When she lived at home with me, she was very isolated. I can't drive at night and don't go out as often as I used to.

This year, Marian and Kim hosted a Christmas party. She gave everyone an assignment, and people were delighted to come. She never would have dreamed of such a thing when she lived with me. I made all of the decisions.

—Josephine Maloney

Benefits of Planning Early

Even before you can realistically visualize your child living outside of your family's home, we recommend that you begin *planning* for him to move out. Benefits of planning early include:

1. Services, funding, and program models change, and being open to learning about what might be possible keeps you in the loop and prepared to develop your unique situation when and if you choose to use it in the future.
2. It will be a relief to your other children and family members to know that you are researching possibilities.
3. It will offer a way for your other children and involved family members to be a part of the decision process.
4. It will allow you to plan for financial resources.
5. It can prevent family gifts and contributions from disrupting your child's public benefits.
6. It will give you the benefit of being part of creating a long-term solution rather than being forced into a setting as the result of an unanticipated crisis.
7. It will enable you to enjoy your family member's next stage of life and gradually become accustomed to the idea of independence to the greatest extent possible.
8. It will allow you to make plans for your own situation and deal with that adjustment in the same way you might deal with other family members leaving the home and the "empty nest" reality. It gives you time to develop a plan with your spouse or other family members as to your new lifestyle.
9. You can develop a concrete image of what you and your child feel would be the best model of residential service. You can take enough time to ask all your questions and allay your fears through gathering knowledge and experience. You will make the unknown familiar in your mind and therefore help other family members and your child to understand the possibilities.

How Will You Know When You and Your Child Are Ready?

How will you know when you are ready to consider residential arrangements outside of your home? The answer to that question is as varied as individuals are. Trust your instincts as to when to begin the discussion. Throughout the school years, you will ideally develop connections with other families, which will naturally lead into conversations regarding "what's next." You may be living in a small town with few others who receive special education services. If that is the case, we encourage you to connect with local associations such as county or state chapters of the National Down Syndrome Congress, the local ARC, the autism support center in the area, or the school's parent organization, even if there isn't one specifically for children with special needs. Many of these organizations have a service for connecting families to one another. Inevitably there will be someone who can lead you to another family with similar interests. Attending housing conferences is an excellent way to get connected with other families, as they typically provide names of conference participants.

You will be surprised to find the enthusiasm and interest of many families once you embark on this path of outreach. Most families are seeking to connect and learn from others. We have found that these types of connections through small groups have created more housing opportunities than nearly any other source of development.

How Do You Begin the Discussion?

When your child is of school age, you are concentrating on getting the best and most comprehensive services to help him with his physical, academic, and life skills development.

As your child approaches adolescence, you will be concentrating on creating social connections so that he will no longer rely solely upon your family as the source of friendships and activities.

As your child begins the transition years in school and a transition coordinator is assigned, you also start to think of your child as an adolescent with friends of his own and preferences and interests. Initiating or even embracing such new opportunities will not come naturally for many children with disabilities or their parents. You may need to coax your child, constantly finding and presenting opportunities in different formats, so that during the teen years he begins to have a vision of himself as a young adult with some expansion to his life beyond his family. Do not let your child's lack of enthusiasm for new experiences deter you from continuing such efforts. Keep in mind that your child has been used to you as the primary source of protection, security, and entertainment. It is the situation with which he is familiar.

Each child's personality is different, as is his tolerance for change. However, setting the stage for new experiences is the first step in preparing your child for a future outside of the family home.

1. ***Offer opportunities for social experiences in which you are not present.*** Your school system can probably suggest recreational and social opportunities, as well as names of other families who have a similar interest. Even if your child is hesitant about participating in such activities, insist on it so that he can get accustomed to the idea of other people and other situations. You may have to ease into the activities or offer your child incentives so that he becomes accustomed to the new experiences. The goal is for you and your child to look forward to new routines and social activities. Even if you get resistance, keep trying it again. It will all be worthwhile, as these parents express:

   > My daughter was 30 years old when she moved out of my house and into a residence. We all had apprehensions. But, after our first weekend visit, we knew we had made the right decision."

   > Your agency [TILL] has meant peace of mind for me, knowing that my daughter is so well cared for. Many times, I take her home to my house for overnights, and the next day she tells me that she's ready to go home. That makes me feel great that she calls her residence HOME."

These changes in attitude did not occur overnight. They were the result of a great deal of preparation over the years using the strategies outlined in this chapter.

Consider involvement in sports such as a bowling group or Special Olympics, trips with other families, weekly events with a few others to activities such as movies or concerts, or starting a small group for a weekly restaurant outing to a local pizza shop, a trip to the library, etc. If formal events do not occur in your area, then consider starting a small cooking group in your home and rotate with different families. These types of activities create a routine that your child and you become accustomed to and look forward to. If such activities do not exist, then you will need to initiate them with other families.

2. ***Obtain an assessment from an agency or specialist that deals with adult residential services.*** While your child is in school, you will have many evaluations related to his academic potential. However, obtaining a residential assessment from an agency knowledgeable about residential options and what is required for participation in them will offer you insight into some areas you can work on while your child is at home. It will also guide you in thinking about different models of residential options. These assessments are discussed more fully in Chapter 3.

3. ***Begin to discuss the possibilities of your child living outside of the family home with others in your family.*** This may have been a topic of conversation throughout the early years, but when your child enters adolescence, begin such conversations more frequently and more formally. Include siblings, grandparents, and other relatives who are a part of your child's life. The more homework you do in getting everyone to see the same vision you have for residential living, the easier it will be for your child to think of himself as living in such a situation.

4. ***Begin visiting residential programs currently operating in the areas you might consider.*** Most states list the agencies that are contracted to provide such services through the specific Developmental Disabilities agency responsible for licensing community based programs. A good place to search on the Internet is under government agencies, most of which are listed with the name of the state and then the word "government" (for example, Massachusetts government). Once you have obtained the name of the licensed agencies, a shortcut to narrow your search is to check the agency's website to determine who provides services for the diagnosis and age group and location in which you are interested. At that point, you may contact the agency directly and ask for the intake worker or referral staff who can direct you to the appropriate person.

It is the rare agency who would not welcome an inquiry into their services and a request for a visit to a program. Agencies have requirements as to privacy, but this should not preclude informational visits. Just as with researching any new service or resource, the best referral is one that comes from a current user. A good source of such names can be pediatric hospitals or medical groups, as well as your local ARC or developmental disabilities public agency.

5. ***Join a group of families who are thinking of establishing residential services.*** Even if this is not of interest to you in the immediate future, the more exposure you have to

different options, the better prepared you will be to frame the "ideal" vision of your child's residential setting. The local ARC or any social group in which your child is involved can help you find such groups. You can also call the private agencies directly. An agency that prides itself on developing innovative residential services will put you in touch with others, if you give permission for sharing your information.

6. *The question as to whether to include your child in all of the planning and visits to residential settings cannot be answered in the same way for all children.* You need to use your knowledge of your child's tolerance for uncertainty and the level of anxiety he might feel when talking about something as abstract and in the future as an adult residential setting. Your child should be central to the planning and be included in as meaningful a way as possible. However, you need to determine whether information that is not concrete and immediate will aid or hinder the process.

    We believe that the best preparation for many individuals is to engage in activities, new routines, and connections rather than in specific conversations about the future that may seem too abstract to understand. Once a potential roommate or small group is being considered, then meetings and activities held on a regular basis will make the process much easier and natural when the time comes to make the move.

7. *If you are not ready when "experts" tell you that you should be ready, take a step back and reflect on what would make you ready.* Perhaps you feel that you always want your child to remain with the family. If that is realistic and possible, given your family constellation, then make a definitive statement that the decision has been made. There is *nothing wrong with such a decision,* and you can revisit it if and when situations change.

8. *If other involved family members do not agree with your decision, remember that you have the primary responsibility to do what you feel is right for your child and you should continue to follow those instincts.*

Become an Advocate for Residential Planning

In addition to preparing your child for an eventual move out of your family home, you will also need to spend time advocating for him at school and with public agencies. To help your child develop the skills needed for independent living and to successfully transition out of school, you will need to advocate strongly for his needs at IEP meetings. To increase the odds that there will be appropriate settings and services for him to transition to, it may help to ask the school's special education department, as well as your local developmental disabilities service office, to advocate for residential planning. The more local your connection to the school system or disability office, the better your chances of enlisting their support to advocate for your child's needs.

1. *Include residential goals in your child's education Transition Plan.* If your child is still in school, you can include residential services in the transition plan for life after school. Under the federal Individuals with Disabilities Education Act (IDEA), a transition plan for adult services is required for all students who receive special education services.

The plan must be written by the time the student is age 16 (14 in some states). The legal definition of transition services—which can include living arrangements—is a "coordinated set of activities for a student which promise successful movement from school to post-school activities." The services are developed by a team that includes the members of the IEP Team (parents, teachers, therapists, school administrators, etc.). You can also include others who will assist with the transition from school to life after school, including a transition coordinator from the state agency (see below), job coach, etc.

2. *One way to use the transition plan is to help your child gain skills that will assist him to live as independently as possible outside your home.* If you have already had a residential assessment done (see Chapter 3), you can incorporate the recommendations in the transition plan. You can specify skills he will need to acquire, such as cooking, laundry, budgeting, using public transportation, and learning home safety skills (dealing with emergencies like fire, loss of heat or power, strangers at the door, etc.).

3. *You can also use the transition plan to advocate for residential services if you think those will be necessary.* If your child already attends a residential program and you are fairly certain your state will pay for such services when he is an adult, you can ask someone from your child's school to advocate for the kind of placement you are seeking. This could include things like the optimum staffing ratio, the maximum number of residents, special training for staff, etc. While there is no guarantee you will receive all the services you are seeking, you will have a written document signed by your child's IEP team that memorializes your goals and provides a roadmap to attain them.

> 66 Our town generously agreed to pay for a residential placement for my autistic son Richard beginning at age 12. The school has a wonderful ABA program and a high level of staffing at the residence (2:1 when the children are home and 1:1 when they go out into the community). This has worked very well for my son, who can be aggressive and self-injurious.
>
> "As Richard approached age 22 and was getting ready to graduate, I was extremely apprehensive that there was no comparable program in my state, where the staffing ratio in group homes is more like 4:1, at best. A friend told me that his daughter escaped several times from her group home and became lost. Fortunately, my son's school stepped up and advocated for Richard. They said he needed a 2:1 ratio during most times of the day and that all staff should have ABA training. They were very specific about what would be needed in an adult residence to keep him safe (door alarms, fenced-in yard). The state agreed and there have not been any real problems so far."
>
> —father of a young adult with autism

4. ***Include residential services in the Individual Service Plan (ISP).*** If your child has completed his education and is receiving state-funded services, he will participate in the annual ISP process, which is required by federal law. (In some states, this may be called an Individual Program Plan or a habilitation plan.) The ISP Team typically includes the parents, the case manager from the state agency that pays for the services, someone from the day or vocational program, therapists, job coach, and anyone else you want to include.

The ISP is essentially the adult version of the IEP, with one key difference—unlike the federal special education law, which mandates education services for children up to age 22, there are no guarantees to services for individuals who have completed special education. (The exception is for people who were parties to a class action lawsuit, who are assured certain protections that were outlined in the settlement, such as the right to live in a community residence instead of in a nursing home or state-funded institution.) The bottom line is that even though your child may qualify for state-funded services under the criteria in your state, the state is not required to provide them.

Even though there is no entitlement to residential services for most adults, you can and should include residential services in your child's annual ISP. If your adult child has left school but is still living at home, a residential program can be a goal, and you can include specific supports and services your child will need to achieve the goal. If your child is already living outside your home, you can include anything your child needs to make home life successful and satisfying (for example, a lower staff ratio so he can participate in community life or meet health goals by exercising or losing weight; assistance staying connected to friends and family, etc.). Even though the ISP goals do not have binding legal authority, you can refer back to the written plan that was endorsed by the ISP team if your child is struggling and needs more services.

Legal Steps You Can Take to Prepare for Residential Living

1. ***Consider guardianship.*** When your child reaches legal adulthood (age 18 in most states), he will be able to make his own decisions about medical care, education, where to live and work, and other important matters. If you feel that your child cannot reliably make sound decisions in these areas, you should consider guardianship. If you are uncertain whether your child needs a guardian, you can gather opinions from your child's physician, other treatment providers, school personnel, and others who know your child well. You could also have a guardianship evaluation. An attorney can explain the laws and procedures in your state. See Chapter 7 for more information about guardianship.

2. ***Identify the state agency that will provide services when your child is an adult.*** When your child reaches age 18, you should link to the state agency that will provide services when he is an adult. This will depend on the nature of your child's disability (intellectual disability, blindness, mental illness, etc.). In most states, your school's special education department will assist you with this. Typically, once a state agency has been identified, a representative from the agency (called a transition coordinator) will attend your child's IEP meetings. You should work closely with the person to

find out what services are available and to ensure your child will receive the optimum amount of services when he is no longer in school.

3. ***Position your child to take advantage of government benefits.*** It can be expensive to support an adult with a disability, but there are public benefit programs that pay for some or all of the cost. Some programs only provide benefits to those who have very limited income and few assets. For example, in order to receive Supplemental Security Income (SSI), which is covered in Chapter 4, a person may not own more than $2,000 in resources, including custodian accounts. Similarly, some states place limits on the amount of resources a Medicaid recipient may own. To assure eligibility, make sure your child does not accumulate more than $2,000 in his name. If you have generous relatives who want to give monetary gifts, ask them to contribute to a trust for your child's benefit. Trusts are covered in Chapter 9.

4. ***File applications for state and federal housing programs.*** When your child is age 18, you can help him apply for state and federal housing subsidies. Subsidized housing, which pays part of a person's rent or mortgage, can make living apart from the family affordable. Many programs have long waiting lists (up to eight years in some communities). By applying early, your child may reach the top of the list when he is ready to move out. Housing subsidies are covered in Chapter 4 and the Appendix to Chapter 4.

What You Can Do at Home to Prepare Your Child for Independence

Throughout their years together, families establish routines and practices that work for them and assign different roles to each family member. With age and maturity, these routines change, as do the expectations for the parents' involvement in decision making. A child with a developmental disability may experience a different learning curve than other children in your family, but nonetheless, you should expect that those changes will occur.

Many of the suggestions listed below may be difficult to achieve while your child is still living at home because they require creating "artificial" situations to teach skills. But they are worth the effort. Your child may initially resist learning new chores. However, as with any learning experience, repetition creates familiarity and learned responses. Some examples can include:

1. Teaching basic household chores such as laundry, use of a microwave oven, stovetop, household appliances, use of cooking utensils. Often parents take on these chores themselves for the sake of expediency, but your priority should become teaching those skills in preparation for leaving, even if the quality of the work might suffer initially.

2. Buy basic ingredients for simple meals. Find a few nutritious meals your child enjoys, even if they are prepared meals, and devise a shopping list that includes quantities, costs, and location in the supermarket. Create a situation in which your child can eventually purchase and prepare the entire meal, regardless of how simple it might be.

3. If possible, leave for an overnight stay or short vacation. Arrange for someone to stay with your child and give him or her instructions about some of the daily skills you have been working on.

4. Your child's ability to get around the community will depend on your location and access to public transportation and amenities. If they exist within a reasonable distance, then begin a travel program as early as possible. If your child is still in school, ask for a travel coach and program to work on this with you. The actual travel is not as important as the skill being taught and the accompanying discussions of "what if" scenarios, their consequences, and teaching your child what to do. For example: What do you do if you get on the wrong bus? Where should you sit or stand if the bus is crowded? Who do you ask for directions?

5. Staying safe in the community. Find out whether there are personal growth or similar community safety classes offered by the local ARC or school. If not, determine whether there is interest among families and consider starting a class. The purpose is to prepare your child for making good decisions when he is out in the community. Depending on your child's needs, he may be in a setting that will offer 24-hour supervision. However, regardless of the staffing arrangements, your child can learn to have some control over decisions that affect his daily routines. Discussing decision making gives him the understanding that he is part of decisions that affect his life.

All of this work helps to make the prospect of living outside of your family home an exciting one, rather than a daunting one, for both your child and your family. The process takes time and needs to be carefully planned out. It is a big step, and the enormity of the decision should not be minimized. For families who have always been there to support, protect, and encourage their child with a disability, it is an enormous transition to suddenly shift to viewing their child as living elsewhere. It is equally so for your child, who has always relied on the comfort, support, and ease of family life. It is a process that can't be rushed but can be nurtured as you look for the small cues that indicate your child is ready. It will all be worth it, however, when you hear your son or daughter say or express nonverbally, "I am too busy to come home this weekend. I have plans with my friends."

Chapter 2
Residential Options

There are many models of residential options currently available for adults with disabilities, both nationally and internationally. Many families choose an existing option in their community. Others create their own option, either alone or with one or more other families. There are no limits to the possibilities that can be developed when we harness the energy and enthusiasm of families, professionals, and the individuals themselves as we collaborate to develop models of residential support arrangements.

Community Residences—How We Got Here

Community residences for people with disabilities are a fairly recent development. Historically, the primary model of care in the United States for people with intellectual disabilities was the large state-run institution. The number of people living in such facilities peaked in 1967 at around 230,000. But by 1977, this number had decreased to about 154,000, and in 2009, only about 33,000 residents remained in state-run facilities. Currently, of the approximately 600,000 people in the United States with developmental disabilities who do not live with their families, 75 percent live in community residences with one to six people.* Eleven states have closed all their facilities with sixteen or more residents. The trend is to support people with disabilities to live in the community—by themselves with support, or with extended families, foster families, or peers in small group residences.

How did we go from large institutions to community residences in such a short period of time? The change came about due to a combination of factors: a change in attitude toward people with disabilities, strategic lawsuits brought by concerned parents and others, and changes in public policy and the use of public funds.

---

* Braddock, D., Hemp, R., Rizzolo, M., Haffer, L., Tanis, E., & Wu, J. (2011). *State of the States in Developmental Disabilities 2011.* Denver: University of Colorado, American Association on Intellectual and Developmental Disabilities.

Public Awareness

The precipitating factor for change was probably public awareness of the poor conditions in most institutions. The institutions, which dated back to the nineteenth century, were probably opened with the best of intentions and may have provided humane care in their day. But as time went on and the population increased, most facilities became overcrowded, understaffed, and dirty. In some facilities, residents were routinely abused by staff and other residents.

The public was largely unaware of this situation. That changed in 1965 when Robert Kennedy, then a United States Senator from New York, made unannounced visits to the Willowbrook State School and the Rome State School. The media widely covered his reaction to the overcrowding, filth, and odors. There were more revelations about Willowbrook in 1972, when Geraldo Rivera exposed the squalid conditions in a series of televised reports secretly filmed at the facility.

The dismal conditions in institutions were not limited to New York State. In Massachusetts, Burton Blatt, a Boston University professor, and Fred Kaplan, a photographer, secretly photographed the back wards of several institutions in New England. The book Blatt produced in 1966, *Christmas in Purgatory*, showed emaciated adults and children living in filthy, overcrowded conditions. The exposure of these conditions shocked the public.

Strategic Lawsuits

With these revelations, the climate was right for reform. However, state officials who ran the institutions lacked the ability and will to make any real changes. Family members of the residents, and even some residents themselves, turned to the federal courts for help, challenging the conditions in the facilities on constitutional grounds. They found a receptive audience. Two examples:

- In 1972, parents of residents at the Belchertown State School in Massachusetts brought a lawsuit against the state, alleging, among other things, that the overcrowded, unsanitary, and understaffed conditions amounted to "cruel and unusual punishment" under the U.S. Constitution. As a result of the lawsuit, Belchertown and four other state-run facilities were placed under the supervision of the federal district court. Conditions in the facilities improved dramatically under the twentyone-year-long tenure of the court-appointed monitor and Judge Joseph Tauro. Eventually Belchertown and most other state-run facilities in Massachusetts were closed.

- In 1974, Terri Lee Halderman and other residents of the Pennhurst State School in Pennsylvania filed a similar lawsuit alleging that their confinement against their will deprived them of liberty without due process under the Fourteenth Amendment. In 1977, when federal district court judge Raymond Broderick issued his opinion in the *Halderman vs. Pennhurst State School & Hospital* case, it was considered the most far-reaching legal event in the field of intellectual disabilities to date. Although the decision was eventually overturned by the United States Supreme Court, Pennsylvania state officials settled the case and agreed to offer community services to all residents. The school was later closed.

The successes in Massachusetts and Pennsylvania inspired parents and individuals in other states to bring similar lawsuits. In many cases, officials were forced to move residents out of institutions into smaller residences.

Academics and Social Services Professionals

Another voice for change came from academics, social workers, mental health professionals, and others concerned with the care of people with disabilities. Beginning in the 1960s, they began to hear about new models of care for people with disabilities in Europe and Scandinavia. Norway and Sweden, in particular, were leaders in providing humane care to people with mental disabilities. The Scandinavian residences—although not quite like the group homes of today—were small, home-like, beautiful, and well-run. This was by design. The Scandinavians believed that people with disabilities could—and should—participate in all aspects of life. In order for them to be "normal," they had to be given the opportunity to have "normal" experiences, which meant living, working, recreating, and enjoying life alongside normal people. This could not be done in an institution.

Influential thinkers like the psychologist Wolf Wolfensberger wrote and lectured widely on the topic of "Normalization" and generated excitement in the American professional community about what could be accomplished when the institutions closed.

Changes in Federal Funding

Even with the mandates from the federal courts and pressure for reform from the public, real change would not have been possible without altering the way services were paid for. Before the 1970s and the court-mandated closures, the state facilities were funded with a combination of federal and state dollars. Most of the federal funds came from the Medicaid program, which only permitted the money to be used in institutions. When institutions began to close in the 1970s, federal money was not immediately directed into community residences as we know them today. Instead, a new model was developed—a sort of mini-institution called the Intermediate Care Facility for the Mentally Retarded (ICF/MR). These state-operated facilities, which housed sixteen or more residents, satisfied Medicaid's requirement that funds must be spent on institutional care. If the states wanted smaller residences, they had to bear the cost themselves.

This changed in 1981, when Congress revised the Medicaid statute to create the Home and Community Based (HCBS) Waiver. It allowed Medicaid funds to be used to support people with disabilities in their own homes. The statute "waived" the requirement that Medicaid funds could only be used in institutional settings. HCBS spending grew from $2.2 million in 1982 to $25.1 billion in 2009. Today, federal funds make up about 55 percent of spending for community services for people with intellectual disabilities.

Mental Illness

The vision that people with disabilities could leave the institutions and be fully integrated into daily life extended to those with mental illness as well. The deinstitutionalization of people with mental illness began earlier than that of those with intellectual disabilities. In the early 1950s, new drugs were being developed that addressed the symptoms of mental illness and helped people function better. This resulted in the discharge of large numbers of people with mental illness from institutions. However, they were essentially released to fend for themselves, without any long-term follow up plans, supports, and supervision. This resulted in widespread homelessness among people with mental illness. Despite advances in medicine and new drugs, this problem has yet to be solved.

Families

No discussion of how we went from institutions to community care would be complete without mentioning the extraordinary efforts of parents of children with disabilities. In the 1950s, the Association of Retarded Children—the precursor to the Arcs of today—was founded by families who refused to accept that their children with mental disabilities would not receive education and training like other children. They fought from that day forward, and they continue to advocate for the best opportunities for their children. Many others have joined voices and collectively made great advances, resulting in thousands of examples of creative arrangements. You, the reader, will continue to generate more ideas as we define what can be accomplished—not what cannot be done.

Models of Residential Arrangements
Which Model of Support Is Best for Your Family Member?

Each residential model can be located in a variety of locations; they can be operated and managed by families or by private not-for-profit or profit agencies; they can be self-managed by the individuals. Each can serve people with varying diagnoses and varying medical, behavioral, or physical needs. The criteria which define each model are the staffing structure, the number of people who live in any one setting, and the rules or expectations for supports defined by the families, individuals, or managing entity. The model chosen should be determined on the basis of the individual's needs, abilities, and personality.

Any of the models can be supplemented by Personal Care Management (PCM) supports if the individual is eligible to receive such supports and they do not duplicate what is offered by the primary public funding source, if there is any. **Personal Care Management** supports are services that are provided on an hourly basis and determined to be medically necessary to allow a person to live semi- or totally independently. They cover such needs as assistance with daily activities, personal care needs such as dressing, grooming, and bathing, and life skills such as cooking and cleaning. The eligibility determination is done through the state agency that administers Medicaid assistance in your state. PCM supports are discussed in Chapter 6.

To assist you in identifying the model that best suits your family member's situation, each model discussed below is organized on the basis of a few distinguishing criteria:

- Structure of the staffing supports and scheduling
- Number of people living together
- Level of independence of the resident(s)

Group Residence

Typically, several people live together and share staffing, structured activities, and routines that accommodate the entire household. The home can be of any shape and size, provided it is large enough to house the number of individuals living together.

Most states have regulations regarding the number of people who live together. The average group residence in most states consists of four to six people living together. The local zoning ordinances may also have restrictions on the number of people living together. However, group residences that are operated by nonprofit organizations are considered to be single family residences according to state building codes. This means that any restrictions that are put on a single family home (e.g., minimum lot size) are also placed on group residences, but no more than what is expected for a single family residence. The pictures included in the Appendix to Chapter 2 show some typical group residences.

The staffing in a group residence is set and is typically handled on an eight-hour shift basis covering an entire 24-hour period. Although staffing may not be necessary for an entire 24-hour period (depending on the residents' needs), the work schedule is calculated on the basis of a 24-hour period and on providing staffing for all or any part of a full day and night. Staff are scheduled to work no more than 40 hours per week, unless overtime hours are built into the staffing pattern. The paid staff may be supplemented by live-in companion staff, if the housing accommodates such an arrangement.

Group homes can be located in rural, urban, or suburban areas, or can be formed as a farm or a collective living arrangement. Typically, the number of people who live together is dictated by the state funding source, if it is supported and/or licensed by a state agency.

Supervised Independent Living

Supervised independent living typically involves one or more person(s) who lives independently and receives support from an outside staff person who works at set times during the week on specific objectives. This residential arrangement can occur in an apartment, a condominium, a single family home, or the person's home. This arrangement is designed for people who have some independent skill level and can manage and benefit from less than 24-hour supervision. In some instances, if the housing arrangement allows it, a companion can live with the person and offer "natural supports" and companionship without the expectation that he or she will be available at all times of the day and night.

Shared Living

Shared living is defined as living with an existing family unit other than one's own family. A family is recruited and trained to live with a person with a disability in the family's home and then incorporates that person into their life routine and structure. Accommodations are made to meet the person's needs, but basically, the person is moving into an existing family unit. The family can be a traditional nuclear family or a single-person family, with or without children. Additional supports and staff can supplement this model as needed. Typically, one to three people can live in any one shared living home.

In most shared living situations, the primary caregiver in the family is paid a stipend in acknowledgement of the fact that they are providing more than just a nurturing home setting; they are also expected to work on teaching goals and life skills. The amount they are paid depends on the area and the arrangements that are made for such a model. The stipend is typically paid as a consultant arrangement and therefore the individual is expected to file his or her own taxes. Refer to Chapter 6 for information on these filing requirements. In many states, these payments are not subject to federal income taxes. The state agency responsible for developmental disability services will direct you as to the requirements of your state. In addition to receiving a stipend, the caregiver usually receives funds from the person with disabilities, who typically pays a portion of her room and board to the provider through her SSI or other public benefits.

Common Characteristics of These Models

Each model can:

- be located in rural, urban, or suburban settings
- have a variety of different staffing patterns and supports associated with their operation
- serve people with a variety of diagnoses and be grouped according to different compatible age and ability groups
- be referred to differently in different states and have a variety of funding sources associated with them, often tied into reimbursement models from the federal government (and in some states can be supplemented by state funds as well as federal)
- be owned and operated and managed in various ways, including but not limited to: the families can own the home; the individuals living in the home can own it; it can be owned by an agency with expertise in developing and managing residential settings; it can be set up as a cooperative or a condominium trust; it can be owned by an independent party not connected with the residential arrangement and rented to the residents

None of the above conditions defines the model of the residential arrangement. They simply define the ownership and management style that will be chosen once you determine which model of support is suitable for your situation.

Group Homes

This is the most common of the models. It has existed in the U.S. since community-based services for adults with disabilities began in the early 1970s. It has become accepted as the default method of services in the eleven states that have closed their large institutions or as coexisting models in states that still maintain institutions.

When group homes were first developed, they were thought of as "halfway houses," in keeping with similar models that existed for people with substance abuse or mental illness. It quickly became apparent that such a term was not appropriate for people with developmental disabilities because they were not there as "halfway" to somewhere else, but rather would continue to need supports in long-term homes indefinitely. Individuals lived in group homes to learn, to progress, and in some cases to move to a different level of support over time.

When deinstitutionalization first began, group homes typically housed up to sixteen people. Over the years, that number dwindled to the current number of four or five. In some cases, there are fewer than four or more than five, but the average number is five. In part, the number is dictated by the local zoning definition of a family and of a single family dwelling.

A group home setting typically has direct care staff who work with the individuals throughout the day and night as needed, assisting them with routine activities of daily liv-

The ability to prioritize what is important in a residential arrangement is expressed well by the parent of a young woman who lives in a group setting, as follows:

I know there is quality when...

I know there is quality in Becky's life when:

- She refuses Saturday lunch with me because she is having lunch with her boyfriend.
- We go for a walk in the local park on a Sunday afternoon and a fellow walker says "hi Becky." It is someone she knows from attending local church services.
- One of the women on her inclusive bowling team invites her to a meal at her house.
- At the voting place four years ago, she was not listed at her current address (she'd moved a few months before), and a former neighbor at the desk said "didn't you use to live at 25 Main Street?" Becky responded "yes" and was allowed to vote.
- She has work or volunteer jobs in the community where she is valued for her contribution.
- She has a boyfriend who makes her laugh and who she makes laugh.
- She has Wilbur, a guinea pig, to care for and love.
- She makes needlepoint and pottery for gifts to family and friends.
- She has the funds to buy a second TV for her bedroom, to take a vacation trip to Cape Cod or to Disneyland, and to belong to CURVES.
- Her three sisters agree that Becky lives life far closer to her potential than any one of them.
- But quality also exists in more mundane areas:
  › Her apartment and workplace are safe.
  › She has good, nutritious food to eat.
  › She has regular medical checkups and monitoring.
  › She has stable staff who have known her as an individual for a long time, who trust her and whom she trusts, and who allow her to experience the risks of ordinary life like the rest of us.

—**Quincy Abbot, organizational management professional
(From Independent Non Profit, Oct. 2004.)**

ing including personal hygiene and grooming, budgeting, shopping, cooking and preparing meals, recreation, community involvement, and relationships. Work and vocational assistance is typically handled through different sources and is not included in the group home arrangement. As the residents become older, some individuals may remain at home for activities during daytime hours as well, but typically, that is not part of the services offered in a group home setting. Staff may offer support during part or all of the 168 hours in any given week.

The number of staff members depends on the number of people who live in the home and their assessed needs. This number need not be permanently set. As needs change (due to people maturing, learning new skills, and aging), so might their need for support staff change.

The home can include an apartment or unit of some size to allow for a live-in staff person or couple or family. This set-up has the benefit of saving money on overnight staffing. It also provides a safety net at all times, even when staff are not "on duty," as this is the live-in person or couple's primary residence and they therefore care for the home on a personal level.

Where the home should be located depends on a few critical factors. First and foremost, it depends on who is being considered for the group home, their affiliations with certain towns and cities, and their family's desire to keep the home within a certain distance for them to be able to visit. The other criterion determining location is whether the individuals can use public transportation and local stores and amenities independently. If they need assistance and need to be driven by staff, then placement in a more urban setting with such amenities may not be as important.

If you are forming a new group home with a few other families, keep in mind that the location will be the one priority that will be nonnegotiable for most families. For example, some families and individuals may be perfectly compatible housemates but insist that the home be within a certain mile radius of their family home. Or, for one reason or another, some families will exclude certain towns. If that is the case, then regardless of compatibility, the grouping won't happen. The more flexible families and individuals can be about the specific location, the easier it is to consider other important criteria for organizing compatible groups. It is one of the main reasons we suggest throughout the book that you not purchase a home before confirming a minimum number of families who are committed to forming a group. Otherwise, you may find yourself with a piece of real estate that may not suit the needs of the final grouping of people and you will then be faced with a financial burden without a purpose for it.

Here is an example of one group who had known each other all through their children's school years:

> The group had discussed a plan in which five of them would get together as their children graduated from school and would jointly purchase a home in which their child would live "forever." One family took it upon themselves to purchase a home in a town that was close to their son's family home. They took a financial risk in doing so, but felt the other families would be happy with the choice and would also be pleased that they had expended the upfront costs for the initial purchase. Unfortunately, two of the families decided they were not ready when the time came, and backed out of the plan. Another family was not satisfied with the location of

the home, as they felt it was too urban and busy an area, and they were afraid their daughter would not be ready for such a move. That left only two families, the buyer and one other.

The families contacted our agency and requested that we recruit three other individuals. Since the home had already been purchased, we were more limited in our search than if we been able to seek compatible housemates without the restriction of location. In six months, the agency was only able to locate one family that was interested in the home and its location and had the means to pay privately, since they were not prioritized for public funding by their state's developmental disability agency.

The owner of the home could not continue to maintain the expense of the home without any income stream to pay for the mortgage and had to sell the home.

A group home can be established as a condominium in which all residents own their personal living space and a share of the common area. It can be owned by one family whose family member may or may not reside in the home. For example, a family may want to buy a unit or be part of a trust for a later time when their child is ready to move in. The home can be owned by an agency that also manages the property and provides the operational support to the program. It can be a rented condominium, a rented single- or multi-family home or apartment, or several apartments together to accommodate the entire group. In other words, the management structure and ownership of the home is not a determining factor in the model of support one designs.

Supervised Independent Living

In some states, this model is also known as residential supports, independent community support, in home supports, individual supported living, and other similar labels. Some states refer to this model as a life share model as well, but for the purpose of clarity in this book and to assist the reader in designing their appropriate residential model, we are referring to this model as supervised independent living.

This model can include one or more people living together, either both males and females or just one gender. It can be located in a rural, urban, or suburban setting. Typically, people who are served in this model are somewhat independent and might be able to use or learn to use public transportation and shop at local stores. Therefore, the residence is often in a location that allows for that kind of independence, even if those skills need to be taught or the person needs to be accompanied initially.

The setting may be owned or rented. Sometimes it is the home where the person previously lived with her family, who have left her the home in their estate. The home can be an addition built onto the current family home and set up as separate space with its own entrance. This can be similar to an "in-law" apartment. As with all such situations, there are potential problems if separation is not clearly delineated between the main house and family and the new arrangement.

The supervised independent living model can offer many benefits. As with all other models, it can change as needs and skills change. The purpose of the model is to provide sufficient supports to people to allow them to gain additional skills toward greater independence. Typically, the types of skills that are worked on with support staff are:

- budgeting and money management to ensure sufficient funds for daily needs;
- meal planning, shopping, and cooking;
- personal care, grooming, and hygiene (with a view that these skills are needed for vocational and social reasons);
- personal organization of space and possessions;
- transportation skills;
- community safety skills;
- interpersonal relationships

A staff person is recruited to live in the home or a condo or apartment in the same complex, if that is the staffing model chosen. The person is typically not paid for the hours worked, as it is their primary residence, but they may receive a small stipend. The free housing is considered to be a great incentive for such an arrangement and is often appealing enough to attract and retain such a person.

Such a live-in model offers supervision even when paid staff hours are not scheduled. In addition to the live-in person, additional support staff may be employed and scheduled for various times of the week to work with one or more of the individuals on specific objectives in the areas noted above. If the option of a live-in is not needed or chosen, then hiring an outside support staff person to work on these skills is the other way to achieve the supports needed for growth and supervision.

An advantage of this model is that changes to the number of hours of support can be made more easily as warranted by the individual's growth or other circumstances, without having to upset anyone else's supports or routines. It can be truly individualized.

Hybrid Settings

Another type of setting that straddles the line between a supervised independent living setting and independent living is an example which the author's agency developed and manages. It is a three-story apartment building located in an urban area of Massachusetts close to many universities, which makes it an ideal location for student housing. The agency purchased this small apartment building with the intent of creating housing for people needing assistance in life skills such as budgeting, meal planning and cooking, and organizing personal space. One apartment is set aside for a live-in resident counselor who is not paid but receives room and board in return for overall monitoring of the building, and providing security and support to the tenants when needed. The counselor also encourages and participates in some of the holiday celebrations, plans some weekend outings, and attends a weekly cooking and tenant group meeting held by an outreach support person.

Since the location is in a desirable area for students, it seemed like an ideal opportunity to rent apartments to people with special needs as well as college or graduate students, thereby making the setting truly integrated. In its first year of operation, the four single-bedroom apartments were rented to individuals supported by our agency. Two of the four three-bedroom apartments were rented to college students and the other three-bedroom apartments were rented to individuals with special needs known to our agency.

During the year in which the college students resided in the building, they were loud, threw parties, and did not contribute to the sense of community of the building. They were being typical college students, but our tenants felt they could not have their friends over when they wanted to because the community room was often occupied by the students. Although the college students never denied them access to the room, they did not feel comfortable or assertive enough to claim it as their own. As a result, the individuals with special needs who had been very excited to live with "cool college students" requested that we not renew the students' leases and instead allow their friends to move into the building when apartments became available.

It was a reminder to us all that although it can be worthwhile to try out things such as integration that sound good, it is important to reevaluate the situation after you try it rather than continue with it despite drawbacks learned from the experience. In this case, we changed our tactic and decided to rent apartments in the building only to people with special needs. Some tenants move on to more independent settings after a time, while others live there over the long term.

Shared Living

This model offers a great deal of flexibility, but has to feel like a good fit for both the family and individual. It is referred to by many different labels, including specialized home care or foster care, depending on the state and federal funding structure. Regardless of the label, the criteria defining this model are: 1) that a family is recruited and trained, and 2) then incorporates the individual into their existing home and family structure. The "family" can be a single person, a traditional nuclear family, or a single person with a child. The family is paid a stipend that covers the room, board, and training support that is necessary for the individual. In some states, it can be supplemented by Adult Foster Care funds, which offer federal supplemental funding for medical needs.

All shared living arrangements operate as a family, with the family providing the supports needed. Typically, there are no hired staff whose job is to support and teach the adult with disabilities. Rather, the person with disabilities is treated like a family member. However, if a state agency is approving and paying for this model, then an Individual Service Plan is required to outline goals and objectives for growth. The family is expected to provide the teaching opportunities to implement these goals.

Some families of individuals with disabilities hesitate to consider this option for fear of the implied message that they are not able to provide their child with the needed supports, yet another family can. However, there are many reasons that this arrangement may be a good option. First, the person with disabilities may have stopped learning and growing because her parents are too used to doing things for her. Second, the family may need to pursue other options for themselves and move on to sharing in their child's life rather than being the primary and sole care giver. Third, a shared living provider might offer skills (such as a nursing background) that may be very helpful to the child.

In our experience, when the right provider is recruited, it can result in an extended family from which everyone benefits. Shared living can be an excellent option in which the individual thrives in a setting that offers the safety and security of a family. In many cases, the biological family is able to keep a vital role in caring for the individual, yet is not the primary source so that the person is essentially supported by two families. Later in this book, we offer some vignettes of shared living arrangements that have been very successful.

As with all other models, shared living can take place in an urban, suburban, or rural setting. It can include one person or up to three individuals. However, most states place restrictions on whether a second or third person with disabilities can be added to a shared living arrangement, and, if so, when they can move in.

Communities

Families may decide to create a small community based on a common purpose, product, or mission. Communities are a larger undertaking than creating any of the group or individual models we describe in this book. If a number of families have sufficient interest and energy, however, then creating a community or joining an existing one is an option to consider.

There are many examples of communities around the country and worldwide that have existed for a long time:

- the Kibbutz model in pioneering Israel,
- the communities developed on the basis of the Irenicon/L'Arche concepts,
- intentional communities for different groupings such as multigenerational groups, and, more recently,
- the farming and ecological communities developed in the United States.

Most of these communities are based on models of living that were economically and socially beneficial for the organizers. They embodied necessity with the benefit of natural supports through multiple generations and groups of people gathering for a common purpose.

The oldest communal farmstead still in operation in the United States is Gould Farm in Western Massachusetts, opened in 1913. Today it offers short-term stays to adults with mental illness. Bittersweet Farm in Ohio and Camphill Village in New York are examples of communities that were formed for people with special needs around a common purpose of living and teaching skills in the communal setting. Farmsteads are a popular model for people with autism in particular. The therapeutic benefits of life and work on a farm are well-documented. Participants can be physically active by growing crops, tending to animals, woodworking, and performing the many daily chores that farm life necessitates. Farmsteads may offer day and residential options. A good source of information about farmstead programs is the consortium Agricultural Communities for Adults with Autism (http://ac-aa.org).

Communities can be designed to offer therapeutic environments in which the residents are engaged in purposeful activities that are integral to the operation of the community. Examples are farming, animal care and boarding, crafts, plants, vegetable and other food products, and bread and bakery production. Typically people with and without disabilities live together in these communities, and all adults, both with and without disabilities, pitch in to help with whatever activity sustains the community. The common purposes are limited only by imagination and market research as to what can be sold or consumed by the community itself.

In another form of group living, a campus is created without the necessity of a common product or service. On these campuses, all services and supports are offered within a defined acreage of land, and housing, day supports, and recreational facilities are typically located on the campus. Some of these programs have extended beyond their campus settings to include offsite housing and vocational training as the residents have progressed or gone beyond the age groupings for which the campus was originally intended.

L'Arche Model. The L'Arche homes and programs operate as a community model in which people who have disabilities live with people without disabilities in an atmosphere of friendship and support. There are currently seventeen L'Arche communities in the United States. Among L'Arche's stated missions are to provide lifelong support for people with disabilities and to "make known their gifts" (http://larcheusa.org).

Cohousing. Cohousing is a type of collaborative housing in which residents actively participate in the design and operation of their neighborhoods. Cohousing residents are consciously committed to living as a community. Typically, residents live in single family homes

What Is Important to YOU in a Residential Setting?

Developing and/or choosing a residential setting outside of the home for your child depends in part on your being clear and honest as to what is important to you as a family member. Including your child in the decision is critical, but it is equally critical that you have a clear understanding of **your** priorities. Otherwise, there may be a conflict between what you want and what the program has to offer. Complete this questionnaire yourself and also give it to other family members to complete without consulting with one another. Compare your answers to see if there is a discrepancy in your priorities.

Rank these 14 goals for your family member in order of importance to you, with #1 being most important and #14 being least important. If you feel that some are not of any importance, note them as 0.

- ❏ To be independent
- ❏ To have friends
- ❏ To be safe
- ❏ To get married or have a significant other in his or her life
- ❏ To live in a place that is clean at all times
- ❏ To learn new academic skills or at least maintain current skills
- ❏ To have a large, beautifully decorated room
- ❏ To have contact with me and/or other members of our family each day
- ❏ To be active and involved in social/recreational activities
- ❏ To have staff who are of the same gender
- ❏ To have roommates or housemates with similar interests and/or ability levels
- ❏ To be with people who have no behavior problems
- ❏ To be able to observe his/her religion in the home/apartment
- ❏ To be well dressed at all times

clustered around a pedestrian street or courtyard. There is usually a common house with a dining room, kitchen, lounge, recreation area, and laundry room. Residents have the option to eat communally several times a week. Cohousing communities can work well for people with disabilities who might otherwise be socially isolated. They can participate in all aspects of cohousing life but should have enough support so they are not dependent on other members of the community. There is information about cohousing at http://directory.cohousing.org.

Selecting a Neighborhood and Dealing with Neighbors

A discussion about residential settings would not be complete without mention of neighbors and neighborhoods which the various models fit into. Since deinstitutionalization began in a concerted and full scale movement in the early 1970s, various legislative advances in most states have been made to ensure that people with disabilities are not discriminated against when moving into cities, towns, and communities. However, legislation can go only so far in protecting the rights of individuals. If a neighborhood or street wants to prevent or delay a group or individuals from moving into their neighborhood, there are many ways they can do so without blatantly violating the law. Even if they are not ultimately successful, the expense of obtaining legal assistance to protect rights and the delays in moving in can be very costly in time and money.

In my (Dafna's) experience of establishing over 90 residential settings in numerous cities, towns, and states over the years, there are a few measures that can assist in the process of being accepted into a neighborhood. We want to caution the reader that sometimes there may be no way to be accepted at first. Instead, your goal may have to be for the residents to be tolerated until neighbors get to know them and appreciate the value they add to the fabric of the neighborhood.

First and foremost, it is important to note that resistance to people with disabilities moving into neighborhoods is based on stereotypes similar to those about any other "unknown" group. The discrimination is based on fear of the generalizations rather than on first-hand experiences. Also, neighbors may fear that resale property values will decrease, or that there may be danger to their families due to uninformed understanding of disabilities and the labels associated with them. (Sometimes this occurs because the occasional unfortunate occurrence is publicized, making it seem as if these problems are the norm rather than the exception.) There is no way to dissuade that kind of belief until the individuals with disabilities move in and prove them to be myths.

Based on that knowledge, TILL (Dafna's agency) chooses not to announce a move into a neighborhood when seeking a home or condominium. We verify that there are no prohibitions against a home being established—meaning that the zoning is proper for the residential setting—and we abide by the number of residents permitted for single family homes. These are the only guidelines that need to be followed in Massachusetts. The zoning and building department regulations of other states should be researched before locating a residence.

In nearly every situation that the author's agency has experienced, neighbors have heard about the impending move and have called their local legislator or the agency directly. We advise that one person at an agency act as the communications person when such calls are received. The message and response to questions has to be consistent, reassuring, and informative and ensure that confidential information is not violated. Offering to provide reference numbers of other neighborhoods in which the agency has programs is useful provided you have established such references (which we strongly recommend). Offering to meet with a group of neighbors in person is seldom advisable, since the people who will attend and be vocal are the ones against the move. In some instances, you can gather supporters, but in reality, meetings such as those rarely change any opposition views. In some areas, public funding agencies mandate that preliminary neighborhood meetings be held and legislative notices be submitted. Those need to be followed if they are required.

Over the past twenty years, there have been very positive changes in the acceptance of residential programs by neighbors. The intent of this section is to remind readers that continuing to make progress in this area is as much our responsibility as it is society's at large. Keep in mind that some of the complaints that providers of residential services might receive are nothing compared to what you might experience as a neighbor on your own street. The difference is that your disgruntled neighbor does not have access to an agency or a state authority responsible for monitoring your home. Neighbors of group homes have a way to "complain" to many sources, whereas other neighbors have to work it out individually. The following example illustrates this point:

The author's agency purchased a home for four women with developmental and physical disabilities in a suburb 15 miles from Boston, Massachusetts. Cosmetic as well as adaptive renovations were done to accommodate a wheelchair user. This included building a ramp that was tucked between two homes and not visible from the street. The ramp led to a deck, which needed to be raised by two feet to allow for the proper slope from the ramp and street and into the home. It connected directly to the kitchen from the outside driveway. The previous owner had two teenage boys and two young adult nephews who lived in the home. The parents were divorced and it is believed that there had been a good deal of family turmoil.

Upon seeing the new ramp, the next-door neighbor enlisted the help of an attorney and the building inspector. Her complaint was that she would now be able to see our deck from her second-floor window. The agency had pulled all the proper building permits and were within their rights to do the renovations. The neighbor simply did not want the home there and created a great deal of noise to prevent us from moving in. We spoke to the building inspector, who was apologetic about having to make the calls to our agency. We spoke to but refused to meet with the attorney, as there were no grounds upon which to meet. We also spoke to the neighbor and invited her to see the renovations. We offered and proceeded to plant some six-foot trees on the property line, which would grow to cover her sightline in a few years' time. We had no obligation to do so, but felt it was a wise move in the interest of our residents as well as her family. She was not satisfied, but did not have any other recourse after our actions.

We are happy to report that we have only heard from the neighbor once, when she complained to the building inspector about our parking for a meeting. There have been no complaints from her husband, who has even attended our holiday party.

If you decide to develop your own residential setting, we recommend the following:

- Do your homework to ensure that the home or condominium the residents will move into is properly zoned for such a use.
- Obtain any permits needed for renovations or construction.

- Designate one person as the contact for your group to provide information. Make sure this information is clear, describes your mission and purpose of this particular home, and allays fears about behavior and diagnosis, but only to the extent that it does not violate confidential information about residents.
- Prepare a few written materials about your agency that you can share with neighbors, funders, and legislators. Have a website which provides information about your longevity and reputation.
- When possible, gather references from other neighborhoods or families who can speak to your being a good neighbor.
- Try to move as quickly as possible before giving neighbors a lot of time to become anxious and gather opposition to the project.
- Consider whether you are making a responsible decision in selecting your site. For example, even though you are legally allowed to move into a new housing development where most residents are new families with young children who congregate in the streets, ride bikes, etc., does it make sense to move five adults with developmental disabilities into such a neighborhood?

Most importantly, after you move in, **BE A RESPONSIBLE NEIGHBOR**. The fact that laws have been written to prevent discrimination does not eliminate the responsibility of being a good neighbor. Your home will be a role model that will ease the way for other arrangements until perceptions are totally changed about the value of people with disabilities moving into a community. We define being a responsible neighbor in the following ways:

- Keep the exterior of your home attractive.
- Keep your landscaping attractive.
- Do not put trash in a neighbor's area.
- Do not leave discarded furnishings or other items outside beyond the pick-up times for such items.
- Shovel your section of the street as needed.
- Offer to help neighbors with their trash, lawn, or snow removal if they need such assistance.
- Do not leave outside lights on if they shine in neighbors' houses, especially at evening hours when staff changes might be occurring.
- Make sure car alarms are not set off accidentally and left running.
- Invite neighbors to open houses and holiday celebrations.
- Let neighbors know if you will be having a large gathering that will affect parking.
- Do not park in other people's spaces and block access to their homes.
- Find subtle ways to get to know your neighbors and to let them get to know you and the people who live there.
- Have staff monitor people who might like to wander into neighbor's houses to ensure that they do not do so.
- At all times, ensure the safety of your home as well as your neighbors' if there are people who live in the home with potential behavioral outbursts.

Group Home Model Planning Story #1— Family Initiated

Twenty years ago, four families approached our agency with a wish to create a home for their children, who were about to graduate from high school. It was unlikely that they were going to receive state funding, since they did not meet any of the high priority qualifications for placement such as homelessness, a risk to themselves and others, etc. The families also had a dream of creating a home where their children could be active members of their community and in which the families could participate in the design, model, and ongoing life of the house, yet not be responsible for the management and daily operations.

They sought our agency after researching others to find the right fit in terms of philosophy, stability, staff retention and training, creativity, and general "chemistry" between the families and the upper management. It took two years of planning before the home opened. In the process, a clear list of responsibilities for the project was defined so that everything got done with little duplication of efforts. Small committees of two or three parents were self-appointed to find the home, furnishings, renovations, and community support.

Our agency was responsible for locating and assessing additional residents who would be compatible with the initial four people; developing a budget that allowed for sufficient staffing and operations; obtaining housing grant funding for building a live-in staff apartment and renovating the large, sixty-year-old Colonial home; and creating a corporate model that allowed for home ownership by each resident.

It was decided that it would be best to have a condominium trust model, allowing each person to own his or her bedroom, shared bath, and a portion of the common area space.

An advisory committee of all families provides an ongoing method of communication and planning between the agency, the house, and the families. Over the years, five of the original residents have left for various reasons. Two moved to more independent settings run by our agency; one left to get married and continues to need minimal outreach support to ensure good money, nutritional, and vocational management with her husband; one developed extensive medical needs that required a more intense medical setting; and one moved to another state to be with her extended family. The other major change was that five years ago the families asked our agency to buy the condominium units from each of them at the price they had paid for the units. The reason was they no longer wanted the burden of ownership if a replacement for their child's unit was necessary and they did not want the burden associated with ownership of any property—namely, decisions about replacement reserves, taxes, insurance, etc.

Our agency purchased the units and has continued to operate the residence for the last five years with the families' input and cooperation. Nothing has changed because the mission of the home has remained the same. A memorandum of understanding was written, guaranteeing to the families that it continues to be their children's home with all the same expectations of operations remaining the same.

Take Away from This Example of a Family-Initiated Group Home Model

1. Decide whether you want to manage the program independently without the assistance of an existing agency that provides such services as part of their mission and purpose.

2. If you want to seek an agency, look for one that is a good match. Use the Agency Checklist in the appendix as a guide.
3. Find an agency that has a strong presence and can provide new residents for the home as people's needs change.
4. Make sure you outline specific responsibilities for each party involved in the development of the program.
5. Provide an assessment of needs for each potential resident before accepting him or her into the home. Use the Compatibility Checklist in the appendix as a guide.
6. Do not try to develop the home "forever," but, rather, enjoy the changes that will occur over the years of growth for each person. Flexibility is key in order to allow people to grow and change with life cycles.
7. Choose the best model for the group's financial status and stage of life at the time of development. For example, the same family-initiated model can be transferred, as this example shows, and the form of ownership does not have to disrupt the person's life.

Group Home Model Planning Story #2

The mother of a young adult with Down syndrome from Connecticut contributed this story:

My child grew up with children from four other families and we always talked about their living together as adults. We did not know how we would do it, but our children came of adult age at the beginning of the self-determination and deinstitutionalization movement, which paved the way for creative thinking about community models.

When our five children were fifteen, we decided to start looking for a house. We had all lived in the same town for years, so we were well known in our small community and by the school system, local businesses, and religious community. We discovered that the rectory of one of the churches was going to be up for sale since it was no longer needed. It was a nice house, but needed extensive repairs. It was well located in an area that was very familiar to our children. We eventually bought the house from the church and spent the next year figuring out the best ownership option.

None of us were in a financial position to simply own another home. We are happy if we can manage our mortgages on our primary residences, let alone come up with the extra money it takes to support a child with special needs at home. We got advice from an attorney who donated his time and who guided us into forming a real estate trust with all five families as trustees. We also worked hard on getting donations from the local businesses, and on getting a grant from the local housing agency to upgrade the property. With support of local realtors, contractors, and attorneys, we were able to get the house ready for rental within a year. Since our children were not ready to move in for quite a few years, we rented the house to accumulate some money, and put the funds into a reserve account until we were ready to make this a group home.

We worked with our local funding agency, who said they could not fund any one of our children, since they did not meet the state's priority status. Our children were not homeless, they were relatively "easy" to take care of in terms of behaviors and medical needs, and we were relatively young and able to continue their care. However, the state was willing to give us start-up funds of $50,000 for the initial operation of the house. If we were successful in getting volunteer staff and other donation money to operate the house, they would consider continuing that level of funding in future years.

After four years of renting the home we decided to make the move. Four of the five families were still interested in having their sons and daughters move in. The fifth family wanted to remain on the realty trust but wanted their daughter to continue living at home with them.

We worked together as a group, meeting constantly to make decisions about everything from furnishings for the kitchen to repairs by some of the families, who were contractors by trade. Everyone in this small town felt some ownership in this project and was very supportive of it. During the five years that we operated the house, we must have held fifteen spaghetti suppers and other forms of fundraisers to pay for the staffing and activities. We kept the house open Monday through Friday and our children returned home on weekends and holidays.

Although our group home was a huge success at first, we eventually realized that we could not keep up the pace of getting volunteer assistance, local fundraisers, and the professional clinical support needed to manage some of our children's behaviors. We also realized we were getting in over our heads with regard to employee benefits, labor regulations, relief staffing, and programming for our children to ensure that they were continuing to grow. Initiating the effort was a wonderful experience, but sustaining it for a lifetime became an overwhelming prospect.

We began seeking the assistance of an agency who would take over the house and ensure its permanency. We interviewed many agencies in the area and visited many programs. We agreed on one agency that had some experience and an interest in creatively managing such a venture. The most important factor in our decision was finding an agency that was flexible enough to incorporate this independent, family-driven model within their agency structure and ensuring that the house would continue to operate with family input.

After eight years of working with the agency—who brought in a fifth resident to get the house open on a full-time basis—we asked the agency to buy the house from the realty trust, as we no longer wanted the burden of ownership, repairs, taxes, insurance, etc. A memorandum of understanding was put in place stating that the agency could not remove any of our children from the house without our agreement. Removal would occur only if changing needs warranted such a move and we would work with the agency on an alternative arrangement for our child.

We have continued our family gatherings but only for holidays and anniversary celebrations, as we do not feel that we need to monitor the agency because of its consistency in management and open door communication.

Take Away from This Example of a Group Home Model

1. Form your group of families from people who have a common interest and goal and keep working at defining the vision into reality.
2. Use the community connections you have established.
3. Use the local resources for their fundraising abilities, as well as their personal interest in implementing your mission and vision.
4. Seek the support of an outside agency for management when and if you feel the time has come to do so. Use the Agency Checklist in the appendix to find a compatible match.

5. Make sure the finances can work by developing a solid budget based on the right number of people living together. This home is intended to last a lifetime.
6. Consider other ownership options as your group's life situations change.
7. Consider making changes to the ownership and/or corporate structure of the home as your life situation changes.
8. Work with an agency that has a source of referrals for new house members, as needed.

Supervised Independent Living Model Story #1

A parent of a young adult with autism from Massachusetts offered this story:

Now that our other children are grown and have moved away, my husband and I plan to leave our home to our son with high functioning autism when we downsize over the next few years. We developed an excellent transition for this arrangement by converting the attached garage in our home into a two-bedroom in-law apartment. We hired one of the aides at the school where my son used to attend as a companion to our 26-year-old son and gave him free room and board in exchange for living in the unit.

Our home is close to public transportation and has a lot of amenities within walking distance. This is great for our son, as we plan for him to learn to travel routine distances independently and to continue in his part-time job at a local supermarket. Our son can become quite isolated unless he is encouraged to deal with other people. He also needs very specific, clear, and consistent routines for every aspect of his life; any deviations cause him to get anxious and potentially loud and disruptive. He also needs incentives to engage in activities other than computer and video games. It is very important that the person living with him is patient, calm, and consistent, and that he understand our son's learning style. We hope to eventually find another roommate to live with him once we move out of the main house.

This arrangement has been working for three years. However, although it has been successful, it has not been without its bumps. This is mainly due to changes in the companion and the realization that more staffing is needed. One person simply cannot fulfill all of our son's needs, especially since he is not getting paid beyond receiving room and board. Although we found some very good applicants, we have been through two companions and hired several part-time staff to assist with some of our son's training needs. We are tired of recruiting and supervising and managing the personnel issues. Therefore, we have decided to work with an agency to manage the staffing and take over our responsibilities to ensure some permanency and relief for us.

Our son is at the point of being willing and ready to consider another roommate and we are going to work closely with the agency to locate a compatible person. We are also ready to move to a smaller home in a nearby town and are working with an attorney to make sure that our son's benefits are not lost when we transfer ownership of our home to him.

Take Away from this Example of Supervised Independent Living
1. Assess your family member's needs well and make sure you have sufficient staffing to cover those needs.
2. Assess your own time and ability to put in the effort before undertaking the operation of such a project.

3. If you work with an agency, ensure that you will have continued input into the items that are important to you, such as selection of a roommate, selection of staff, etc.
4. Work with an attorney and financial planner to make sure that transfer of ownership does not conflict with the family member's long-term benefits.
5. Make sure that the location of the home is beneficial for your family member's lifestyle and can enhance his abilities over time.

Supervised Independent Living Model Story #2

The mother of an adult son with Asperger syndrome who is supported by the author's agency writes:

I am a single, divorced mother with one son who is 39 and has Asperger syndrome and some developmental delays and mental health issues. Michael is an expert in several esoteric topics, including the Civil War and all manners of weapons that were used in every war from the creation of time through to contemporary days. He has a degree from a local community college and as far as his intellectual abilities are concerned, he could easily comprehend the course work of a much more difficult college curriculum. However, his social abilities and his obsessive need for order did not allow him to be successful in most college settings.

He has been in several different apartment living situations that included two or three others, as well as group home settings in which there was structured staffing with set times for meals, activities, daily routines, and the like. In each of these situations, I was initially sure I had found "the answer." It gave me peace of mind to know that someone was looking out for his safety and wellbeing. However, as he continued to be unhappy and not thrive in any of these settings, I realized that perhaps I needed to think about another model that dealt with the reality of what he would accept—regardless of what *I* wanted and thought he needed.

I found an agency that worked with independent living models and got an assessment of Michael's skills and interests. It was more of an inventory than an assessment, but it led to a discussion about what level of support and living situation made sense for him. Together we decided on a one-bedroom apartment with fifteen hours of outside staffing to come in during the week and work on his personal grooming, apartment organization, cooking and meal planning, and weekly schedule, including taking his medications consistently. The agency hired the staff person and helped me to find the apartment. I furnished it with items that I have been trying to get rid of for years from my own personal home moves.

I must say that Michael is happier and calmer than he has been for years. He seems to enjoy the privacy of his own company. Although it seems like a lonely existence from my point of view, he is visibly less stressed by not trying to socialize with others on a daily basis and compromise his need for order and consistency. The staff person is very clear and "undemocratic" about the condition of his apartment and the order in which it must be kept. He also introduces people to my son gradually from his other job assignments so that they have dinner with others at least weekly without my son feeling like he has to be in a social setting in which he is uncomfortable.

Take Away from This Example of Supervised Independent Living

1. Don't be afraid to make a change if you feel the model you have established is not working.
2. Seek an agency that can deal with unique models of service.
3. Until you are sure that the model fits, look for a physical setting that allows you to make a change without committing financial resources permanently (such as by purchasing a home or condominium).
4. Assess honestly whether what is important to you is the same as what is important to your family member.
5. Determine who will pay for the services and whether you can continue with the ongoing supports that will be needed.

Shared Living Model Story

A mother and father shared their story with Dafna when attending a conference on housing supports in Rhode Island:

We wanted our daughter to live with another family so that she could continue to have the benefit of the kind of family life she had known all her life with us. My husband and I are in our 80s, and, even though we are in relatively good health, we realize we have to make plans for the time when we are not able to care for our 47-year-old daughter. She is a mild mannered woman with Down syndrome who needs assistance with most aspects of personal grooming and daily care. She has some of the "typical" medical problems associated with Down syndrome, and therefore needs to have cardiac and respiratory monitoring as part of her life.

We could not see her moving to a group home with strangers, although our local funding source told us they might be able to place her in a group home when an opening arose. Instead we wanted to help pick the people she would live with. We also wanted it to be in a quiet, rural setting since she has always lived in a small town thirty miles from the nearest large urban area.

We began inquiring at our church and local senior center to see if anyone knew of families who would be interested in having our daughter live with them. After a year and many connections that led us from one person to the next, we met a couple who had just moved into the area and had two small children. The wife had grown up with foster children as part of her family, so she was used to the idea. They had moved into a farm house, which they were in the process of renovating, and the idea intrigued them. They were also very interested in the extra money that such an arrangement could bring to their family, especially since the wife had decided to stop working outside of the home for a few years.

We spent six months getting to know one another. We included the area funding agency in our discussions and got their commitment for funding this kind of model. The state agency advised us to go through a local human service provider agency rather than do an independent choice model in which we would receive the money, pay the provider, and oversee the service. [See Chapter 3 for an explanation of these funding models.] Even though we liked the idea of being in charge of it all, it made sense to go through an agency, which could offer a level of distance between the payments and the oversight. It took an additional three months, during which our daughter made visits to the family over dinners and weekend activities and had a few overnight stays. She was particularly happy when she could be part of decorating her own new room.

We must admit it was much harder for us than we had imagined when our daughter moved out. But not so for our daughter, who has begun to call this new home her "other home" after one year. The family has found our daughter to be a delightful addition to their family and have begun to talk about adding another person to the shared living situation. We are nervous about this option, but feel we need to be open to the idea, as it might be a good addition to our daughter's life and offer more companionship. The agency and the funding agency have assured us that any new person being considered will not have disruptive behaviors that will detract from our daughter's quality of life.

Take Away from This Example of Shared Living

1. Consider all models of service.
2. Use your own contacts and see if that leads you to what you want to achieve.
3. Be diligent in making sure that the shared living family unit can meet your family member's needs.
4. Trust your instincts with regard to the model you feel your family member needs and make sure you are truly taking your family member's needs into account, not just yours.
5. Be honest with yourself in assessing how you would feel if your adult family member begins to think of a new family as her family as well.
6. Be willing to consider changes to the shared living model such as other people being included into what you thought might be an exclusive setting for your family member alone.

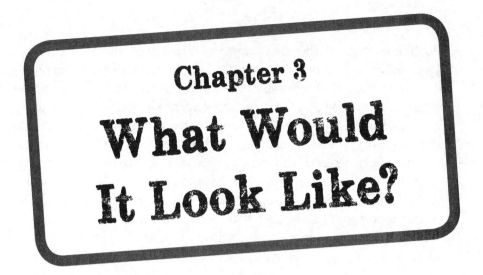

Chapter 3
What Would It Look Like?

In Chapter 2 we discussed the exciting possibilities for unique and creative designs of residential arrangements. Although it is beneficial to have so many choices, the variety can be overwhelming and leave families perplexed as to where and how to start in implementing a plan. We are devoting this chapter to presenting specific steps that will help you proceed sequentially in planning residential services.

Step One—Do Your Homework

1. *Meet with other families who are at the same stage of interest in residential arrangements as you are.* Do not be concerned at this stage with their family member's abilities or interests but rather with whether the families have a similar interest level in developing residential services. Determining compatibility and funding sources will come at a later stage. At this initial stage you are looking to develop a group of people who share the same interest in exploring residential services.

2. *Determine which state agency is responsible for providing services to your child when he leaves the educational system* and becomes part of the adult services system at age 22. If your child is still in school, this determination will be made by the transition team with your input (as discussed in Chapter 2). Every state has designated an agency to be responsible for people with developmental disabilities. In some states, that agency is a unique, independent one. For example, in Massachusetts it is the responsibility of the Department of Developmental Services (formerly known as the Department of Mental Retardation). Before it was an independent state agency, services fell under the Department of Mental Health as a division of the larger agency. In almost all states, those services fall under a larger umbrella of Health and Human Services.

These state agencies receive funding annually through the state budget. Families, agencies, and other interested parties advocate year-round for adequate funding to ensure that new funds are put in the budget to meet the needs of adults with disabilities, as well as to ensure that funds are not cut, which would limit what is already in place. It is no different than all the advocating for education or community safety needs, libraries, local aid, etc. which occurs constantly and throughout the country.

Once you determine which state agency is responsible for providing services to your child based on diagnosis, then that agency becomes the potential funding source for those services. You need to remain in constant communication with them to ensure that eligibility is determined. If you start this process while your child is still in school and have been active during the transition years, then the state agency designated as responsible for potentially funding those adult services will be determined prior to his graduation from the educational system. If you have not begun working with a state agency before graduation, then you need to determine which state agency is responsible for adult services based on the disability diagnosis of your child. See the box below for an idea of all the steps involved in determining eligibility with your state agency.

How the Eligibility Process Works in Massachusetts

A specific example from the state of Massachusetts might be helpful in helping you understand what might be involved in seeking services in your particular state. In Massachusetts, the Department of Developmental Services (DDS) serves individuals with intellectual disabilities. Those individuals have varying degrees of disability. In order to qualify for supports from DDS, an individual must complete an intake process. Adults must be living in Massachusetts and must have a diagnosis of intellectual disability as defined in Department regulations. (This definition can be found on the DDS website.)

Applications for DDS eligibility can be submitted directly to any DDS office or through the website. Applications are then sent to the Department Regional Eligibility Team (RET), and an eligibility specialist contacts the applicant or designated party. During the eligibility process, the individual is interviewed and documents regarding the diagnosis must be gathered. If an applicant is found ineligible, he has the right to appeal the determination. If found eligible, the information is forwarded to the appropriate DDS area office to determine the individual's prioritization for available supports.

The next step in the process is administration of the MASSCAP (the Massachusetts Comprehensive Assessment Profile), which is designed to assess what services are needed and how urgently the services are needed. The MASSCAP distinguishes between requested services and assessed need. Services available through the DDS are grouped into three categories: 1) supportive services, including family and individual support, employment support, and DDS-funded day supports; 2) community living services such as intensive family support and more intense individual

3. ***Work with your potential funding source.*** Even if you have not gotten a commitment from your state agency's funding source, it is essential that you make your needs known to them. If there is a state or municipal agency that is responsible for providing supports and services for your adult child based on his diagnosis, then ensure that you are well known to them and that you clearly articulate your interest in residential services. You need to maintain that relationship with the funding source on a constant and ongoing basis. Public officials are bombarded with unmet needs throughout the year. Even in the best of funding and budgetary fiscal years in any state, there typically is not enough funding to provide the necessary supports for people who are already in the system, as well as those who are just entering it.

  The fact that a state agency may tell you that there is not funding available does not mean you should accept that as a reality in the future. State budgets change

supports over 15 hours per week; and 3) residential services, which range from 24-hour services such as group homes to shared living and individual residential support services.

  The need for services can change over time due to the changing needs of the individual, the family, and the caregiver. In those cases, families make the changes known to DDS and request that a new MASSCAP be administered. If the person qualifies for a requested service, he is put on one of two lists. Priority 1 for a service means that the provision, purchase, or arrangement of a support is necessary to protect the health or safety of the individual or others. For most Priority 1 situations, service planning will be initiated within 90 days. Priority 2 for a service means that the provision, purchase, or arrangement of the support is necessary to meet one or more of the individual's assessed needs. DDS will then engage in active planning with the family and individual for those services while waiting for the prioritized services and funding for them.

  A third priority means no priority is assigned for a requested service. This means either that the individual does not qualify for the service based on the assessed need or that the request is for a service at least two years in the future. Decisions regarding prioritization for services are only made when a service request is received. If no request is made, no prioritization determination is issued.

  How the eligibility process works in Massachusetts is similar to how it works in other states, which all have a designated agency and a process for determining eligibility and prioritization for services. It is incumbent upon families to do their homework in order to determine the appropriate state agency and then to remain in active contact so that they are not overlooked when services become available.

constantly, as do needs identified throughout any given year. Maintaining a personal relationship with the proper person at the funding source will ensure that your needs are not forgotten or overlooked. Remember, funding officials and case managers are interested in providing services but need to be reminded frequently of your needs and interest in residential services. You need to make yourself a priority and there is no better way to do that than by making your presence known on an ongoing basis.

If you are not satisfied with the responsiveness of your designated contact person, it will be up to you to find someone else within the agency who will attend to your needs. Even if you are not expecting to use public funds for your child's residential arrangement, becoming qualified for services is essential for the future, as it may entitle you to supports, day programming, etc., which you may wish to use in the coming years.

4. ***Make sure your child's needs for residential services and day services are clearly documented in the Individual Transition Plan (ITP)*** before the age of 22. Adult services are provided "a la carte," as opposed to children's educational services, which are an entitlement until the age of adulthood as defined in your state (typically age 21 or 22). This means that each adult service—residential, day, vocational training, and support services, including respite for you or funds for your child to participate in recreational activities—is provided separately and is often funded through different state budgets and accounts and sometimes through different agencies.

5. ***Find out which agency(s) is responsible for which supports in your state.*** This information is available on the state agency's websites. ***Apply for all services for which you are eligible,*** even if you do not need them immediately. Establishing your child's name on a waiting list will allow you to have an entry date in requesting services. Sometimes a state will be subjected to a lawsuit in the future, which will entitle people who are on waiting lists to receive services. This has happened in many states and only people who were registered for services prior to the consent decree date were eligible for services.

Anecdotal experience illustrating the points above: Massachusetts was under a consent decree to provide residential services to the plaintiffs, who were defined as any families who had never received services from the state for their adult age children after they left the educational system. This *Boulet* consent decree, also known as the "waiting list" lawsuit, resulted in a five-year period, from 2001 through 2006, during which residential services were developed and offered to all people who were on waiting lists prior to the date on which the decree was filed. There was not a way to predict that this consent decree was going to take place and that the plaintiffs were going to be successful. However, families who had not registered for services prior to the consent decree were not eligible. It applied only to individuals who had already been known to the state agency of the Department of Mental Retardation and had been determined eligible for services even though they had not received the residential or day services from the state. Families who had decided that they were never going to be funded for services and therefore did not apply to the state to become qualified and eligible for services were not considered for funding when the *Boulet* suit was implemented.

The second lesson to bear in mind from this lawsuit is that by the time the plaintiffs agreed to the terms of the consent decree, many people included were not interested in residential services for a variety of reasons. Individuals who were known to the Department of Mental Retardation were therefore offered services as "substitutions." Again, there would not have been a way to know of such an occurrence in the past, but those who had kept their relationship current were gladly offered the new openings when the opportunity arose.

Step Two—Be an Educated Consumer

1. *Contact service provider agencies who provide residential services to individuals who have similar needs/diagnoses to your child.* Most states have a registry of such listings of agencies. Listings of licensed agencies are available through various websites which can be found on the state websites responsible for licensing private service providers or through the local ARC or other advocacy groups. You can start with agencies whose mission statements specify they provide such services and offer them in locations that are convenient for your family and your child. You may later discover other agencies that do not currently provide services in your area of choice but share a philosophy that agrees with yours. However, for this initial step, use the resources that already exist. Ask whether you can visit some existing programs and meet with key personnel who develop or manage residential services. Such meetings will give you an initial "feeling" for what to look for and questions to ask, and an ability to check your intuitive sense of what feels right for your particular situation. Ask the questions noted on pages 48 and 50.

2. *Speak with other families who have had residential experiences with provider agencies.* Call your local advocacy organization to find out whom to contact. As with all such research, finding a good match for your interest and your personality and philosophy is in part science and in part art. Obtaining information about an agency's reputation is very helpful in determining with whom you want to work as well as what residential supports can look like.

Step Three—Obtain a Residential Assessment

By the time your child has completed his education, you will probably have gotten many assessments, evaluations, and specialized consultations and recommendations. The type of assessment that is valuable in determining which model of residential supports is appropriate for your child is one that combines interviews with key people with formal assessments for community living. This evaluation may or may not use standardized assessment tools. The most valuable part of a residential assessment will come from the practical experience of the professional doing the assessment.

Where Can I Get Such an Assessment?

Some families choose to work with a *psychologist or social worker* who is knowledgeable in performing such assessments. A word of caution: note that professional credentials are not an indication of someone's experience with community based residential services. As with your research into agencies and residential support models, you need to be assertive in asking about the professional's specific experience with community based services since you are not seeking another evaluation that will simply describe your son's diagnosis, with which you are probably all too familiar by this time.

Comprehensive assessments vary in cost and can range from $500 to upwards of $3000. The higher cost does not necessarily indicate a more comprehensive or valid assessment. Assessments that include professionally administered, diagnostic tests tend to cost more, however. The best way to determine where to go is to ask what components are included in the assessment and whether the professional has experience on a practical level with community based services.

If you do not need diagnostic tests, then you may want to get the assessment from an *agency that provides residential services.* They typically have a coordinator or director on staff who has a combination of practical and evaluative skills. Most importantly, they usually know what is needed for success in the community. When considering using an agency that provides services, ask whether they only do assessments for people who will use their own services, since that is not what you are seeking. If they do not provide assessments as part of the range of their agency's services then you may not get an objective assessment of what your child actually needs; rather, you may be directed to services or residential arrangements that that particular agency already provides.

You may decide to use a *testing service,* but again a word of caution is in order. Remember that you are looking for practical experience, not simply diagnostic labels for your child's disability, which you undoubtedly have by the time you have reached this stage.

What Information Does an Assessment Provide?

A residential assessment can be done by a social worker, a psychologist, or a counselor experienced in evaluating safety skills, personal care skills, and psychological, emotional, and personality needs, as well as interest inventories and questionnaires aimed at assessing learning styles to determine your child's potential for learning community safety skills. The evaluator would begin by meeting your child. The questions and process used would obviously depend on his cognitive level and ability to communicate. At TILL, we use questionnaires such as "When I Move Out" as an entry point into the discussion about community living. That questionnaire is included on the next page. Your child's responses to such a questionnaire can provide insights into his view of living outside your home. It may also reveal his wishes and dreams, which must be taken into account, even if they do not necessarily seem realistic to you.

A good practical assessment will provide you with insight into your child's potential to learn skills necessary for successful community living outside of the family home. It will include a practical set of questions to assess comprehension as well as the ability to grasp and be taught issues that can affect safety and mobility in the community.

The comprehensive assessment should include:

- Dialogue or meetings with key family members, siblings, grandparents, parents, and others significant in the person's life and knowledgeable about his personality.
- Dialogue and input from the educational system, if the person was in school recently. If it has been many years since school, obtain the written records, but bear in mind that it could be very outdated information and not a true indication of current ability.

When I Move Out . . .

When I move to my own apartment/house/condo, the VERY first thing I want to do is:_____

_____ .

If I didn't have to listen to my mother or father or other people who are authorities in my life, I would: _____
all of the time or most of the time.

My favorite food is:_____ .

When I get to do what I want to do, I choose to: _____ .

When I am alone in a house or condo or apartment, I feel: _____

_____ .

When I think about moving out of my family home, I worry about: _____

_____ .

I wish I had a: _____ .

I would like to move to my own place just like my sister or brother or friend did or will in the near future. True / Not True (circle one)

Moving out of my family home is my idea. Yes / No (circle one)

If it is not your idea, then whose idea is it? _____

If I had lots of money, I would buy: _____ .

I would love to go on a trip to: _____ .

My favorite movie is:_____ .

I enjoy playing video games. Yes / No (circle one)

I like to be alone: sometimes / all the time / never (circle one)

I look forward to getting my own meals. Yes / No (circle one)

- Dialogue and input from individuals familiar with the person's work or vocational situation.
- Meeting with the person for whom residential services are being developed. The information gathered should provide an indication of personality, ability to live with others, and compatibility with others, as well as the individual's wishes and dreams. This is a critical piece of information and one that should provide an outline for the type of residential support.
- Standardized assessment of abilities, interest inventory, and personality assessments. In some cases, you may ask the agency to describe their internal assessment tool. Although it is not standardized, it may provide even better information, as it is based on their practical experience in developing residential services.

At the end of the assessment, the interviewer should have an indication of your child's self-care skills. You should know the answers to these questions:

- Can your child safely remain home alone for any period of time? How would he deal with strangers at the door, telephone calls from people soliciting money, repair people, etc.?
- Can he plan reasonably nutritious menus, shop for food, cook, and clean up?
- Can he clean, do laundry, and keep his living area reasonably neat and organized?
- Can he manage his medications?
- Can he attend to his own hygiene, such as bathing, brushing his teeth, and other personal care?
- Can he safely use appliances, such as a stove, oven, microwave, hairdryer, etc.?
- Can he evacuate in case of a fire or other emergency?
- Can he manage his own money and budget so that he will have some money left at the end of the week or month?
- Can he get around independently in the community using public transportation, a wheelchair, walker, or special transportation for people with disabilities?
- If he can't do the above now, what is his potential for learning? What kind of training and staffing is needed to provide that training?

If your child does not possess these skills, it should not prevent him from moving into a residential setting. This is to be used as a guide to determine what training and exposure can be offered before a move occurs. More importantly, it can guide your decision as to the amount of staffing and support that is necessary in the residential setting.

The interviewer should also have an indication of your child's personality, compatibility, and ability to live with others based on questions like these:

- Does your child do best with other people his own gender, or does he get along equally well with both genders?
- What is his personality like; e.g., shy, outgoing, cooperative, possessive, teasing, temperamental?
- Does he get along with some types of personalities better than others; e.g., noisy people, talkative, animated, sedentary, etc?
- What kind of environment does he do best in; e.g., quiet, structured, limit setting, etc.?

- Does he enjoy playing a "helping role" with housemates and therefore might like being with housemates who are less independent?
- How does he view himself; e.g., as nondisabled and therefore does not want to live with others with any visible disabilities?
- Is he physically frail or emotionally vulnerable so that certain roommates should be avoided? e.g., those who might push him accidentally or otherwise, boss him around, borrow his things?

If it is determined that it is not appropriate for your son or daughter to live alone, then consider some of the issues in grouping compatible housemates so that you can be an active voice in making this decision. Issues to consider when grouping people are:

- Age span—typically within a 10- to 15-year span makes sense, but as is true for others without special needs, the variability in behavior and attitude based on chronological age is vast. Don't rule out a larger age span, but use it as a general guide. Age span is especially important with one's first experience out of school, since someone who is 22 has a vastly different set of life experiences than someone who is 42.
- Mobility—not necessarily a factor to consider, but it can affect the type of activities the program's participants can be involved with, as well as the environmental arrangement and cost for adaptations.
- Location—the one factor that is truly nonnegotiable for many families, as they often want their family member to be close to them, as well as close to work or social connections.
- Cost—willingness or ability of potential families to pay for services, either publicly or privately.
- Number of people living together.
- Readiness of other applicants to move into the new arrangement.
- Readiness of the potential residential candidate and the individuals who would be living with him. Often the two don't coincide, but if they seem like a compatible group, then keep working with the hesitant individual by exposing him to the future idea of community residential arrangement. Setting a time limit, regardless of how long, will aid the process, unlike offering an undefined time in the future, which may never occur.

Step Four—Decide Who Will Develop and Operate the Residential Arrangement

The decision as to who will operate the residential arrangement for your family member should be made on the basis of your personal situation, how much time you want and can devote to the management of such an arrangement, your administrative talent for doing so, your financial capacity, etc. Most families seek an outside professional agency that specializes in operating such services so that they can continue to be a loving support to their family member yet not have the primary responsibility for staffing and management.

Some families wish to operate the services themselves and may form a corporate entity to operate it, such as a profit or nonprofit corporation. Some states have developed models of funding that allow families to develop their own models of service and manage them by using a fiscal intermediary agency. This intermediary agency takes care of the financial administration of services and pays bills, yet all decision making and hiring is done by the family together with the individual in need of services, if appropriate. For example, Massachusetts has developed a model called Agency with Choice (AWC) that operates in this way. New Hampshire has developed a similar model called Consumer Driven Services (CDS). This method relies on the family and individual to make decisions about services and changes as they are needed. You need to be prepared to be a very active participant in the recruitment, supervision, and management of support staff, even though payment for those services will be handled by a financial intermediary agency.

In thinking about which choice is right for you, consider the following issues in your personal situation:

- How much time do you have to devote to this venture?
- What else are you giving up in your life to do this?
- What will be the impact on your other family obligations? How will it affect extended family members or other children (depending on their ages and needs)?
- Can you handle staffing and recruitment tasks as staff members change and leave?
- Can you handle supervising the staff and create a work environment that encourages staff retention and growth?
- Do you want the liability inherent in employing personnel and the complications of owning real estate? Consider that it could cause undue risks for your personal situation and family.
- Do you have the funds to manage and cover expenses during vacancies if the arrangement involves others? To cover expenses when your child has increased needs due to age or medical needs, even if they are temporary?
- Do you have the funds to cover out-of-pocket expenses such as upfront real estate costs, vehicle repairs, etc. while you are waiting for reimbursement from funding sources or other families?
- Can you be objective enough to ensure that your family member's needs do not take precedence over the others in a group situation? If not, this would create inequities that are not beneficial for the long-term cooperative nature of such an arrangement.
- Can your family member truly be part of a cooperative arrangement that you manage without feeling that he has special rights or privileges or the ability to use his greater status to complain about others?
- Do you have a source for new referrals of others who might fit into this arrangement to avoid vacancies, which would be both programmatically and financially difficult to manage?
- Would you have the flexibility to change real estate arrangements if your family member, or others, if it is a group arrangement, need a different setting due to physical needs, growth in relationships, or a change in vocational opportunities? Would moving cause a financial hardship so that you might keep the physical setting longer than the needs warrant?
- Do you have a mechanism that will enable you to recruit, hire, discipline, and supervise staff, as well as offer them benefits and a salary structure that will support growth and successful performance?

■ Can you be objective enough to allow someone to remain in the arrangement while he or she experiences a temporary need for more behavioral or medical supports, even if you deem it to be detrimental to your family member?

Weigh all the issues above when considering this decision. Make a list articulating what you would hope to accomplish if you were to operate the arrangement by yourself or with a group of other families. Having control in decision making is the answer families most often give when asked this question. If that is your goal, then consider putting together a management agreement with an experienced agency of your choice to outline the type of decision making the families want to retain.

Another alternative is to choose a very active role in the way the program operates, yet not have the total responsibility for daily operations, legal requirements, labor laws, etc. In this case, you can work with an existing agency with which you have done the research as outlined in this chapter. If you choose this option and the provider agency is willing to work with you in this way, then consider putting together a management agreement with the agency. We provide a sample management agreement in the Appendix to this chapter.

You may decide that you want to start your own corporation and take on all the responsibilities on your own or with a group of families with a similar interest. Typically, families decide to take this step when they want to make all decisions regarding staffing (including hiring and firing), grouping of housemates (including asking people who don't fit in to leave), the daily structure, and the "rules" for personnel and job expectations rather than working within the policies of an existing residential agency with policies that guarantee equity to all employees and individuals. In this case, it is best to start your own entity and develop rules unique to this one particular setting. In making this important decision, you should also remember that the decision can be changed during the life of the service.

Choosing a Provider Agency

Selecting an agency to provide residential services to your family member can be a difficult task. There is a lot of information to sort through. Below, we list some questions that are important to cover in doing your research. Some of the items may not apply to your situation and therefore will not enter into your decision. Furthermore, each family has different concerns—which is why it is important to be clear about your views and priorities before starting your research.

A good place to start is by talking to as many people as you can about the agency that you are considering. What is the agency's general reputation? What experiences—good or bad—have any of these people or their family members had with the agency? If there have been problems, has the agency resolved them reasonably promptly to the family's satisfaction? If they were in your position, would they choose the agency as a residential provider, or would they continue looking?

In your interactions with the agencies, keep in mind that they will show you their best programs and only refer you to satisfied families. They want to put their best face forward. But even if an agency is being selective, it is difficult to create the illusion that it is well run and respected if that is not the case.

Last, if you own the property that your family member will occupy and are hiring an agency to run the residential program (as opposed to moving into housing that the agency owns), your focus will be a little different and there will be additional questions to ask.

The Big Picture

- **Mission statement**—What is the agency's mission statement? Does it mirror your values?
- **Size**—Some families prefer the intimacy of a small agency where they know everyone and everyone knows them. But there can also be advantages to a larger agency. If a residence is no longer a good fit for your son or daughter, there may be an alternative within the agency. This could mean less disruption and the ability to maintain contact with friends and familiar staff.
- **Location**—You will probably want your son or daughter to live reasonably close to you. Also consider how close the agency's main office is to your home or workplace. You might want to get involved as a Board member, volunteer for a committee, or attend agency-wide events. If so, you will probably be more likely to participate if you don't have to travel a long distance.
- **Specialty**—Find out how much experience the agency has had working with people whose needs are similar to those of your family member (autism, schizophrenia, head injury, etc.).
- **Age of the residents**—Some agencies are geared toward serving residents who are in their 50s, 60s, or even older, while other agencies have a more youthful population.
- **Experience**—Find out how long the agency has been in existence. Usually it is better to select an agency that has a proven track record of providing good quality residential services instead of a start up.

Visits and Meetings

- Visit some of the agency's homes. Are they clean and comfortable? Do the residents seem happy? Can you envision your family member living there?
- Meet with some of the managers and administrators. Keeping in mind that everyone will probably try hard to make a good first impression, what kinds of feelings do you get from them? Do you have confidence in the agency?
- If possible, meet with people who are working, or have worked for the agency as direct care staff. Ideally, you should talk to them away from the job site. You can get a good idea of the quality of services from employees and former employees.
- Consider attending an agency-wide event, if that is possible. You can learn a lot by watching how the residents interact with one another, and how the residents and staff interact. Do you see loving bonds and attachments, or boredom and indifference?

Daily Life

- How do families stay informed about the resident's health, sleep, behavior issues, etc.? How are any issues communicated?
- What are the agency's systems for handling medical, behavioral, or other emergencies?
- If your child is sick, can he or she stay home alone? Typically, residential staff begin working after 3 pm; however, other staffing arrangements can be made.

Ten Commandments to Follow When Planning Residential Services

1. It is never too early to start planning.

2. Be ready to compromise; you will not be able to have all of your ideal preferences in one setting.

3. Don't buy the real estate before you have a plan in place. As tempting as it is to seize a real estate opportunity, it will limit your chances of putting together a compatible group because each family has their own idea of a "perfect" location and setting and it may force you to settle on including people who may not be compatible for the setting, yet want the location.

4. Do your homework in researching and "shopping around" for the provider agency that "feels" right to you and shares your vision of residential living.

5. Establish your priorities of nonnegotiable items in a residential setting as well as those that are of less or no importance to you.

6. Obtain a residential assessment to assist you in understanding your child's readiness and skills for living outside of your home.

7. Be realistic about your long-range ability, time, resources, and reasons if you are considering developing and operating the residential program yourself rather than going through a provider agency.

8. Focus on what is essential for you and your child in a future residential arrangement; don't be distracted by the endless possibilities of models that exist.

9. Listen to your instincts about whether the timing is right for a move outside of your home. Keep an open mind about options, but readiness is a process and you and others who are part of the decision making need to feel that the timing is right.

10. Resist the urge to design a residential arrangement based on feeling that you know your child well and therefore know what is best for him. It is a role you have probably played since your child's birth—but remember, you are planning for his or her future, not yours. Include your child in the design and decision.

- Who takes the residents to their medical and dentist visits?
- How does the agency support its residents to practice their religion, attend services, and celebrate religious holidays?
- How are special dietary needs and food requests handled?
- Who does the menu planning, what kinds of foods are prepared and offered, and are there sample menus you can look at?
- How does the agency handle personal interactions and intimacy between the same gender and with the opposite gender? What are its policies on sexuality and privacy?
- What are the agency's views on human rights? How does the agency support the residents to make their own decisions?

Community Involvement

- How does the agency teach people to be involved in the community?
- Can you see examples of community recreation, volunteer experiences, trips, sports, or whatever else you hope your child will be involved in? What happens if one person does not want to participate?
- How does the agency deal with the neighbors and maintain neighborly relations?

Family Involvement

- How does the agency involve families in residential life? Are there get-togethers at the house, agency-wide events, picnics, cookouts, holiday parties, etc.?
- Does the agency have any policy about overnight or weekend visits with the family, either encouraging or discouraging such visits?
- If a parent were sick and unable to see his or her child, would someone bring the child to visit the parent? Has this ever happened?

Management

- What are the agency's hiring practices and procedures? How does their staff retention rate compare to similar agencies'? What, if anything, do they do to try to recruit and retain quality staff?
- What is the agency's track record? You can find out if the agency is doing a good job by checking its annual reports with the state licensing agency. These should be available on the Internet in most states. The reports will tell you how the agency compares to others in the state in key areas such as human rights, staff training, and overall quality of life in its residential and day programs. Five years of reports should be sufficient.

Obstacles You Might Encounter When Planning Residential Services

Despite all of the advances that have occurred over the past forty years in community based services for people with disabilities, there are still obstacles that stand in the way of such development. We are listing them below because it is best to be forewarned about what you might encounter. That way you can be prepared to deal with problems, and also be pleasantly surprised when the outcome is positive.

When presenting a vision you might have for your family member's residential arrangement, you might hear from other families or from public sources the following reactions:

Public Funding Sources' Concerns Can Include:

Q. Our regulations and state waivers do not allow us to do creative planning.
A. Ask to see the regulations, look them up online, or ask to speak with an authority who knows the regulations well. Often public officials cite limitations that do not exist when probed further.

Q. We don't have enough staff to work with you on this.
A. Reiterate that you will be doing all of the leg work. If expressed properly, your enthusiasm for the new project will be transmitted to the public official and convince him or her that others in the geographic area can benefit from your collective hard work.

Q. We don't know anyone else who has been successful in doing this kind of creative planning.
A. This is where your networking and research to date will come in handy. Prior to approaching the public agency, do your homework and talk to the local family resources, to schools, and to private provider agencies to see other models that have been tried and that work successfully.

Q. Cost sharing with you will "Open a Pandora's box" and everyone will expect it.
A. This is a very real concern for public funding sources, but it is important to advocate for your particular situation and reinforce the case that in reality you are helping others by developing models that will distribute funds to others as well.

Q. The state has no obligation to pay for adult residential services.
A. That is likely to be true in most states; however, the fact is that states have made a commitment to fund adult services. Your advocacy is merely reinforcing the principles of individuality, least restrictive alternatives, and the language that nearly all 50 states use, which encourages community residential models.

Q. Your plan is not available to everyone.
A. Emphasize politely but firmly that all services are not available to everyone, as needs differ. Again, the point is that by working with you at a planning stage, a more costly service can be avoided in the future.

Q. People without financial resources can't access the service. Public sources need to ensure equitability in service procurement and therefore can't support your idea.
A. This is a similar point to the one above, but we encourage you to be firm in insisting that equality is not achieved by depriving everyone of services. It needs to start somewhere, and your energy and community connections can pave the way for others.

Some of our readers might feel that they are not best suited for this kind of advocacy. If so, you may prefer to join with several other families or consider working with an advocate or an agency with whom you want to work long term to best articulate all of the points.

Families' Concerns Can Include:

Q. We won't be able to afford it forever.
A. This is one of the major reasons we strongly recommend that financial planning start as early as possible and with a qualified financial planner and attorney specializing in this area. Also see Chapter 4 for an overview of the financial issues and funding ideas.

Q. My other children will suffer if I use so much of our family's funds for this one child.
A. The answer once again lies in financial planning.

Q. I don't know other families who would be interested.
A. Your networking to date will be useful at this point. Furthermore, you may be able to affiliate with an agency that has other families who are of a similar mindset.

Q. Will I have to pay forever once I start to pay for it privately?
A. Our experience shows that indeed, once families begin to pay for services for their child, it is hard to get the state to take over the financial obligation. However, if your family circumstances change and can be documented, the funding source will often pay the costs. In this case, it actually works to your advantage. Once an adult with disabilities is in a residential setting outside of the home, it is highly unlikely that his services will be terminated. Therefore, the public source must find a way to sustain that residential arrangement. As with all situations, continued communication is key. Families need to continue to remain in touch with their public sources to ensure that their family member is not forgotten, even though their residential situation is in place for the immediate future.

Q. If I proceed with this idea, the public service providers in my area may be alienated and not provide any supports to my family member.
A. Presenting your ideas and maintaining good communication with public agencies responsible for services for people with disabilities is key. Remember, these agencies are comprised of people who want to do the right thing and to provide as many services as possible, but they often have limited resources and must make difficult decisions about allocating them. If you continue to communicate with them even when you do not need them, it will allow your situation to remain in the forefront in a very positive way. Invite them to holiday celebrations, inform them about your family member's successes, and, if you are working with an agency, make sure that the agency has a good system for communicating with the public sources.

Q. Some members of our extended family (in-laws, grandparents, ex-spouses) don't agree with our plans.
A. There are no easy answers to this problem other than to continue trying to convince everyone to reach consensus. At some point, however, you need to come to terms with the reality that 100 percent agreement may not be reached. It may be helpful to ask a counselor or other mediator who is well versed in family matters to facilitate a meeting to lay out the issues and help dissenting parties come to terms with the situation. Hopefully, you can agree on an action plan that allows everyone to proceed forward. The focus must remain on what is best for the adult with disabilities, not the individual members' personal agendas.

Resolving disagreements can be particularly complex if one party in the family is a financial partner in the adult arrangement. You need to stay focused on how to get that partner's cooperation with what you know to be the best plan. If you can provide recommendations from a professional outlining the best plan for adult services, it introduces a level of objectivity that cannot be obtained from you. If that does not work, then you may be faced with the difficult decision of whether you want to use financial assistance from that family member or not.

Provider Agencies' Concerns Can Include:

- Families are too demanding.
- It takes too much work and effort to develop new models.
- The public funding sources will never consider us for funding if we begin by paying privately for services.
- What if we fail? It will ruin our reputation.

If the agency presents you with these kinds of issues, you have not chosen the right agency—one that will embrace and welcome the opportunity to work in uncharted territories. Find the agency in your area with a reputation for innovation and working well with families as part of their team.

Our response and experience to all of the above obstacles is:

> ## DO NOT TAKE NO FOR AN ANSWER.
>
> Society has come this far because families and innovative provider agencies have refused to accept the status quo. This is not a time for the faint of heart. Persistence and tenacity will get us to the next stage of more creative, unique, individualized options with funding streams that encourage new opportunities and that will grow as people grow and change.

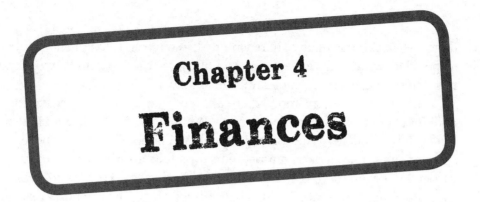

Chapter 4
Finances

Perhaps you have an idea of which living arrangement would be best for your child. You might have a specific location in mind and have some potential roommates or staff lined up. You might even have a commitment from the state agency that assists your child to pay part of the expense.

A key question in any living arrangement will be, what will it cost? This chapter explains the financial aspects of the different living arrangements. We itemize the various cost factors in each arrangement and provide worksheets to help you develop a budget.

Once you have an idea of the cost, another key question is, how can I pay for it? In addition to providing a home that is separate from the family home, you must pay someone to do everything the family did before your child moved out.

This chapter is for families who want to set up a private residential arrangement. We show you how to combine public benefits with private resources so that your child can move out. We don't mean to suggest that this is within everyone's financial reach. If your child needs 24/7 care (as Barbara's son does), the cost would probably be prohibitively expensive. But if your child needs less support, you may be able to piece together a satisfactory residential arrangement by combining your resources with public programs that pay for rent, staff support, food, and utilities. We give many real-life examples of families who have done so.

No Entitlements to Housing Services

Unlike children with qualifying disabilities—who are all eligible for special education at no cost to their families—adults with disabilities aren't automatically entitled to publically funded services and supports.

This chapter would not be necessary if there were enough housing and support services for all adults with disabilities who need them. If that were the case, a person who was completing her special education program at age 21 or 22 could move to an attractive residence when she was ready. There would be enough staff to help her live as independently as possible while keeping her safe. And of course there would be work opportunities and the chance to do something meaningful all day....

But as most parents know, there are few guarantees for services for adults with disabilities in twenty-first century America. While the Individuals with Disabilities Education Act (IDEA) mandates a free and appropriate public education for children with disabilities, there are no similar federal entitlements for adults after they have completed special education. Moreover, there is a critical lack of housing services. According to a recent report, there are more than 88,000 adults with disabilities on waiting lists for housing. This does not include individuals waiting to move out of housing that does not meet their needs and those living with their aging parents.*

With the lack of federal entitlements, each state must find its own way to solve the housing problems of its residents with disabilities. The federal government does encourage states by making federal dollars available through the Medicaid program. But this money does not pay for housing costs—those dollars must come from the states. As a result, each state has its own programs, initiatives, and priorities. The services your child will receive will depend on factors such as the health of the economy in your state; the priorities in your state (family living as opposed to group living); and having the "right" diagnosis (for example, in Massachusetts, autism is not considered to be a mental illness, and therefore adults with this diagnosis may not receive services from the Department of Mental Health). Luck and timing can also play a part. If someone is on a waiting list for housing and an opening comes up for which she would be the right fit (age, compatibility, geography, etc.), she might be given priority over someone who has been waiting longer.

What does this mean for families as a practical matter?

- Since each state's programs and rules are different, you must learn about the initiatives offered in your state. A good way to find out is to attend housing conferences and workshops sponsored by groups such as the Arc. You can learn what other families like yours are doing.
- If your child has been accepted by your state office of disability services, you should work closely with your child's case manager to find out what residential services are available.
- You can work with a nonprofit agency that runs residential programs for adults with disabilities whose needs are similar to your child's. Find out what programs and services suit your child best.
- There are some additional suggestions in Chapter 1.

Cost Factors

Every living arrangement has costs associated with a few key components:

- Staff and personal assistance
- Housing
- Transportation
- Food and house supplies

---

* University of Minnesota Research & Training Center on Community Living, *Residential Services for Persons with Developmental Disabilities Status and Trends Through 2008,* August 2008.

- Staff training
- Management
- Residents' personal expenses

Staff

The cost of staff is usually the most expensive item in any housing arrangement. In Chapter 1, we recommended that you obtain a residential assessment. The assessment will tell you, among other things, the number of hours per week of assistance the person will require in order to live apart from her family. Knowing the amount of assistance will help you decide which arrangement is realistic: living alone, or living with a live-in companion, a family, or a group. The costs and methods of payment differ depending on the living arrangement. There is also information about staff in Chapter 6, where we explain who works with people with disabilities, their background, training, and duties.

Direct Support Staff

As the name suggests, direct support staff work directly with people with disabilities in their homes. They provide assistance with activities such as preparing meals, cleaning, bathing, dressing, and taking medication, and do whatever else is needed to help people in their homes. Direct support staff are usually paid on an hourly basis and work up to 40 hours per week. The rates vary by state and by location within the state. Some states dictate the minimum amount that the state, as well as residential providers who have contracts with the state, must pay support staff. The rates are published on the state websites. In some cases, individuals and agencies pay more than the minimum rate in order to recruit and retain preferred staff. For purposes of the examples later in this chapter, we assume that staff are paid $10 per hour.

In addition to paying the agreed-upon hourly rate to your employee, you are also responsible for withholding federal income tax, state income tax, Medicare tax, and the Social Security payroll tax (FICA). Most states also require employers to pay worker's compensation and unemployment insurance. In our examples, we assume that such taxes and insurance increase the employer's costs by 13 percent.

Some agencies that employ direct care staff give their full-time employees fringe benefits such as medical insurance, dental insurance, contributions to a 403(b) retirement plan, and life insurance. Most individuals who employ support staff directly—as opposed to using an agency—do not provide fringe benefits. However, if you choose to provide such benefits, we estimate that they would add 15 percent to your employment costs.

Companions

Companions, sometimes called live-in aides, usually receive free rent in exchange for their services, and some also receive a monthly stipend. A companion can provide assistance to someone who does not need 24-hour care. Some typical duties can include food shopping, preparing meals, light housekeeping, and filling prescriptions and making sure the person takes them. There is a sample job description for a live-in companion in the Appendix to Chapter 6.

Most importantly, a live-in provides company for someone who may not form relationships easily. A companion can allow a person to have a somewhat typical roommate experience as opposed to a more childlike experience living with a family, or even living in isolation. The companion may go out to the movies or go shopping with the person with disabilities rather than just providing assistance.

Some states have Medicaid waiver programs (discussed below) that pay companions and live-in aides a stipend that is not subject to state or federal income taxes. However, if you hire a companion or live-in aide privately (as opposed to going through the Medicaid program), you must determine whether you have created an employer-employee relationship that requires you to withhold taxes and pay for unemployment insurance and worker's compensation insurance. An accountant can help you with this. In the examples later in this chapter in which a family hires a live-in aide or companion privately, we assume that the person is an employee. Accordingly, we add 13 percent of the person's salary as an employment cost.

Respite and Relief Staff

Most companions and live-in aides are free from their responsibilities one weekend per month, and most also receive two weeks of annual vacation after they have worked for a year. Respite providers take over during these scheduled breaks, and also when the companion or aide is sick or is called away for an emergency. If the respite worker is filling in for a companion or live-in aide, the respite worker usually stays at the resident's home. If the respite worker is filling in for a caregiver family (Shared Living Model), the respite can take place in different ways. If the family is going away, the respite provider can come to the resident's home, minimizing disruptions to the person's daily routine. Alternatively, the person with disabilities can stay at the respite provider's home. This can provide a mini-vacation for the person with a disability.

Another way to provide respite is through the networks that some family care providers form with one another. If a family needs respite, someone from the network can fill in. They either pay one another or exchange respite services. The network can give the individual with a disability more social connections and also provide the caregiver with a support network.

Family Care Providers

Family care providers in our shared living model receive a monthly payment that covers the housing, food, and personal services they provide to the person with a disability. Some states offer shared living programs that are managed by residential service providers and funded through the Medicaid program. Family care providers do not pay federal or state income taxes on the money they receive through these programs. The resident typically contributes a portion of her public benefits (SSI, SSDI, Veterans Benefits, etc.). In Massachusetts, participants pay 75 percent of their income from public benefits to the care provider.

Housing

Housing costs for the physical site are usually the second largest budget item. These costs include:

- Rent or mortgage, real estate taxes, and homeowner's insurance
- Common area charges for a condominium
- Utilities such as gas, electricity, heat, and water, as well as cable television, telephone, and Internet charges

■ If you or the resident own the property, you must budget for real estate taxes, insurance, repairs, maintenance, landscaping, and snow removal. You should budget for major repairs (roof, painting, etc.) and periodic replacement of appliances and major systems (heating, cooling, water heater, etc.). Many people keep a capital reserve fund for such contingencies.

There is a worksheet in the Appendix to help you estimate the annual costs of housing items.

Transportation

You should include transportation in your budget. The resident may need to be taken to work, to medical appointments, and on errands, or she may need daily bus or subway fare to get to work or to a volunteer position. Some groups take trips together on the weekends to the movies, restaurants, or outlet shopping.

Some group residences use a van for transporting the residents. It could be leased or owned by the residential provider, by the families who own the property, or by another entity (trust, LLC, etc.). You should include the cost of financing, insurance, gas, registrations, inspections, and maintenance.

Some companions and live-in aides use their own vehicle to transport the residents and to do errands. They typically receive a mileage allowance. The rate, which depends on prevailing gas prices, is currently about 40 cents per mile. You should make sure there is adequate liability insurance in case of an accident involving personal injury. Many standard automobile insurance policies do not cover work-related transportation, so there is often an extra premium for this kind of coverage. The employer usually pays the premium. If the companion or live-in aide does not own a vehicle, the family could rent one and list the person as an additional driver.

In some communities, there is accessible van or bus transportation specifically for adult with disabilities. The service may be free, low-cost, or provided on a sliding scale depending on one's income. Applicants would need to show they qualify by providing evidence of disability benefits (SSI, SSDI, Medicaid, etc.). You can find out about such services in your community by searching the Internet or contacting a local disability provider (the Arc, Easter Seals chapter, etc.).

Food and House Supplies

In our examples, we estimate the cost of food to be $10 per person a day for individuals who live alone, and $8 per day for those who share meals. If staff will eat with the residents, you should include their food in the budget. Also include household supplies, such as paper products, trash bags, cleaning items, and laundry supplies. In our examples, we estimate that these items would cost $1 per person per day, regardless of whether the person lives alone or with a group. You should also consider the cost of purchasing and periodically replacing dishes, utensils, cookware, and small appliances (toaster, coffee maker, food processor, etc.).

The Appendix contains a complete list of items you might need to set up a house.

Staff Training

Most staff who take care of people with disabilities receive periodic training in first aid, cardiopulmonary resuscitation (CPR), and handling blood-borne pathogens. You might want the staff to have additional training in areas such as applied behavior analysis (ABA), skill building, using adaptive devices, communication, or working with individuals with autism or Asperger disorder. The employer usually pays for this training.

Management

There can be a lot of paperwork associated with hiring staff and managing a residence. You can do it yourself or hire an agency. In our examples, we estimate that an agency would charge an administrative fee that is between 6 and 15 percent of the budget. The particular percentage would depend on the state where the residence is located and the size and complexity of the arrangement (single person versus a group, number of employees, etc.).

The management tasks include:

- Supervise staff. Someone needs to recruit, train, hire, and (if necessary) fire the staff; check references and perform criminal background checks; make sure staff come to work; and assure that staff are doing their jobs properly.
- Pay staff. This involves writing paychecks and withholding payments for federal and state income taxes, FICA, and Medicare taxes. You may also have to purchase worker's compensation and unemployment insurance.
- Pay bills, including rent, mortgage, utilities, cable television, etc.
- Periodically file reports with any state and federal agencies that provide housing, staff, food, and utility assistance to the person with a disability.

Residents' Personal Expenses

All residents will have personal expenses for clothing, medical insurance, out-of-pocket medical costs, dental care, toiletries, recreation, work-related travel, leisure activities, or the like. These are not strictly residential expenses, because the person would have to pay them regardless of whether she lived with her family or had moved out. Thus, we did not include these items in our sample budgets at the end of this chapter. However, you should be aware of them and include them when you are calculating the person's living expenses. There is a worksheet in the Appendix to help you calculate a person's daily living expenses.

Sources of Funds to Purchase the Residence

Let's say you have plans to buy a property for your son or daughter—or you are part of a group of families who want to purchase a property together. How will you finance the purchase? Housing can be expensive, and even middle income families can be priced out. Fortunately, if you don't have the ability to finance the property yourself, there are many affordable housing programs that encourage homeownership by low-income people, including those with disabilities. This section describes some of these programs.

If you are exploring financing for the first time, a good way to start is to attend a housing seminar in your state. Many disability groups such as the Arcs offer conferences and workshops on housing. You can learn about resources in your state and hear success stories from families who have achieved homeownership.

If you are further along in the process and are actively seeking a grant or loan, you can hire a housing consultant. These specialists can identify promising sources of public funds and assist with applications. Your local office of community development, Arc, or similar organization can probably put you in touch with someone who has worked with families in your situation.

Buying a Single Unit

Let's say you are buying a property for your son or daughter to live in. It could be a condominium, single family home, or shares in a housing cooperative. There are some public and private programs (described below) that assist people who are buying their first home. In order to qualify, your son or daughter must be the homeowner. You—the parent—cannot qualify because the property will not be your primary residence. Thus, an initial decision you must make before you apply for financing is: Whose name will be on the deed?

Deciding who will own the property can be complicated. In Chapter 5, we cover the various factors you must consider. These include your son's or daughter's ability to receive public benefits, including Section 8 rental assistance, after the purchase; the income tax benefits of home ownership (deductibility of mortgage interest and real estate taxes); and protection of the property from creditors. Your child's capability to manage her finances and sign legal documents is another factor. If your child has an intellectual disability or serious mental illness, the property should probably be owned through a trust.

Person with a Disability as the Borrower

Let's say you have weighed the options and decided that your son or daughter will be the homebuyer. Below we list some programs that assist people with disabilities to become homeowners. There is more information about these programs in the Appendix.

- *First Time Homebuyer Loans.* These loans, which are underwritten by the federal government, are offered through many banks, mortgage companies, and other lending institutions. They are targeted at low-income people who are buying their first home. Since most people with disabilities have low income, they can qualify. The programs offer below-market interest rates and waive some of the usual requirements for loans, such as minimum down payment, salary requirements, and credit history. Some programs also reduce or eliminate application fees, attorney fees, and closing costs. It is relatively easy to find a participating lender. Most banks that have mortgage programs participate or can put you in touch with a lender who does.

- *HOME (Home Investment Partnerships Program).* Every state has a HOME program that awards grants and loans on a competitive basis to low-income homeowners, including those with disabilities. These could be low- or no-interest loans, or "forgivable" loans that are discharged if the borrower continues to own the property for a specified length of time (such as ten years).

- *Community Development Block Grant (CDBG).* The CDBG program provides federal funds to all the states to benefit low- and moderate-income people, including meeting housing costs. The funds can be used for homeownership (down payment and closing costs), repairs, and accessibility modifications.

■ *USDA (U.S. Department of Agriculture) Section 502 Direct Loan Program.* A source of public funds for homeowners who live in rural areas is the 502 Direct Loan Program. This program offers mortgages to low-income homebuyers in rural areas. A rural area is a non-urban community that has a population of 20,000 to 25,000 or less. The funds can be used to build, repair, renovate, or relocate homes.

■ *Section 8 for Homeownership Program.* This program allows current and new households receiving Section 8 assistance to use the monthly subsidy toward payment of a mortgage instead of rent. (The Section 8 program, which pays rental assistance to low-income individuals, is covered later in this chapter and in the Appendix to this chapter.) The Section 8 for Homeownership Program can be used for single-family homes, condominiums, and cooperatives. Some, but not all, sponsors offer this program.

Parents and Others as the Borrower

If you—not your family member with a disability—will be the borrower, you cannot access these affordable housing programs because the property will not be your principal residence. Thus, you will have to look for alternative sources of funds. These include:

■ *Mortgage on Your Residence.* You could use your primary residence as security for the loan by refinancing an existing loan to obtain additional funds or by taking out a second loan in the form of an equity line of credit. One benefit to this approach is that the mortgage interest and real estate tax payments you make are deductible for income tax purposes.

■ *Commercial Loan.* You could obtain one of the commercial loans that are available to people who buy investment real estate. The loan would be secured by a mortgage on the property your family member will be occupying. You would report as income any rent your family member pays, and you could deduct the mortgage interest, utilities, taxes, insurance, and other operational costs on Schedule E of your federal and state income tax returns. Unlike families who use their residence to finance the purchase (previous example), you might be able to depreciate the property, which would further reduce your income tax liability.

Buying Property as a Group

Perhaps you plan to pool your resources with other families to buy a residence for your children with disabilities. Obviously, this is a significant undertaking that will require a large investment of money, time, and resources. We cannot overstate the importance of planning ahead for future years. Even though you may be able to afford the initial purchase price, you need to consider how you will operate the house in upcoming years. After all, a 22-year-old might live another 50 to 60 years or more. How will you—or more likely, your estate—be able to afford the mortgage payments, taxes, insurance, utilities, and repair bills? What if you need to expand the property to add another bedroom or office, or increase the living area? How would you finance it?

Anticipating future costs is a concern even if you are buying a single unit. But the potential problems are magnified with a group because the owners are financially dependent on one another. If one person or family cannot meet its obligations, the project can fail.

Another point that we emphasize throughout this book is that you must be realistic about the amount of personal support that your family members will need in order to live in the residence—and you must have a sound plan to provide it. This can be problematic when you are planning for one person, but when you are planning for a group, the potential difficulties increase exponentially. If one person has a problem and needs extra help, it can drain resources from the group. Staffing costs can easily overwhelm a budget. If your finances are exhausted paying for staff, there will be less available to pay for occupancy costs.

We are not trying to discourage you from joining with a group of families to buy a home or persuade you to abandon your plan. It's just that we have seen group living situations fail due to excessive cost, unanticipated expenses, caregiver fatigue, and family stress. We want you to protect your investment and give your project the best chance for success.

With these caveats in mind, here are ways that we have seen groups of families finance their residences.

- *Private Financing.* In our experience, most families who are buying a residence as a group obtain a commercial loan. The interest rates are higher than those for residential loans, but this is unavoidable. You can't qualify for the lower residential rate because the property is not your primary residence. If you are going to renovate or improve the property, you will need a construction loan. A contractor you hire will oversee the project and report to the lender, who will then release funds as they are needed to complete each phase of the project.

  If your long-term plan is to convert the property to condominiums or a housing cooperative, the individuals who will occupy the property or their families will purchase the units or shares. (Condominiums and cooperatives are covered in Chapter 5.) As the units are sold, the proceeds are used to reduce the commercial loan. When the property is fully occupied, the loan can be discharged.

- *Public Programs.* Perhaps you are planning a large-scale project that will involve renovating, enlarging, or even building a residence from the ground up. In addition to purchasing the property, you might incur expenses for architects, attorneys, and contractors, and for out-of-pocket items like insurance and building permits. There are public funds available to finance these kinds of projects. In addition to providing the down payment, some of them pay for development costs, and some even pay a repair allowance for up to 40 years.

  Unlike private financing, however, the public funds for larger projects are limited, and the process to obtain them is extremely competitive. You will be vying for financing with nonprofit agencies and for-profit developers that have a track record of developing and managing affordable housing. Experts say that lenders are more likely to select an applicant who is proposing to build a multi-unit property or even an apartment complex as opposed to a single building.

A good place to start your search for financing is with a local housing consultant who has experience with affordable housing for people with disabilities. The consultant can review your project and tell you whether it is economically feasible. If it appears to be and you want to go forward, the consultant can prepare the applications for funding. You will be responsible for paying the consultant's fee whether or not you are the successful bidder. However, some public financing programs allow consultant fees to be included in the project budget, so you will effectively be reimbursed for your advances. In addition to working on funding, a consultant usually assists with other aspects of the project, such as coordinating with the architect, attorney, engineer, or other professional you may be hiring.

The following are some public and private sources of funds your consultant may explore. There is more information about these programs in the Appendix.

■ *State Housing Finance Agencies* (HFAs). Every state operates an HFA, which is authorized by the federal government to sell tax exempt bonds for a variety of different public purposes, including assistance with homeownership and making properties accessible.

■ *The USDA (United States Department of Agriculture) Rural Housing.* If your project is located in a rural area, the *Section 515 program* can be used to purchase, build, repair, or renovate a group residence. The *Section 521 program* can provide a project-based operating subsidy that covers the difference between 30 percent of the tenants' income and the monthly rental rate that is approved by the program.

■ *HOME (Home Investments Partnerships Program).* HOME funds can be used to finance group housing, including single occupancy units, studio apartments, or multi-bedroom units. There is also a limited amount of tenant-based rental assistance available. Assistance is awarded for a two-year timeframe but can be extended if HOME funds are available.

■ *Community Development Block Grant (CDBG).* Similar to the HOME Program, CDBG provides loans and grants to nonprofit groups, housing developers, landlords, and other agencies as a grant or loan that must be paid back.

■ *Section 811 Supportive Housing for Persons with Disabilities.* Section 811, which is administered by the Department of Housing and Urban Development (HUD), assists nonprofit agencies to create supportive housing projects for people with disabilities, including group residences. The funds are provided as a grant that bears no interest and does not have to be repaid as long as the housing remains available for at least 40 years for very low-income people with disabilities. The program also includes an operating subsidy that pays the difference between the residents' contribution toward rent (usually 30 percent of their income) and the HUD-approved operating cost for the project.

The competition for HUD §811 funds is intense, and they are usually only awarded to nonprofit agencies with a strong track record in developing affordable housing. The application process is lengthy and expensive, and even if you are successful, it can take several years from the time you apply until you have the funds in hand.

Sources of Funds to Operate the Residence

By the time you have added up all the components of residential living, the cost may seem financially out of reach. However, there are several public benefit programs that help people with disabilities live apart from their families. This section explains the most common public benefit programs, and there is additional information about them in the Appendix. If the person does not qualify for public benefits, or if the benefits do not cover the entire cost, the family may be able to make up the shortfall. Thus, residential living can be paid for with public funds, private money, or a combination of both. The most common sources of funds are:

- Assistance from the state office of disability services
- Medicaid
- Housing subsidies, including the Section 8 program
- SSI and SSDI benefits
- SNAP (food benefits), fuel assistance, and utility subsidies
- Assistance from one's family or a trust

What Are Personal Support Services?

Many people with disabilities need help with routine tasks of daily life. Depending on the state, the person who provides the assistance may be called a Personal Care Attendant (PCA) or Personal Care Assistant (PCA). The person can help with personal support activities such as:

- Bathing
- Grooming (brushing teeth, shaving, etc.)
- Getting dressed and changing clothes
- Passive range of motion exercises
- Eating
- Planning meals, preparing meals, and cleaning up
- Toileting and physical assistance with bowel or bladder care
- Housekeeping, such as light cleaning, laundry, and organizing the home
- Shopping for food, toiletries, clothes, etc.
- Driving the person to medical appointments and running errands
- Mobility needs, such as transfers, walking, or using equipment to get around
- Medication management, such as helping the person fill prescriptions, organize the medication, and making sure the person takes it

Every state has a Medicaid program that pays for personal support services. However, not every state pays for every kind of personal service.

In many states, the Medicaid program allows the person with a disability to interview, hire, train, and pay the PCA. This permits the person to hire someone she likes and to train him or her in the ways she needs help. If the person with a disability cannot do this, a surrogate or representative can do so. In other states, an agency hires, trains, and employs the person. Regardless of who does the hiring and training, the person who receives the services must work with an agency that is eligible to bill the state's Medicaid program for the services provided.

Assistance from the State Office of Disability Services

For many people with disabilities, the largest amount of financial assistance comes from the state office of disability services. Each state has its own rules and procedures. Typically, a person must have a disability that meets specific criteria under the state's laws. Some states have income and asset limits.

Even if a person meets the disability and financial criteria, there is no guarantee she will receive residential services. There are no entitlements to these services under federal law. This is true at the state level too, although some states must provide community residences to certain classes of individuals who have benefitted from lawsuits brought on their behalf. For example, in Massachusetts, the state must provide community-based residences for individuals with developmental disabilities who are residing in state institutions but want to live in the community, as well as those who are inappropriately placed in nursing homes.*

Once a person has been approved for residential services, the state typically pays a non-profit agency to furnish the services. A few states run programs that place the money directly in the hands of consumers. This allows the person with a disability to decide how to spend the money on housing, personal assistance, job support, or other necessary items and services.

Medicaid

Medicaid is an important public benefit program for people with disabilities because it pays for staff to provide personal care services. Personal care assistants help with activities such as bathing, dressing, eating, housekeeping, and taking medication. The Medicaid program does not pay for housing. However, it can pay for support services that allow people to live in the community, such as personal care, day programs, supported employment, and case management. In most states, SSI recipients receive Medicaid automatically as part of their SSI benefit. (See the box on page 65 for more information on personal support services.)

Housing Subsidies, Including the Section 8 Program

Even if an adult with disabilities receives SSI or SSDI benefits (discussed below), she will need financial help to pay for housing. According to *Priced Out in 2010,* there is no rental market in the country where a person who receives SSI can afford to rent an apartment. As a national average, a person receiving SSI needed to pay 112 percent of her monthly income for a modest one-bedroom apartment. People with disabilities were also priced out of smaller studio/efficiency units, which average 99 percent of monthly SSI.**

Fortunately, there are housing subsidy programs that pay for all or part of a low-income person's monthly rent or mortgage. The federal Section 8 program is the largest housing subsidy program. Most participants pay about 30 percent of their income for rent, and the public housing authority (PHA) or other agency that administers the program pays the remaining rent directly to the landlord. To qualify for the Section 8 program, an individual must have low income. There is no asset limit, but if the participant owns assets that

---

* As the result of *Ricci v. Okin,* a Massachusetts court case that lasted from 1972 to 1993, individuals who were formerly residents of state institutions must be offered community residences upon request. In another Massachusetts landmark case, *Rolland v. Cellucci* (1999), over 1,700 individuals with intellectual disabilities who had been placed in nursing homes without medical necessity were moved to community residences.

** *Priced Out in 2010* by E. Cooper, A. O'Hara, & A. Zovistoski, is published by the Technical Assistance Collaborative, Inc. (TAC) and the Consortium for Citizens with Disabilities Housing Task Force. The publication is available on TAC's website: www.tac.org.

generate income (interest and dividends), the income can increase the person's rent. Similarly, if a person is the beneficiary of a trust that makes regular distributions, the distributions can be treated as income. Some agencies run Section 8 programs that pay a portion of the participant's mortgage and related housing costs (real estate taxes, homeowner's insurance, utilities, etc.).

Section 8 vouchers can be "portable" or "site-based." Someone who rents an apartment or condominium, or who lives in a housing cooperative, can obtain a voucher that will pay part of the rent. This kind of voucher is portable—if the person moves, she can use the voucher for a different property. A group residence can receive a site-based voucher that covers all the residents. If a resident moves out, the new resident would be covered by the voucher, while the former resident would lose her voucher.

If you are buying (as opposed to renting) a property and plan for your family member to participate in the Section 8 program, you must carefully consider who will own the property. It is usually best for a trust to own the property. The person with a disability cannot own the property directly in her own name if she will be using Section 8 funds to pay the rent, because the same person cannot be both a landlord and a tenant. The rules also prohibit a close family member (parent, child, grandparent, grandchild, sister or brother) from owning the property unless the housing authority makes an accommodation. (These rules are covered in the Public Benefits section of the Appendix.)

SSI and SSDI Benefits

The Supplemental Security Income (SSI) and Social Security Disability Insurance (SSDI) programs pay a stream of income to eligible adults with disabilities. In 2013, the maximum monthly benefit for the SSI program is $710 for an individual ($1,066 for a couple), although a few states voluntarily supplement the benefit. The SSI benefit is reduced in any month that a person receives unearned income such as interest or dividends of more than $20, or earned income of more than $85. SSI will also be reduced if a person receives any cash, or help with food or housing benefits. Recipients may not own more than $2,000 in countable resources ($3,000 for a couple).

In many states, SSI recipients automatically receive Medicaid insurance. This is explained in the Appendix to this chapter.

Social Security Disability Insurance (SSDI) is an insurance program that you qualify for by paying Social Security taxes during your working years. Social Security counts each quarter that you work as one credit. The number of work credits needed for disability benefits depends on your age when you become disabled. Generally you need 40 credits, 20 of which were earned in the last 10 years ending with the year when you became disabled. However, younger workers may qualify with fewer credits.

The Social Security Disability program also pays benefits to the disabled adult children of disabled, retired, or deceased workers. The monthly benefit is based on the worker's earnings record. There is no asset limit for the SSDI program. The monthly benefit is not reduced due to earnings, but if a recipient earns more than $1,040 in any month ($1,740 for a blind recipient), Social Security could deem the recipient to be not disabled and stop benefits. (The amounts quoted are for the year 2013. In most years, the amounts increase due to inflation.) SSDI recipients qualify for Medicare after receiving SSDI for 24 months.

In a typical scenario, a young adult with a disability will start out receiving SSI benefits at age 18, subject to the $2,000 resource limitation. Then, if one of the parents retires or becomes disabled (or dies) and begins to draw Social Security himself, his child with disabilities will automatically qualify for SSDI benefits, which are often higher than the SSI payment. If the SSDI payment is lower than the SSI check the person was receiving, he can receive both SSI and SSDI.

SNAP (Food) Benefits, Fuel Assistance, and Utility Subsidies

The federal Supplemental Nutrition Assistance Program (SNAP)—formerly called food stamps—helps low-income people buy food. Individuals with disabilities in any living arrangements can qualify. People in group living usually receive the lowest amount because the SNAP program counts the income of the entire household and then prorates the benefit according to number of household members.

All states have programs that assist low-income people with utility and fuel costs. To qualify, a person must own or rent her home. This means that people in group residences may not qualify.

See the Appendix to this chapter for more information about the SNAP program, utility assistance, and fuel assistance.

Wages

Adults with disabilities can contribute their wages to the cost of housing. However, wages are not a significant source of income for most people with disabilities. Moreover, if a person with a disability is working, her wages will often reduce or even eliminate the SSI or SSDI benefit that she would have received if she were not working. We discuss SSI, SSDI, and work in the Appendix.

Assistance from One's Family or a Trust

Some people with disabilities receive financial assistance from their families. The assistance can range from a token amount—such as an occasional bag of groceries—to the full cost of a private housing arrangement. Some people receive assistance from a trust. This could be a trust they funded themselves from an accident settlement or an inheritance, or a trust that was funded by a parent or other family member.

If an adult with disabilities receives regular financial assistance from her family or from a trust, it can be hard to avoid a reduction in public benefits. With SSI, for example, the monthly benefit is reduced on a dollar for dollar basis if an individual receives more than $20 in cash in any month. If an SSI recipient receives a gift card (such as a Visa gift card or gift card to a grocery store or to Sears), the value of the card is counted as income if the person can use it to buy food, or if the card can be resold. And if an SSI recipient receives outside assistance with housing costs (rent, mortgage, utilities, water, or common area charges for a condominium), her SSI benefit can be reduced by up to one-third of the monthly amount.

This raises the question: How does Social Security keep track of recipients' finances? One way is through voluntary reporting. All recipients are supposed to report changes in income and resources within ten days of receipt. Another way is through periodic reviews. The agency may ask a recipient to come to the office and bring records such as pay stubs, W-2 forms, and bank statements. At the meeting, the recipient might also be asked if she has received any gifts or financial assistance of any kind from her family, friends, or a trust.

Besides having her SSI benefits reduced, a person who receives regular financial assistance may also face a rent increase if she receives a housing subsidy (such as Section 8). As explained earlier in this chapter, participants in the Section 8 program pay a portion of their income—30 percent in most cases—as rent. The program can count as "income" any amounts the person receives on a regular basis. If the person's family or trust pays her monthly rent or utilities, or gives her spending money on a regular basis, this would be considered "income" that would increase her rent share. There is additional information about the Section 8 program in the Appendix to Chapter 4.

If a family member is relying on you for financial assistance, you should plan for what would happen if you can no longer provide the assistance due to financial reversals, your disability, or your death. We cover this topic in detail in Chapter 9.

Reducing Costs by Sharing Expenses

For some people, the cost of living alone may be out of reach financially. One way to reduce costs is to share expenses with other people with disabilities who have similar needs for assistance. Roommates and housemates can divide housing costs, and they may be able to share staff as well. For example:

Beth wants to live in her own apartment, but needs someone to stay with her overnight. She also needs help with cooking, food shopping, budgeting, and cleaning. Her family locates someone who is willing to live with Beth, in exchange for free rent and a stipend of $1,000 per month.

Beth's Monthly Budget:
- Rent and utilities for a 2-bedroom apartment—$1,200
- Cable TV/telephone/Internet—$175
- Stipend for live-in assistant—$1,000
- Taxes on stipend (13%)—$130
- Food and house supplies—$300
- **Total—$3,055**

Beth finds a roommate who has similar needs for assistance. Beth's assistant agrees to help both of them for an increased stipend of $1,500 per month. They rent a three-bedroom apartment that can accommodate the live-in assistant.

Budget for Beth and Her Roommate:
- Rent and utilities for a three-bedroom apartment—$1,500
- Cable TV/telephone/Internet—$175
- Stipend—$1,500
- Taxes on stipend (13%)—$195
- Food and house supplies—$600
- **Total—$3,970**
- *The cost per person is $1,985 per month.*

Beth and her roommate could further reduce their costs by obtaining Section 8 vouchers. They would each pay about 30 percent of their income as rent, and the local housing authority would pay the balance of the rent directly to the landlord. Their landlord would have to agree to participate in the Section 8 program. Beth and her roommate would also need an accommodation from the public housing authority that would permit them to rent a three-bedroom apartment for two people.

Beth or her roommate might also qualify for a Medicaid-funded program that would pay the caregiver's stipend. In most states, there are nonprofit agencies that operate programs that pay a caregiver to provide services in a person's home.

Sample Budgets

The following are some sample budgets for different living arrangements. In most of the examples, we assumed that the person has Medicaid or other health insurance that pays for medical, dental, prescription drug, and vision costs. These expenses would be the same whether the person is living with his family or in his own home.

Story #1: Supervised Independent Living— Public Funds & Family Contribution

Jeff, age 35, uses a wheelchair due to injuries he received in a car accident. He lives by himself in a fully accessible one-bedroom apartment in a complex for the elderly/disabled. He receives 21 hours per week of staff assistance for help with dressing, bathing, food shopping, and housekeeping. Jeff receives SSI, Medicaid, and a housing subsidy.

Jeff's Monthly Budget:
- Staff—$912
- Rent (including utilities)—$1,500
- Cable/telephone/Internet—$175
- Transportation—$40
- Medical/dental (Medicaid pays)—$0
- Food and house supplies—$330
- Personal expenses—$165
- **Total—$3,032**

Jeff's Income:
Jeff receives some public benefits that reduce his living expenses. Still, he does not have enough money to support himself, so his family pays for his cable/telephone/Internet charges.
- SSI benefit—$710 per month
- Medicaid—Medicaid pays for 21 hours per week of personal care assistance. Jeff pays nothing for this service.
- Housing subsidy—Jeff pays 30 percent of his income as rent. The balance of the rent is subsidized by the local housing authority.
- Food—Jeff receives $100 per month in SNAP benefits.

Jeff's Adjusted Budget:
- Rent (including utilities)—$213 (30% of the $710 SSI benefit)
- Staff—$0

- Cable/telephone/Internet—$0 (family contribution)
- Transportation—$40
- Medical/dental (uninsured)—$0
- Food—$230
- Personal expenses—$227
- **Total—$710**

Story #2: Supported Independent Living—Privately Funded

Cindy, age 29, lives with a companion (a graduate student) in an apartment that Cindy's father rents for them. The apartment is near public transportation. Cindy is quite independent. She can stay home alone and take public transportation to her part-time job at a museum and to her volunteer position at a local animal shelter. Cindy's companion receives free room and board in exchange for living with Cindy. In addition to keeping Cindy company, the companion helps Cindy with food shopping, money management, keeping the apartment neat and organized, and ensuring that Cindy takes her medication. A residential provider Cindy's father has hired pays Cindy's bills and oversees the arrangement.

Cindy's Monthly Budget:
- Rent and utilities—$2,000
- Cable/telephone/Internet—$175
- Transportation—$50
- Food and house supplies (2 people)—$670
- Medical/dental (covered under her father's plan)—$0
- Agency fee—$450 (15% of budget)
- Cindy's personal expenses (entertainment, personal items, etc.)—$300
- **Total per month—$3,545**

Cindy's Income
Cindy has some income to offset these expenses, and her father makes up the shortfall.
- Wages—$280
- SSDI benefit—$950
- Family contribution—$ 2,415
- **Total $3,545**

Potential Ways to Reduce the Family's Contribution:
Cindy could apply for a housing subsidy, such as Section 8. Since she needs a two-bedroom apartment for herself and her companion, she would have to ask the local housing authority for a reasonable accommodation to permit her to live independently with support. If her current landlord will not agree to participate in the Section 8 program, she would have to move to a different apartment.

Adjusted Cost: Cindy would pay 30 percent of her income ($369) as rent. The housing authority would pay the balance of the rent directly to the landlord. This would reduce Cindy's total monthly expenses to $2,014, and her family's contribution to $784.

Story #3: Supported Independent Living—Privately Funded

Peggy, age 30, needs 24-hour assistance due to a seizure condition .She has a live-in companion who is home whenever Peggy is home. The companion is free from her duties for one weekend per month and two weeks in the summer. There is relief staff during these times. Peggy's family leases a car for the companion to use and adds the companion as an insured driver on the policy.

Peggy's Annual Budget:
- Stipend for companion—$24,000
- Relief staff (1 weekend per month, and 2 months summer vacation)—$7,000
- Taxes for companion—$3,120
- Taxes for relief staff—$910
- Rent and utilities—$24,000
- Cable/telephone/Internet—$2,100
- Food and house supplies (2 people)—$8,000
- Vehicle lease and gas—$6,400
- Agency fee (15% of budget)—$7,150
- Peggy's personal expenses—$2,000
- **Total—$84,680**

Peggy's Annual Income:
- Peggy receives SSDI benefits of $900 per month ($10,800/year)
- Peggy's family contributes $73,880

Potential Ways to Reduce the Family's Contribution:
Peggy could obtain Section 8 benefits and then pay only 30 percent of her income as rent. However, she might have to move to a different apartment, because the local housing authority would probably not approve a two-bedroom apartment that costs $2,000 per month, even though it includes utilities.

Peggy could qualify for about $100 per month in SNAP (food) benefits (the Supplemental Nutrition Assistance Program).

Another way to reduce costs would be to add a roommate. The roommate could share the costs of staff, rent, utilities, and transportation. There would need to be a larger apartment to accommodate both women and their live-in companion.

Story #4—Shared Living—Publicly Funded

Erica is a mild mannered, pleasant young woman, aged 25. She is very willing to cooperate with anything that is asked of her but shows little initiative or preferences for recreational or social interests. She needs prompting and assistance with most daily living skills, although it is assumed that she will learn to accomplish many of these somewhat independently once she knows the routines of the household. Since she recently moved in with a shared living family, they are working on developing those skills as she gets accustomed to living without the parental assistance that she got at home. Erica's program is managed by a local nonprofit agency that receives funding from the state office of disability services. The agency monitors the family to make sure that Erica is well cared for and that the money is benefitting her.

Erica lives with a couple and their two young children. The couple pays for all food and shelter items. Erica attends a state-funded day program and receives free transportation between her home and the program. The couple takes Erica on vacations with them. They receive funding for respite care, which allows them two weeks' vacation and one weekend a month without Erica. During these breaks, Erica stays with another family who belongs to a local respite provider's network. Often the providers in this network exchange respite care for one another or they are paid for their time, depending on whether or not an exchange of time is feasible.

The couple receives a stipend of $18,000 per year from the agency that manages the program, and they are expected to pay for all food and personal care costs for Erica. The state also gives the family a clothing allowance of $400 per year for Erica. Under the program rules, Erica contributes 75 percent of her monthly SSI benefit of $710 to the family. She uses the remaining $177.50 for her personal expenses.

Story #5—Shared Living—Privately Funded

Peter, age 27, is easy going, fairly independent, and needs minimal assistance with his daily routines. Peter's parents are deceased, but they left funds for him in a special needs trust that is managed by his sister. Peter, unlike Erica (Story #4), does not qualify for a shared living program in his state, so his trust pays his living expenses. Peter lives with a couple and their two children. He attends a publicly funded vocational day program five days a week, and he receives free transportation between home and his program. The family is free from their responsibilities to care for Peter for one weekend each month and for two full weeks each year. During these breaks, Peter stays with his sister and her husband.

Peter's Annual Budget:
- Stipend for the family—$24,000
- Taxes for the family—$3,120
- Respite for family—$7,000
- Peter's personal expenses—$2,000
- **Total—$36,120**

Peter's Annual Income:
- SSI—$8,520
- Contribution from Peter's trust—$27,600

Story #6: Group Living in Agency-owned Housing—Publicly/Privately Funded

A three-family residence is the home to five men with disabilities. Two residents live on the first floor, three residents live on the second floor, and a live-in couple and their two children live on the third floor. The property, which is owned by the agency that runs the program, is accessible by public transportation. The live-in family receives free rent in exchange for being available overnight, and they are paid to provide 25 hours per week of assistance to the residents. Some residents pay privately for additional personal assistance from outside staff to help them with money management, hygiene, and nutrition.

Annual Residential Budget:
- Live-in staff—$0 (exchange for free room and board)
- Additional support provided by live-in staff—$13,000
- Fringe benefits (15%)—$1,950
- Taxes for additional staff (13%)—$1,690
- Staff training—$1,000
- Rent—$24,000
- Travel reimbursement for live-in staff—$1,250
- Food and house supplies—$18,250
- Group activities—$3,000
- Agency fee (15% of budget)—$9,471
- **Total—$73,611**
- *Divided by 5—$14,722 per resident*

Residents' Income:
All residents receive SSI or SSDI benefits, and some have wages from employment. Each resident has a Section 8 voucher that allows her to pay 30 percent of her income as rent. The public housing authority pays the balance of the rent to the agency.

Budget for each Resident:
Each resident pays $14,722 annually. Residents who require additional assistance with money management, nutrition, etc. pay for this privately. The residents also pay their personal expenses such as clothing, toiletries, and work-related transportation. The residents pay for these expenses with the 70 percent of their income (SSI/SSDI and wages) that remains after they have paid 30 percent of such income for rent. The balance is paid by the residents' families or with a grant from the state department of developmental services.

Story #7: Group Living—Privately Funded Program, Privately Owned Housing

Two men and three women with disabilities live together in a single-family residence. The residents are fairly independent and can stay alone for up to three hours. They need reminders to make good food choices, not talk to strangers in the community, make sound purchases, and use the Internet safely. A live-in staff person receives free rent in exchange for being available overnight. Additional staff provide 104 hours per week of services to the residents as a group. One of the resident's families bought the home and pays the mortgage, real estate taxes, and insurance. All the families pay an agency to run the program and handle the administrative tasks (supervising the staff, paying the bills, maintaining the house, etc.).

Annual Budget:
- Live-in staff—$0 (exchange for free room and board)
- Additional staff (104 hrs. per week)—$63,250
- Fringe benefits for additional staff (15%)—$9,500
- Taxes for additional staff (13%)—$8,250
- Utilities—$4,000
- Cable/telephone/Internet—$2,100
- Travel reimbursement for staff—$1,000

- Food and house supplies—$18,250
- Staff training—$2,000
- Group activities—$3,000
- Agency fee—$16,700
- **Total—$128,050**
- *Each resident pays $25,610*

All residents receive SSI or SSDI benefits, and so are able to contribute up to the extent of their benefit and earned income annually toward their costs. Some have wages from employment. They use their income for their personal expenses.

Potential Reductions to Costs

If a resident qualified for state-funded residential services, the state office that supports the person might pay for all or part of the residential services. This would reduce or eliminate the need for that resident's family to contribute to the program costs. In most states, the resident would contribute 75 percent of her income (from SSI/SSDI and wages) to the agency to offset the cost of this support.

Story #8: Group Living—Apartment Building

An apartment building houses sixteen residents and one staff person in four three-bedroom apartments and five one-bedroom apartments. All the residents have the skills to live independently but would not have a very good quality of life if they did so. There is a large living room/ activity room in the basement where the residents can spend time together. The area includes a kitchen where they can cook meals. Typically, the residents cook a group meal once a week. A live-in staff person is on call overnight. Another staff person provides assistance to the residents 20 hours per week. Some residents pay privately for help with budgeting, food shopping, and medication management. On weekends they might go to a concert, local festival, or outlet shopping.

Annual Program Budget:
- Live-in staff —$0 (exchange for free rent)
- Additional staff (20 hrs. per week)—$10,400
- Fringe benefits for additional staff (15%)—$1,560
- Taxes for additional staff (13%)—$1,350
- Utilities for common areas—$1,500
- Travel (mileage for staff)—$1,000
- Food for weekly group meals ($6 per meal per person)—$9,984
- Staff training—$2,500
- Group activities—$3,000
- Agency fee—$18,000
- **Total—$49,294 (without food or rent)**
- *Cost for each resident—$3,080*

Additional Living Expenses:
- Rent—A one-bedroom apartment rents for $1,245 per month, and a three-bedroom apartment rents for $2,200 ($734 per person). All the residents have Section 8 vouchers, so they pay about 30 percent of their income as rent.

- Cable/telephone/Internet—These services are bundled and cost about $175 per month per apartment.
- Food—The residents eat dinner together twice a week. We included the cost of these meals under the program budget. The residents buy food for the rest of the week separately.
- Additional personal assistance—The residents can pay for personal assistance at a rate that varies from $10 to $35 per hour.
- Personal expenses—Residents pay their own personal expenses for transportation, clothes, toiletries, etc.

Annual Income:

All the residents receive SSI or SSDI benefits, and so are able to contribute toward their monthly costs (after subtracting 30 percent of their income for their Section 8 housing vouchers). Some have wages from employment. Residents who receive SSI pay 30 percent of their income ($213 in 2013) toward their rent. Residents who receive SSDI or work pay slightly more (but never more than 30 percent of total income). They use their income for their personal expenses.

In addition, some residents receive $50–$100 per month in SNAP (food) benefits. Some residents receive utility assistance of about $15 per month.

Story #9—Self-Pay with No Public Benefits and Minimal Family Assistance

Laura, age 28 and a high school graduate, has been diagnosed with Asperger syndrome but has never been able to qualify for public benefits such as SSI or Medicaid. Her disability is deemed to be too mild. She insists on living independently, so when she received a Section 8 voucher, she moved out of her mother's home into an apartment, which is not in an especially safe part of town. Laura needs guidance in financial issues, managing her time, and keeping her apartment clean, as well as reminders about hygiene and personal care. Her mother worries about her judgment, gullibility, and safety. Laura rejects suggestions from her mother, who is wondering if she should seek out support at a local college that has a social work program. A friend whose daughter has similar issues arranged for students in that program—both male and female—to befriend her daughter. Laura's mother wonders if this could work for Laura.

Laura earns $950 per month working part-time in retail sales. She relies on programs that assist low-income people: subsidized housing, SNAP food benefits, and utility assistance. Laura's mother pays for her health insurance. She wants Laura to have medical care if she needs it—and she also hopes that Laura will see a social worker or therapist who will accept the insurance.

Laura's Monthly Budget:

- Rent (with a Section 8 voucher)—$285
- Utilities—$50
- Cell phone—$60
- Food (with SNAP benefits)—$200
- House supplies—$30

- Medical insurance—$0 (mother pays)
- Dental care and uninsured medical bills—$50
- Transportation—$60
- Personal expenses—$215
- **Total—$950**

This is an extremely bare bones budget, but typical for a very low-income wage earner who lives a marginal lifestyle. The kinds of public benefits that Laura relies on (subsidized housing, utility assistance, and SNAP food benefits) are available to low-income individuals, whether or not they have a disability. Fortunately for Laura, her mother can help her if she loses her job and can't pay her bills.

Laura's inexperience and gullibility, coupled with her refusal to accept suggestions from her mother, are concerning. We don't especially like her mother's idea of soliciting unpaid volunteers to help her daughter. There is too much potential for exploitation. A better alternative, if her mother can afford it, is to pay a young woman to spend time with Laura. This might be a better use of her money than paying for health insurance. If she can wait until 2014, Laura may be able to get very low-cost or free private medical insurance under the federal healthcare law. She would qualify for a federal subsidy because of her low earnings.

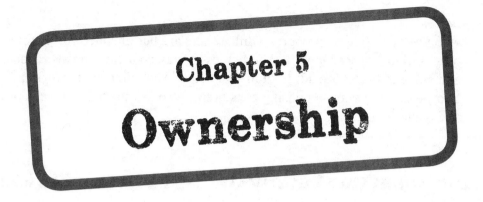

Chapter 5
Ownership

This chapter covers the different ways that individuals and groups can own a residence. The options range from basic (property owned by the person with a disability) to sophisticated (limited liability company or condominium project).

We don't mean to suggest that everyone should buy a property, or even that ownership is best for everyone. There can be advantages to moving into housing that the service provider owns or rents. It is convenient, and there is no cost. The properties are safe and are maintained under state and local fire and health standards.

Reasons to Consider Buying Property

Individuals and their families buy properties for many reasons. For some, moving into agency-owned property may not be a choice—it is simply not available. Other families want the permanence that owning the home can provide. Some individuals seek privacy that is not available in group living.

The main advantage to owning the property is control. You can personalize the property to suit your taste. You can decide who will live there, and you can choose the staff who will work with your child. You don't have these options with agency-controlled housing. Let's say you don't like the house manager, or the staff are not doing their jobs. If the agency won't fix the problem, your options are limited or nonexistent. The agency—not the residents—gets to choose the staff. Or let's say your child's housemate is disruptive or even violent. If the families own the residence, they can ask the disruptive person to leave. An agency is not always willing to do this.

Owning the property puts you in charge. If the agency is not living up to your expectations, you can fire it and hire a different one. Often the threat of removal can be sufficient to persuade the agency to respond to your requests.

Deciding Who Should Own the Property

When you decide to buy a residence, that can raise the question: Who should own the property? There is no one-size-fits all answer. Some options work well for an individual who lives alone in the property, while others are better suited for a group. Public benefit programs that assist people in their homes (discussed below) are also a factor. The services and eligibility rules are different in every state. You will need to work closely with a local attorney, and possibly a housing consultant, who is knowledgeable about real estate law and public benefits.

Pitfalls When One Family Owns the Group Residence

Sometimes when a group of families plan for their children to live together, one family might buy or donate the property and pay all the carrying charges themselves. While the other families might initially see this as a benefit, it can potentially undermine the harmony of the group—or even cause it to collapse altogether.

Sometimes the financial inequity can create a sense of entitlement for the owner. The hidden (or overt) message is, "You are living in my house, and I can make the rules." This perceived sense of entitlement can extend to major decisions (who can live there) as well as minor ones (menus, décor, thermostat setting, etc.). There is the implicit threat that if you can't get along, you may be asked to leave. At one house, the owners picked up and dropped off their child on their own schedule, without regard to the other residents' plans. Everyone at the group residence had to wait until the owner's child was picked up, and then they had be back in the group residence in time for his arrival.

Even if one family is paying the major expenses (real estate taxes, insurance, mortgage), there can still be a financial burden for the other residents (or the agency) over time. In one case, an owner postponed repairs so that the house became less energy efficient and cost more to heat and cool. Since everyone was sharing utility costs, this increased their expenses. Another owner avoided making a septic repair, resulting in excessive water bills for the agency. Yet another owner postponed necessary roof repairs, and everyone had to live with a leaky roof.

When one family owns the property, it can undermine their adult child's sense of independence. After all, if you are living in your parent's house, how much independence have you truly achieved? In one case, we saw the owner's child take on a bossy attitude toward his housemates, telling them, "you can't do that in my mother's house."

This is not to say that ownership by one family can never work. But for it to succeed, everyone must be aware of the potential pitfalls when they go into the arrangement. Moreover, the owner must go the extra mile to cooperate with the others for the greater good of the group. Your chances of success are vastly increased when everyone shares the same benefits and burdens.

Here are some factors to consider in deciding which kind of ownership is best for your situation:

- *Longevity:* You must make sure that the person you are planning for will be able to live in the property as long as desired. You don't want the arrangement to end prematurely because there is not enough money to pay the mortgage, taxes, and upkeep so that the property becomes unaffordable. There could also be a problem if the owner dies (if it is someone other than the person with a disability), or if a co-owner dies. The property could get caught up in their estate and have to be sold.

- *Public Benefits:* You should maximize all potential public benefits, including SSI, Medicaid, and Section 8 housing. Sometimes a person's housing arrangement can affect his public benefits. For example, if a person receives SSI, his monthly benefit can be reduced by up to $1/3$ if he receives assistance with housing costs such as mortgage, real estate taxes, or utilities. Another important public benefit program is Section 8 rent and mortgage assistance. Section 8 can be tenant-based, which means that the person uses his subsidy wherever he lives; or it can be project-based, which means that everyone in the residence is covered by the subsidy. How the property is owned (in your own name, through a trust, etc.) can determine whether the person with a disability can receive Section 8 assistance. (See Chapter 4 and the Appendix to Chapter 4.) Repayment of Medicaid benefits is another potential concern. When someone aged 55 or older dies, the state Medicaid agency can recover the cost of care it provided while the person was alive by placing a so-called Medicaid lien on the property. In most states, the agency can recover its costs from the person's home if the home was part of his probate estate. (See the Appendix to Chapter 4 for more about Medicaid recovery.)

- *Creditor Protection:* The property should be protected from claims and lawsuits that could be brought against any of the owners—the person with a disability, if he owns the property in his own name, or the parents of the person with a disability, if they own the property for their child or as part of a group. For example, let's say the person with a disability owns the property in his own name and incurs bills he cannot pay (medical, credit card, utilities, etc.). He could be sued and the creditor might be able to force a sale of the property to satisfy its claim.

    One way to protect the equity in your property is through a homestead exemption, which prevents creditors from seizing the equity in your home. In some states, homestead protection is automatic, while in other states the homeowner must file a claim for homestead exemption with the state. The amount of protection is different in each state. (For information about homestead exemptions, see Chapter 8.) However, a homestead exemption will not protect a property that is owned by the parent of the person with a disability or by a group of parents, since it is not their residence. Thus, if one of these owners were sued (car accident, business debt, etc.) the creditor could potentially force a sale of the property to satisfy the debt.

    Besides risks of lawsuits, other possible problems with non-occupant owners are that an owner might need nursing home care that he cannot pay for, or an owner could die and the property could become part of his probate estate and have to be shared with his creditors and relatives. All these events could place the property at risk.

■ *Proper Management:* Some people with cognitive or emotional difficulties may not be able to respond to legal notices or pay mortgage, taxes, insurance, or common area charges in a timely manner. If bills go unpaid, a creditor could obtain a judgment and force a sale of the property.

■ *Financial Considerations:* You may want to take advantage of public programs that provide mortgage assistance, grants, and low- or no-interest loans to low-income homeowners. We describe some of those programs in Chapter 4 and the Appendix to Chapter 4. If you form a nonprofit organization, your group may be exempt from paying real estate taxes. In addition, nonprofits can solicit contributions from the public that donors can deduct on their income tax returns.

■ *Income Tax Benefits:* A homeowner can deduct payments of mortgage interest and real estate taxes on his federal and state income tax returns. Many municipalities offer real estate tax abatements to low-income homeowners.

■ *Flexibility:* The arrangement should be flexible in case your or your child's circumstances change. If you want to sell the property (or your share of it), you should be able to do so easily and—ideally—get your investment back.

With these considerations in mind, the following sections explore some different ways that individuals and families can own the property.

Example 1: Ownership by the Person with a Disability

Jeffrey G., who has a developmental disability and receives SSI and Medicaid, wants to buy a condominium where he can live by himself. A local nonprofit agency helps him with the home ownership process. The down payment comes from a grant from the HOME program. Jeffrey obtains a first-time homebuyer's loan that has a low interest rate. Jeffrey owns the condominium in his own name.

Comments

Buying a home can be extremely difficult for an adult with a disability who has few financial resources. Yet it can be done. A good source of information about people with disabilities owning their homes is the Institute on Disability (IOD) at the University of New Hampshire. The IOD contains archived materials from the Center for Housing and New Economics (CHANCE) and the National Home of Your Own Alliance (HOYO). Although neither group is currently active, their publications contain many inspirational stories and practical strategies for homeownership. To obtain the archived publications, including the *Home of Your Own Guide,* go to www.iod.unh.edu and search the CHANCE publications. There are additional resources on home ownership in the Resources section at the end of the book.

Considerations

- *Public Benefits:* Jeffrey might be able to get Section 8 mortgage assistance if his Public Housing Authority runs that kind of program. However, since he owns the property in his own name, he cannot get Section 8 rental assistance. If Jeffrey received help with housing expenses such as taxes, insurance, or utilities from his family, his monthly SSI benefit would be reduced by up to $1/3$. In addition, Jeffrey's property would be subject to Medicaid recovery if he dies at age 55 or older. In most states, Jeffrey could avoid this result if he owned his home through a trust. (See Example 4.)

  Another potential downside to owning the home in his own name is that if Jeffrey sold his home, he would lose SSI benefits because he would have more than $2,000 in liquid resources. To maintain SSI, he would have to purchase another property, buy non-countable resources (vehicle, pre-paid funeral, etc.), or put the money into an ir-revocable special needs trust.

- *Management:* As the sole owner, Jeffrey would receive the real estate tax, utility, and insurance bills directly in his own name. There could be a problem if he does not always pay the bills on time. A bill payer could help him manage his checkbook. Many agencies train volunteers to help people who are elderly or have disabilities with bill paying. Alternatively, Jeffrey could sign a power of attorney authorizing a parent or other relative to receive the bills and use his funds to pay them.

- *Creditor Protection:* The property would be at risk if Jeffrey were sued over a debt, an injury at his home, etc. He could protect his home by filing a Declaration of Homestead that would protect the equity up to the specified amount in his state.

- *Financial Considerations:* As a low-income homeowner, Jeffrey might qualify for a grant or a low-interest loan to repair his home or make it accessible. He might receive a real estate tax abatement for low-income or disabled homeowners from the municipality.

- *Flexibility:* If Jeffrey's needs change and he decides to sell his home, he will have to sign the deed and other closing documents. There could be a problem if his cognitive capacity declines and he loses the ability to sign legal documents. But he could give someone power of attorney to sign the deed and related documents on his behalf while he still has the capacity to do so.

Example 2: Ownership by a Parent, Sibling, or Other Family Member

Evelyn is 35 years old and receives SSI. Her parents buy a two-bedroom condominium for her and her life share companion. The parents provide the down payment and pay the mortgage, real estate taxes, and condominium charges. Evelyn's parents own the property in their names.

Considerations

- *Longevity:* Evelyn's parents have planned for the likelihood that Evelyn will outlive them by creating a special needs trust for her benefit. On their deaths, the trust will own the real estate. There will be enough money in the trust to pay the real estate costs for the rest of Evelyn's life. They have named successor trustees to manage the trust. See Chapter 9 for more information about special needs trusts and trustees.

- *Income Taxes:* Evelyn's parents can deduct the mortgage interest and real estate taxes they pay on their state and federal income tax returns. This is permitted because they own the property. If they rented the property to Evelyn for a nominal sum, they could claim depreciation for the property. However, this could be counterproductive, because the Internal Revenue Service might require them to pay tax on the amount of rent they could have received if they rented the property at a market rate.

- *Public Benefits.* Evelyn's monthly SSI benefit is reduced by ⅓ because her parents pay her housing costs. Evelyn's parents might be able to participate in the Section 8 rental program. Evelyn would have to apply for and obtain a Section 8 voucher. With the housing authority's approval, her parents would rent the apartment to her. Evelyn would pay about 30 percent of her income to her parents, and the housing authority would pay the balance of the rent directly to her parents.

- *Creditor Protection:* If Evelyn's parents needed nursing home care that they could not afford, the property might have to be sold to pay for their care. They could reduce this risk by buying longterm care insurance. Another option is to own the property through an irrevocable special needs trust. This kind of trust is a separate legal entity that would not be considered their asset for purposes of public benefit programs. We explain these options in Chapter 9.

Example 3: "In-law" or Accessory Apartment in a Relative's Home

After Candace's parents died, Candace went to live with her sister and her sister's husband in their home. Candace used most of her inheritance to build an accessible addition to her sister's home. The addition, which has a bedroom, bathroom, and small kitchen, is considered an "in-law" or "accessory" apartment under the local zoning regulations. Candace will pay a proportionate share of the housing expenses, including mortgage, taxes, insurance, and utilities. Candace's sister, brother-in-law, and their children will assist Candace with medication, food shopping, meal preparation, cleaning, transportation, and money management.

Comments

A person with a disability who rents a so-called in-law apartment in a relative's home has more privacy and space than someone who rents or occupies a bedroom. An in-law apartment, which is also called a "secondary suite" or "accessory apartment," usually contains private space (separate bedroom, bathroom, and kitchen) as well as shared space (living room, laundry room, etc.). The apartment may (but does not need to) have a separate entrance. In-law apartments are regulated by the laws of the municipalities where they are located. Some municipalities prohibit these apartments because they do not meet local building codes and land use laws. Other areas allow a relative to occupy the apartment, but not an unrelated tenant who pays rent.

If you and your relative wanted to participate in the Section 8 program, you would probably have to meet criteria under your town's building code (kitchen, bathroom, separate entrance, minimum square feet, etc.).

Whenever an individual makes a substantial financial investment, the terms should be in writing. In this case, there should be a written agreement that spells out the amounts and kinds of care that Candace's family will provide and the compensation, if any, they will receive. The agreement should also cover contingencies. For example, what would happen if Candace runs out of money, or needs care that her family cannot provide, or if Candace's sister develops health problems and cannot care for her, or if the sister dies or sells the house.

To protect her interests, Candace might receive a promissory note and mortgage on the property for the value of her contribution, or the deed might be changed to give her a life interest in the property.* Alternatively, Candace could have a long-term lease. These options can have significant tax and public benefits implications. For example, if Candace received a promissory note from her sister and later had to enter a nursing home, the remaining value of the note might prevent her from qualifying for the Medicaid program. (Medicaid pays for nursing home care.) Moreover, on Candace's death, the state Medicaid agency might try to recover the benefits it paid on her behalf from the remaining value of the note. This could place the sister's house at risk. In order to avoid these outcomes, it is important to work closely with an attorney in your state who is knowledgeable about real estate, taxes, and public benefits.

Considerations

- *Public Benefits:* Candace's sister might qualify for a low- or no-interest loan, or a forgivable loan to make the property accessible. Most public programs will lend funds to a homeowner to make a property accessible for a non-owner relative with a disability. Candace might qualify for a Medicaid program in her state that would pay her sister to provide care. If Candace does not have an ownership interest in the property, she might qualify for tenant- based rental assistance. She and her sister would need to sign a lease, and the local housing authority would have to waive enforcement of the rule that prohibits most inter-family rental arrangements. In addition, the apartment would have to qualify as a separate rental unit under local zoning regulations.

- *Proper Management:* Candace's sister helps her write checks to pay her bills, including the housing expenses and payments to herself. Since the sister is using Candace's funds to pay herself, there is a potential conflict of interest. Candace should sign a

---

* A life interest, also called a life estate, gives a person (the life tenant) the right to occupy a property for life. If the property is sold, the life tenant receives a share of the proceeds based on his age and remaining life expectancy. In some states, a life tenant is expected to pay certain costs like the real estate taxes and homeowner's insurance, although this can be changed by agreement of the life tenant and the remainder owners.

power of attorney giving an agent the ability to use her funds to pay her bills. Ideally, someone other than the sister or her husband should be the agent. If this is not possible, then the power of attorney should specify that Candace's sister can use Candace's funds to pay herself.

Example 4: Leaving Property to a Trust

Prior to their deaths, Paul's parents created a trust for his benefit. The trust owns the family home where Paul lives and contains enough money to pay the house expenses (mortgage, taxes, insurance, repairs, utilities, etc.) for Paul's lifetime. Paul's brothers are the trustees. When the trust ends, the remaining trust funds will pass to Paul's brothers and their children.

Comments

Leaving the family home to a trust for a son or daughter with a disability can be a sound arrangement. The person can stay in familiar surroundings, and there might be an informal support system of friends, neighbors, and local merchants. You must make sure there will be enough money to operate the house and that the person will have adequate assistance to live in the home. We also recommend that you tell your other children about your plans in advance and obtain their support. You don't want family conflicts or resentment to undermine the arrangement.

Considerations

- *Public Benefits:* Paul might be able to obtain a tenant-based Section 8 rental subsidy. With the housing authority's approval, the trustees could rent the property to him. Paul would pay about 30 percent of his income as rent, and the housing authority would pay the balance of the rent to the trustees. The housing authority would have to allow an accommodation in two respects: the house is larger than Paul needs for himself, and the trustees are close family members. If Paul is receiving SSI, his monthly benefit would be reduced by $1/3$ because the trust is paying the real estate taxes and utilities.

- *Creditor Protection:* Since the property is owned through a trust, it is protected from Paul's and his siblings' creditors. If any of them were sued (for example, for a car accident, medical bill, or unpaid loan) the creditor could not force a sale of the property to satisfy the judgment. On Paul's death, the property can be sold and the proceeds given to the family members who were named in the trust to receive them.

- *Management:* The trustees can receive the bills and pay them from the trust funds. They can also make sure that the property is properly maintained, repaired, and insured.

- *Flexibility:* If Paul cannot live in the house for any reason, the trustees can sell it. The proceeds from the sale would remain in the trust and be used for Paul's benefit.

Example 5: Limited Liability Company

Four families form a limited liability company (LLC) and buy a house for their adult children. The families pay the down payment from their personal funds and obtain a commercial loan for the balance of the purchase price and cost of renovations. The LLC rents the property to their children. The parents (as the LLC members) pay the operating costs (mortgage, taxes, utilities, etc.). The LLC selects an agency to operate the program. The support staff who assist the residents are paid from a variety of sources, including the Medicaid program, the state department of disability services, and contributions from the families.

Comments

Forming a limited liability company (LLC) can be an effective way to own a group residence. An LLC is managed by the members and managers—in this case, the parents. An LLC is governed by the laws of the state where it is located. All states require an LLC to register, and many states require an LLC to have an operating agreement. Even if your state does not require an operating agreement, it is a good idea to have one. The operating agreement can cover important points such as each member's percentage of ownership, their obligations to pay the operating costs, how management decisions will be made, and what will happen if a family wants to leave, a member becomes disabled or dies, or some members fail or refuse to pay their share.

Considerations

- *Longevity:* An LLC can provide permanence. A resident can stay in the property as long as he (or the family member who is an owner) pays his share of the costs.

- *Creditor Protections:* An LLC is a separate legal entity. The property is protected from claims or lawsuits that could be brought against any member. Similarly, an LLC member's assets are protected from losses that might occur at the residence. No Medicaid liens could be placed on the property if a parent or resident needs nursing home care.

- *Public Benefits:* An LLC can rent the property to the residents. The LLC could receive a project-based Section 8 subsidy that would cover all the residents. Alternatively, the residents could obtain individual vouchers for tenant-based Section 8 assistance.

- *Tax Benefits:* The LLC uses the owners' contributions to pay mortgage interest, real estate taxes, and other operating costs. An LLC can "pass through" any tax-deductible expenses to the owners, who report them on their individual income tax returns.

- *Flexibility:* The LLC provides a flexible structure. If a resident moves, the family can sell its shares and get its investment back. The procedure to sell shares, as well as the formula to determine the share price, would be outlined in the operating agreement.

Example 6: Condominium

Six families buy and renovate a large house for their children and then convert the property to condominiums. Each condominium unit consists of one bedroom. The residents share the living room, dining room, kitchen, yard, etc. as common areas. Each unit owner pays the real estate taxes for his unit as well as a monthly fee that covers the common area charges (utilities, maintenance, repairs, insurance, and a reserve fund for repairs). There is a Board of Trustees that runs the property according to management and operating agreements that cover key items such as resale of the units, major repairs, and budgets. If an owner wants to sell his unit, the trustees must approve the buyer. The trustees hire an agency to run the program. There may be live-in staff as well as shift staff during mornings, evenings, and weekends.

Comments

The condominium model has been used successfully for many years by Specialized Housing, Inc., a nonprofit agency located in Brookline, Massachusetts. Specialized Housing helps groups of families obtain financing (public and private) and locate architects, builders, attorneys, and others who can help them develop the property. When the project is complete, the families can (but are not required to) hire Specialized Housing to run the program. There are committees that do things such as approving staff and new residents. If the trustees become unhappy with the agency, they can hire a different one.

Forming a condominium can be a two-step process. Some families initially form a Limited Liability Company. (See Example 5.) The LLC members (the families) obtain a commercial loan to purchase and renovate the property. When the property is ready for occupancy, the partners convert it to condominiums and sell the units. Then the LLC is dissolved because it is no longer needed.

When the LLC is ready to sell the condominiums, each family must decide who will own their unit—the person with a disability, another family member, or a trust. (See Examples 1, 2, and 4.) Most residents own the unit through a trust, but every family's situation is different, and there may be sound reasons for another choice.

Many condominium trusts have restrictions on the amount of profit a seller can receive. The resale price would be set according to a formula that is specified in the condominium documents. A condominium trust for people with disabilities would also restrict who the owner can sell the unit to and require that the trustees approve the new resident.

Considerations

- *Public Benefits:* If the resident does not own the unit he is occupying, he should have a rental agreement with the owner. This will allow him to obtain tenant-based Section 8 rental assistance. The amount of the subsidy would be the single room occupancy (SRO) rate. (We explain this in the Appendix to Chapter 4.) If the condominium is owned by the resident's close family member or through his trust, you might need to obtain a waiver from the public housing authority. In the Specialized Housing condominiums, most residents qualify for Medicaid, which pays for personal care attendants. Another Medicaid program in Massachusetts, Group Adult Foster Care (GAFC), contributes about $650 per month for each resident. Most states have similar Medicaid programs that pay for in-home care.

- *Flexibility:* If a resident wants to move, he can sell his unit. The trustees would have the right to approve the new owner.

Example 7: Housing Cooperative

Three families buy a property that will become a group residence for their children and two other adults with disabilities. Each unit consists of a bedroom and a half bath. The living room, kitchen, dining room, laundry room, and basement are shared areas. Each family (or resident) will own shares in the cooperative that entitles the resident to occupy a particular unit. There is a limit on the maximum price an owner can charge to sell his shares. (This is called a "limited equity co-operative.")

Comments

A housing cooperative is an arrangement in which a corporation owns real estate for the benefit of all the residents. The owners buy shares that entitle them to occupy one of the housing units and have equal access to the common areas. The owners sign an occupancy agreement, which is called a proprietary lease. The units can consist of a single room, a mini-suite with a bathroom, or an apartment.

Owners pay a monthly fee that covers the operating costs, such as mortgage payments, property taxes, insurance, maintenance, utilities, and a contribution to a reserve fund for repairs.

An owner who wants to move can sell his shares. A cooperative for people with disabilities would place some restrictions on the owner's ability to sell. A common restriction would require the seller to obtain approval from the Board of Directors in order to sell to a particular buyer. The Board would want to assure that the new person is compatible with the other residents. Another common restriction limits the maximum price the seller can charge. This is called a "limited equity cooperative." The maximum resale value is predetermined by a formula specified in the cooperative's bylaws. The limit on the seller's profit helps make the shares affordable for subsequent owners.

A cooperative is managed by a Board of Directors that decides all policy matters and runs the community. The cooperative members elect the directors.

Considerations

- *Flexibility:* Shares in a cooperative are considered to be real estate. This can make it relatively easy to borrow money because a lender can secure the loan by placing a mortgage on the property. The loan can be given to the cooperative as a whole (to pay for the purchase, repairs, or improvements) or to an individual share owner. However, it may be hard to obtain a loan in a state where cooperatives are not very common.

- *Public Benefits:* A person who owns shares in a cooperative can receive SSI benefits if he occupies the unit. The cooperative might be able to get approval from the local housing authority for site-based Section 8. If it cannot, a resident should be able to obtain tenant-based Section 8 assistance for his housing shares. The amount of the subsidy would be based on the size of the unit (single room, studio, etc.). If the shares are owned by the resident's relative or by a trust, the resident should have a rental agreement with the owner. Even with the rental agreement, you might have to ask for an accommodation in order to obtain Section 8. The housing authority might not approve a family landlord-tenant arrangement.

■ *Income Tax Benefits:* Co-op owners receive the tax benefits of home ownership. Payments of mortgage interest and real estate taxes are tax deductible on their federal and state income tax returns.

Example 8: Tenants in Common

James and Robert, who both have disabilities but can live independently, buy a house together. A grant from the HOME program provides the down payment, and the remaining funds come from a first-time homebuyers' loan program. They share expenses equally. The state department of disability services pays an agency to provide a limited amount of in-home support. A local homemaker agency provides help with housekeeping, food shopping, and budgeting. James and Robert own their home as tenants in common. That is, they both own one half of the house, but with no rights of survivorship. If either dies, the other person does not inherit his housemate's share of the house. Instead, the deceased owner's interest in the property will pass to the beneficiaries under his will or, if he doesn't have a will, to his legal heirs under the laws in the state where he lives.

As tenants in common, James and Robert should have an agreement that spells out their respective financial responsibilities and covers contingencies such as what would happen if one owner pays more than his share, or wants to sell his interest, or gets sick and can't remain at home. The agreement should be enforceable by (and against) both owners' legal heirs.

Considerations

■ *Longevity:* If James or Robert dies, his half of the property would be owned by his estate. His heirs might be unwilling to pay their share of the expenses for the house, or they might try to force a sale of the property while the survivor is still living there. This scenario could be avoided by having an ownership agreement that describes what will happen if an owner dies. There might also be a potential problem with the state Medicaid agency. The agency would have a claim on the deceased owner's share for the cost of medical care he received over his lifetime, and it could force a sale of the property to satisfy its claim. Upon request, the agency might defer collection until the co-owner dies or sells the property. However, it would be up to the representatives of the deceased owner's estate (usually the family) to process an appeal based on hardship, and the family might not be willing to do this. Moreover, hardship appeals are not easy to win.

■ *Public Benefits:* Owning the property as tenants in common would not interfere with the owners' public benefits. James and Robert might be able to receive Section 8 mortgage assistance if the local Public Housing Authority offers that program.

- *Creditor Protection:* James and Robert should both file for homestead protection to shield their equity in the property from accidents, lawsuits, and debts. Homestead declarations are discussed earlier in this chapter and in Chapter 9.

- *Proper Management:* A bill payer can help James and Robert pay the real estate taxes and utility bills on time. The property should be inspected periodically and repaired as needed. A local disability-related nonprofit group that owns real estate might voluntarily undertake this. Many of these groups have a property committee that periodically inspects their properties and makes recommendations for immediate and deferred repairs and maintenance. Last, James and Robert should consider giving power of attorney to a relative or trusted friend. If either owner lost capacity to sign legal documents, including those related to the house, the agent could take over.

Example 9: Nonprofit Corporation

Four families form a nonprofit corporation whose mission is to provide housing for adults with autism who cannot live independently. The families buy a property together and donate it to the nonprofit. The nonprofit leases the house to the agency that will operate the residential program. The families' children are the initial residents. The operating charges and staff costs are paid through a combination of the residents' public benefits, funds from the state department of disability services, and family contributions. The families manage the property as a Board of Directors.

Comments

A nonprofit corporation must register with the state where it is located. Each state has its own rules governing nonprofits. Most states require you to file Articles of Incorporation and Bylaws that show how the corporation will be managed. A Board of Directors and Officers (President, Treasurer, etc.) run the corporation. Most states require nonprofits to file annual reports that are open to inspection by the public.

A nonprofit corporation must have a general charitable purpose, which means that the enterprise must benefit people other than the initial members. You would have to commit to serve additional people with disabilities who may want to join the group, or those in future generations. Besides registering your nonprofit with the state, you may want to go one step further and obtain tax-exempt status under the Internal Revenue Code. The application process to become a so-called 503(c)(3) organization (named after a section of the Internal Revenue Code) can be rigorous and lengthy. However, if you are successful, there can be many financial benefits (see below).

Considerations

- *Financial:* The arrangement could be structured so that the families receive a charitable deduction on their income tax returns for the value of their donation. Another benefit is that a tax-exempt nonprofit group does not have to pay real estate taxes. It might also be in a better position than a private group to obtain public or private grants to purchase, repair, improve, or maintain the property, or to make it accessible. If you have tax-exempt status from the Internal Revenue Service, you can solicit contributions that donors can deduct on their federal and state income tax returns. (But before doing so, be sure to check your state's rules that govern soliciting donations.) There are some disadvantages to being a nonprofit group, including the amount of paperwork that is required. You have to file annual reports with the state, and you also have to file federal and state income tax returns. Another potential disadvantage is that you would not be able to get your investment back if your family member moved.

- *Public Benefits:* The nonprofit could lease the property to the service provider agency, which could obtain a site-based Section 8 voucher. Alternatively, the residents could obtain tenant-based vouchers.

- *Creditor Protection:* A property owned by a nonprofit corporation would be protected from creditors of any individual family.

Example 10: Housing Donated to an Agency

Mr. and Mrs. B. move out of their home and donate it to an agency that will operate a program for their adult sons, who have developmental disabilities. The agency obtains federal and state grants to renovate and expand the property in order to operate a group residence for the sons and three other adults with developmental disabilities.

Comments

Some families might plan to leave their home to a nonprofit agency at death. That way, they assume, their child with disabilities can stay in familiar surroundings for the rest of his life, and the agency will take care of him. Unfortunately, that strategy is not always sound. The adult with disabilities may need more support than the agency can provide. As we emphasize throughout this book, the lifetime cost to provide personal assistance for someone with a disability almost always exceeds the cost of housing for the person. In addition, there may not be sufficient funds to operate, maintain, or repair the property. Moreover, not every property is optimal for group living. A classic three-story Victorian home in a residential neighborhood might be lovely to look at, but a fully accessible, weatherized, one-story home near public transportation may be better suited for the needs of aging, medically involved, or mobility-impaired adults.

Nevertheless, with advance planning and by working closely with an agency, it may be possible to achieve the goal of your child staying in his home permanently. Keep in mind, however, that an agency is unlikely to commit to serve your child for life. There are too many factors outside the agency's control—your child's changing needs (mobility problems, nursing care), increased staff costs as your child ages, and even the agency's longevity. But an agency that receives a donated property should acknowledge a moral commitment to serve the person, even if it is in a different residence.

In the example above, the Newton, Wellesley, Weston Committee, Inc. (NWW), a nonprofit agency located in Newton, Massachusetts, received a donated property from a family whose twin sons were served by the agency. The house is now home to the sons and three other adults with developmental disabilities. NWW received federal and state funds, including a HUD 811 grant (see Chapter 4 and the Appendix to Chapter 4), to renovate and expand the property. The HUD 811 program includes a 40-year operating subsidy that pays for repairs and maintenance and covers the difference between the rental income and the mortgage. In the NWW property, all residents receive tenant-based rental assistance.

TILL, Inc. (Dafna's agency) also received a donated property. For several years, the agency had operated a family-owned group home for four adults. Rather than continue to manage the property and pay the real estate taxes and operating costs, the families agreed to sell the property to TILL for less than its fair market value. TILL assumed the operating costs and continues to run the program for the residents. (TILL does not pay real estate taxes because of its nonprofit status.) The families have the right to buy back the property if the agency decides to sell it within a specified number of years.

Considerations

- *Financial:* The agency would be responsible for paying the future costs to maintain the property. If it needs to be repaired or renovated, the agency would be in a better position than the family to obtain public grants and forgivable loans. The arrangement could be structured so that the family could receive a charitable deduction for the value of the donated property.

- *Public Benefits:* The agency can obtain a site-based Section 8 voucher for the house. Alternatively, the tenants can obtain tenant-based certificates. Both of these arrangements would bring income into the agency and reduce occupancy costs.

- *Flexibility:* In most cases, once you give up ownership, you have no control over how the property will be used, who can live there, or even if your family member will be able to remain. If there are problems with the agency, you can't replace it with a different service provider. And if the agency goes out of business or is absorbed by a larger agency, any promises that were made may be forgotten. Nevertheless, if you and your family stay involved with the agency (perhaps by joining the Board of Directors or one of the agency's committees), your continuing presence will remind the agency of its moral commitment. In that way, your wishes will probably be respected, and you and your family can influence how the property is operated.

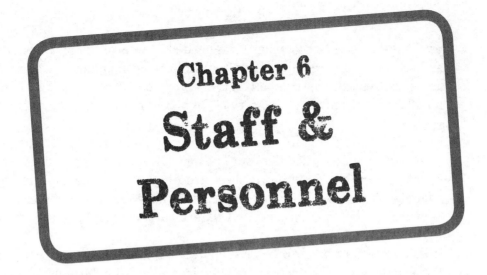

Chapter 6
Staff & Personnel

Staff can be the heart and soul of a residential arrangement. Without competent, caring staff, the arrangement can fail. This chapter explains what caregivers do to assist people with disabilities in their homes and describes their training and their qualifications. Should you hire and employ the staff yourself or go through an agency? This chapter explains the benefits and drawbacks of each arrangement. If you decide to become the employer, we tell you how to select the best candidate for the job. We also explain how to comply with government regulations that apply to employers and tell you steps you can take to protect yourself from liability.

Job Descriptions, Expectations, Qualifications, and Training

Whether you are hiring the staff yourself or working with staff in an existing program, defining what you expect staff to do and the type of person you want to work with your family member will help you find or accept the right person for the job.

Different terms and titles are used for people who provide direct care to others. Terms and titles include personal care attendant, direct care worker, or direct support professional (DSP), which is the term most commonly used. DSPs play an important role in the lives of people with disabilities and their families. Their roles can include many tasks such as personal care, recreational skills, socialization, academic teaching, money management, and general life skills training.

Some of the functions that DSPs might perform depend upon the positions for which they might be hired. These include:

■ *Companion:* A companion lives with an individual with a disability and provides "natural supports" by sharing the household chores and daily responsibilities; eats some or all meals together; offers advice as needed on interpersonal issues, social skills, and vocational choices; and offers friendship and companionship on some joint social activities. Typically the companion is not paid and an exchange for room or room and board is considered an in kind service for his or her time and companionship.

- *Relief:* Relief staff are hired to provide coverage as part of a set staffing schedule to cover for "regularly scheduled" staff people during vacations or sick time, or when unexpected vacancies occur due to staff turnover. Such staff can be hired by an agency or a family. They should be recruited before the need arises so that they can be trained, have their credentials checked, and be ready to provide relief on short notice.

- *Respite:* Respite workers provide support in Supervised Independent Living or Shared Living models to offer the primary caregiver relief from the daily responsibility of care and support. The respite can take place in the person's primary residence, if there is room. It can also take place in the respite provider's home. It is typical to give the primary caregiver a two-week vacation, plus some weekends off during the year. Such arrangements should be made in advance as part of the agreement when developing the residential services. In some Shared Living situations, care providers develop a network of support with a group of care providers and barter respite time with one another. This gives the individual with disabilities more connections as well as a social network for the provider. Care providers can also pay one another for respite if an exchange is not what they choose to do.

- *Direct Care Worker:* A direct care worker is a staff person who works with the individual with disabilities on a daily basis in a group home. Depending on the number of people who live together and the staffing pattern that has been established, there may be more than one DSP to cover a full week of 168 hours. Depending on the residents' level of need, DSPs can help with activities of daily living, personal care, organization, meal planning and cooking, cleaning, or teaching new skills. Most group homes have a residential manager who manages the scheduling, finances, staff supervision, implementation of policies, and general operation of the home. In many agencies, managers also have some direct care responsibilities in addition to their managerial responsibilities.

In many states, there are minimum qualifications for DSPs as well as for managers. At a minimum, agencies typically expect DSPs to have a high school degree and experience in working with individuals similar to those with whom they will be working. There is usually also a minimum age requirement. A sample qualification list for a DSP might be:
- Must be 18 years of age or older.
- Valid driver's license is required.
- Must possess good written and verbal skills to effectively communicate individuals' needs and goals.
- Must be able to pass the Medication Certification Training in English.
- CPR and First Aid training are a condition of employment.
- This position includes providing direct care for individuals, including lifting them, passive restraints, and hand-over-hand instruction.

We recommend that you list the qualities that you want a DSP to have, over and above the minimum qualifications necessary for doing the work. Here are some ideas you can use as a checklist, but you may want to add some of your own:

- Assertive
- Calm
- Committed
- Common sense
- Consistent
- Dependable
- Determined
- Empathetic
- Encouraging
- Honest
- Insightful
- Positive
- Punctual
- Resourceful
- Respectful

Such qualities cannot be determined by reading a resume, but they can be observed and assessed through interviews, observations, and references from previous experiences and connections.

Training

The training a Direct Support Professional receives is as important, if not more so, than the qualifications he or she brings to the job. Most states have minimum training requirements, and many agencies offer elective courses for staff who want to progress professionally. In most states, the following training is required for employees of agencies that have contracts with the state:

- **Medication.** Any DSP who will give medication must complete a course in medication management that is taught by a certified nurse trainer. Such courses, which usually take between twelve and sixteen hours, cover medication safety, signs of distress, medication interactions, how to dispense different kinds of medication, and reporting medication errors. A competency test is required at the end of the training, and only DSPs who pass the test are permitted to give medications.

- **First Aid and CPR Training.** These standardized courses require competency tests and are taught by certified trainers.

- **Physical Intervention.** Training in physical interventions covers all forms of restraints and physical holds. In most states, these procedures can only be used as a last resort if a person is violent and at risk of hurting herself or another person. In Massachusetts, the use of any restraint by an agency employee must be reported to the agency's Human Rights committee as well as to a state body that receives and evaluates such reports.

In addition to providing mandatory training in these areas, agencies may offer elective courses for DSPs. For example, TILL offers elective courses in self-determination, autism, seizures, brain injury, computer technology, alternative communication systems, intellectual development, and development of community and leisure skills.

Staff Retention and Turnover

A common fear on the part of families is the staff turnover rate in residential programs. While it is true that the annual turnover rate for DSPs in the U.S. averages 32 percent and higher, this number must be taken in context. Namely, there are many states and specific agencies that experience much lower turnover rates, averaging 12 percent. The turnover rates for professional staff averages 10 percent, and for administrative staff, 5.4 percent. There are strong correlations to both the age of a DSP and to the salary scale. Not surprisingly, the lower the person's age and the lower the salary, the higher the turnover rate as people move on to other opportunities.

Such turnover rates are typical of many other jobs and industries. There has been a decline nationwide in turnover rates for this field as the profession of human services has expanded and as economic shifts have created more opportunities in health care. Agencies with consistent management and professional staff will be able to uphold standards and good operating procedures since they offer history and experience to programs. This is not unlike in other industries that might experience high turnover rates in their frontline staff, yet offer stability and excellent services because of the stability of their upper management.

The other reality that should allay families' fears is that individuals with disabilities form connections with their peers and housemates that are as strong or stronger than their connections to their staff. The comfort of familiar surroundings and people comes as much from the daily routines and activities and friendships as it does from staff.

Families can assist in ensuring a successful staffing arrangement in the following ways:

1. Be clear about what you expect from the person. Be specific about hours, days, vacation time, holidays, weekends, guests, method and frequency of communication with you, etc.
2. Put the expectations in writing and be sure that you and the staff person have a copy and are in agreement with the arrangement as written.
3. Assume nothing. It is better to be clear than to second guess whether the person has the same values and expectations as you do about cleanliness, dinner time, food selections, religion, etc.
4. Be clear about your priorities. Remember, you can't have everything exactly as you would do it. If that were the case, then you should do it yourself. Decide in advance with the staff person what is nonnegotiable, what is preferable, and what is not important.
5. In a live-in arrangement, offer pleasant, comfortable living quarters, ideally with a separate entrance and a separate bath. Ensuring that staff have their own space during time off and private sleeping arrangements makes it more likely they will stay.
6. Ask yourself if you are being intrusive or merely involved in your visits and communications with your child and with staff.
7. Provide training that is in keeping with the situations the staff will encounter and which allow them to implement the goals of the program.
8. Offer professional growth opportunities for advancement.
9. Offer a good benefit package that includes health benefits and a salary in keeping with the averages of other health care professionals in the region.

Should You Employ the Staff Directly or Use an Agency?

When you are ready to hire a staff person, you must decide whether to employ him or her yourself or go through an agency.

There can be many benefits to using an agency. An agency often has a supply of qualified workers whom they have screened and trained. If they don't happen to have anyone who meets your needs, they can recruit someone for you. If the worker they place with you calls in sick or fails to show up, it is the agency's responsibility to fill the shift. The agency cuts the paychecks and takes care of all necessary withholdings and insurance payments. If the worker is not doing a good job—or you think he or she is not a good match—you don't have to deal with firing him or her. You can ask the agency to send someone else.

One downside to using an agency is the additional expense. Besides paying the worker's salary, you are paying for the agency to handle administrative tasks. You have to decide whether it is worth your time and effort to take care of these chores yourself.

Another disadvantage to using an agency is that you do not have as much control as you would if you hired the caregiver yourself. Let's say you want the caregiver to acquire special training in applied behavior analysis (ABA) to work with people with autism. You offer to pay for the training. You can require your own employee to be trained, but if the employee works for an agency that doesn't think that particular training is necessary, it may not happen. The agency's employee is under their control, not yours. If you hired your own staff, you could decide to specify the age or gender. However, bear in mind that you would be subject to the same choices that an agency has and would want to hire the best person for the job. Sometimes that might mean deciding that gender and other specific qualifications are not as important as the person's overall performance and demeanor.

With regard to gender, there is an interesting dilemma that should be noted. In the authors' experience, parents never say they do not want females working with their male and female children. However, there have been many restrictions on males working with both males and females. Given the stereotypes and societal expectations and realities, this is not surprising, but we caution you to review qualifications and experience over gender.

Another downside to using an agency is that they can refuse to hire—or they can fire—the person you want the most. A person can be an excellent care provider and have a strong bond with the residents. As families, this is what we hope to achieve. But these qualities alone do not always make the caregiver a good employee, at least from the agency's perspective—given that there are administrative requirements and expectations that must be applied equally to all employees.

> Marie was an experienced and beloved caregiver at a group residence for women. But due to a difficult family situation, her attendance at work could be spotty. The agency fired her due to excessive absences. Although the families protested and rallied to her support, the agency refused to reinstate her. If she had been working directly for the families—instead of for the agency—the families might have chosen to keep her despite the problems caused by her absences.

An agency is bound to conform to the staffing patterns that they and the funding agency determine to be necessary for the particular setting. Agencies are bound by many oversight agencies to ensure that they terminate employees who engage in illegal behavior or are negligent in their duties. Most states have requirements to report any type of purported negligent or abusive behavior to the funding agency. An agency will probably have a Human Rights Committee that would review reporting of such incidents and determine fault and consequences.

Basic Requirements for Employers

If you are going to hire an employee directly, there are some government requirements you need to know about, which we describe below. Some of them involve withholding taxes from your employee's pay and buying workers' compensation coverage. Many of us have heard about someone who bypassed these requirements and paid the worker cash "under the table." While it may seem convenient to avoid the red tape, it is not worth the risk. An employer who is found to be in violation of the law can face stiff penalties and be required to pay all the taxes that should have been withheld over the years, plus interest. You could also expose yourself to a lawsuit if your employee is injured on the job, because you would not have any protection from the state workers' compensation system. It's best to avoid informal hiring and observe the rules.

Pay Minimum Wage and Overtime

With the exception of live-in staff, employees are protected by federal and state wage and hour laws. These laws require employers to pay the minimum wage, which is currently $7.25 per hour. You also have to pay your employee time-and-a-half for each hour your employee works beyond 40 hours in a week. Some states have minimum wage and hour requirements that are stricter than the federal amount laws. To find out the rules in your state, contact your state's department of labor.

When you are in the business of providing care for people with disabilities, it can be easy to exceed the 40-hour limit. There can be contingencies and emergencies that you can't plan for—residents get sick and need extra help, staff don't arrive on time for their shift and someone has to stay late, etc. Staff must be compensated for their time whenever they work extra hours or stay late on the job. This is the case even if the caregiver volunteers to do something extra.

> John needs a ride to a regular therapy appointment. Sandra, who works at John's residence, offers to drive John to the appointment after her shift because it is on her way home. This becomes part of her regular routine. Sandra must be paid overtime if transporting John is not included in her 40-hour work week.

Another issue that can come up in residential services is "on call" time. Sometimes employers can require employees to remain available to come to work or respond to a crisis. Such "on call" time does not have to be compensated if the employee can be doing other things while waiting to be called. If she is told to be on call specifically for your job, then she is technically working for you and cannot do other things. Therefore, you need to pay her for hours in which she must be available.

As noted, these wage and overtime protections do not apply to staff who live in the home. Typically, these staff receive free room and board as well as a stipend. Such "live-in companions" are exempted under the Fair Labor Standards Act, which covers many employer-employee relations.*

Make the Required Tax Withholdings

As an employer, you are responsible for withholding federal income tax, Social Security tax, and Medicare tax from your employee's paycheck. The instructions and forms you will need are described in IRS Publication 15, *Employer's Tax Guide,* which is available on the IRS website (www.irs.gov). Most states also have an income tax, so you will also have to deduct the proper amount of state tax from the paycheck. For information, refer to your state's department of labor website. In addition, if your city or county imposes an income tax, you can obtain this information from the city or county treasurer's office. In order to make the required tax withholdings, you will need an Employer Identification Number (EIN), which you can obtain from the Internal Revenue Service.

Don't Discriminate

Most parents do not expect to deal with the issue of discrimination since they have often fought to ensure that their child with a disability is not discriminated against. However, as an employer, you must be sure that you do not impermissibly discriminate against an applicant or employee.

Most employers do not have to worry about federal anti-discrimination laws, because these laws only apply to businesses that have 15 to 20 workers or more. An exception is racial discrimination, which applies to all sizes of businesses, including single-employer businesses. Some states have laws that prohibit discrimination based on color, race, gender, religion, sexual orientation, national origin, pregnancy, citizenship, disability, and age. In several states, one or more of these prohibitions apply to businesses with one employee. A few cities have local ordinances that prohibit discrimination based on sexual orientation. To find out the rules in your state, consult your state's labor department.

In some limited situations, you may be allowed to base a hiring or employment decision on a particular trait. For example, if you are hiring someone to provide personal care for a woman with a disability, you would probably only consider female applicants. Most states that have anti-discrimination laws would make an exception for this situation, but you should check to be sure.

Buy Workers' Compensation Insurance

All states have a workers' compensation system that protects employees who are injured on the job. The system can replace lost income until the employee returns to work, pay medical expenses, and sometimes award a lump sum to compensate for future eco-

---

* "Fair Labor Standards Act of 1938, as amended, 29 USC sec. 213(a)(15).

nomic losses. Most states require employers to buy insurance, although some make it optional. Some states exempt domestic caregivers from coverage.

We recommend that you buy workers' compensation for your employee, even if your state does not require it. In addition to protecting your employee, the insurance shields you from personal liability. If your employee is injured on the job, all compensation is paid from the state fund. The employee is barred from suing you for his losses.

Verify That Your Employee Can Work Legally in the United States

Federal law requires employers to verify that their employee can work legally in the United States. This means that the employee must be a U.S. citizen, a permanent resident alien, or an alien who is authorized to work. The Immigration and Naturalization Service (INS) can impose fines on employers who knowingly employ an illegal alien, as well as for other violations of the law.

You and the employee must both sign INS Form I-9, and you must inspect supporting documents the employee provides. There are time limits on how long you must keep the form (three years from the date of hire and one year from the date of termination). You must also keep the form and supporting documentation separate from other employee files. For more information, go to the website for U.S. Citizen and Immigration Services (www.uscis.gov).

Going Beyond the Basics

Have a Written Agreement

It is essential to have a written job description that covers the duties the caregiver will perform. This is true whether you are hiring a single employee to care for one person or several workers for a group residence. Many problems can be avoided if both parties are clear about one another's expectations.

The job description should spell out general categories of duties the worker will perform, such as "helping the resident make a healthy breakfast and dinner," or "taking the resident to medical appointments." We recommend that you not go into too much detail, because then it could be implied that since you did not include a specific job, it is not required. For example, if you are hiring someone to be a full-time companion for an individual with disabilities, you might list keeping the home clean as part of their duties, and then detail the rooms in the house. If you omit listing one of the rooms because you assume it is implied, then the person can avoid cleaning it and assume that you meant to omit the room. In this situation, it would be better to reference "maintain the home in a clean and safe condition" which should cover the intent of that part of the job expectation. We have included some sample job descriptions in the Appendix. The job description should also include anything you don't want the employee to do on the job—such as smoke cigarettes, have guests, or bring pets to work.

One item that should not be included in the job description is a promise of job security. You must be able to discharge caregivers promptly if they are not doing their job. Therefore, you should insist that the agreement be "at will," which means that you can remove the employee at any time without cause. This is not to say that there should not be any notice requirements. Most caregiver agreements provide that either party can end the relationship by giving a specified amount of notice (such as 60 days). The employer would reserve the right to fire the employee immediately, however, if she is not treating the person in her care properly.

We have included sample agreements for life share (live-in caregiver) and group living arrangements in the Appendix. You might have to modify these agreements to meet requirements in your state. A local attorney who specializes in employment law can assist you with this.

Consider Giving Fringe Benefits

In addition to paying minimum wage and overtime, which is required by law, you might want to consider giving your employee some additional benefits. However, this would be voluntary on your part. Federal law does not require employers to pay their employees when they are not working (sick days, personal days, etc.) or provide benefits such as a retirement plan or life insurance. A few states require employers to provide health insurance, but only one state (Hawaii) currently requires single-employee businesses to do so.

One common practice is to give employees a few days of paid time off when they don't work—sick days, personal days, vacation, bereavement, etc. Some employers give workers unpaid leave to care for sick family members. Ideally, the employee should notify you in advance of using the time. Similarly, many employers give their employees a paid vacation time after they have been on the job for a year. If you offer paid vacation time, the laws in your state might dictate how unused vacation time accrues. Some states prohibit a "use it or lose it" policy under which employees forfeit vacation time if they do not take it within a specified period of time. To find out the rules in your state, go to your state's department of labor.

As administrations change, new employee/employer requirements may take effect, and you must be careful to keep up with any changes that affect single-employee businesses. (If you are working with an agency, they are required to keep up with changing labor and other regulatory laws.)

Develop an Employee Handbook

If you will be forming a business and hiring several employees, you should consider developing an employee handbook that describes your policies and procedures. The more defined the policies are, the less likely there will be inequities in hiring, supervising, promotions, and terminations that could subject you—the employer—to discrimination claims. In addition to protecting you, uniform policies can create a working environment where staff will feel treated fairly.

Note, however, that if you have written policies and procedures, you must apply them consistently and uniformly to all employees. If you don't, an employee could accuse you of discrimination, which is what the handbook was designed to avoid. For example, perhaps a worker might do everything that is required of his job, but the residents don't like him and he is let go. He could claim that the reason is discrimination, not a personality conflict.

If you decide to develop an employment handbook, an attorney who handles employment matters can draw one up for you. The features could include:
- Job descriptions
- Salary schedule that includes cost of living increases and merit raises

- Description of any fringe benefits that you provide, such as retirement, health insurance, paid education courses in the disability field
- Training requirements (CPR, applied behavior analysis, human rights, etc.)
- Disciplinary action
- Grievance procedure
- Sexual harassment policy and reporting procedures
- Drug, alcohol, substance, and smoking policies
- Policies regarding sick time, holidays, leaves of absence, bereavement, personal days, military duty, and jury duty

Protecting Yourself

Anyone who is overseeing a residential arrangement for a person with a disability must be concerned about liability. You must be careful about whom you hire, and you need to supervise them properly. But even when everyone is being careful, accidents can happen. Worse, someone could intentionally injure the resident, a coworker, or an innocent third party. If this were to occur, you could be sued, and your home or other assets could be placed at risk. There are some steps you can take to protect yourself.

Have Adequate Insurance

If you will be operating the residence through a business entity (nonprofit agency, limited liability company, etc.) and have several employees, you can buy commercial insurance that will cover most contingencies involving the residents, employees, directors, volunteers, and the general public. If you are hiring a single employee or running the residence on a small scale, you should consider the following kinds of insurance as needed for your situation:

- *Workers' Compensation Insurance:* Earlier in this chapter, we advised you to buy state workers' compensation insurance that would cover your employee if he or she were hurt at work. The insurance can pay for lost wages, medical bills, and other injury-related expenses. If you do not take out this coverage and your employee is injured on the job, you could be personally liable for his or her losses.

- *Property Insurance:* With the exception of your employees who are covered by worker's compensation insurance, a homeowner is potentially liable to anyone who is injured on their property through their carelessness. This includes people who may be visiting the property (friends, volunteers, mail carriers, etc.) or doing work there (housecleaner, contractor, landscaper, etc.). Thus, property insurance is essential. Check the policy to make sure it covers the kinds of situations we mentioned. If it doesn't, a rider can be obtained.

- *Umbrella Policy:* You should consider an "umbrella" liability policy that would cover more remote contingencies. These could include a worker who hurts a resident or steals money, or even a resident who intentionally injures a worker or another resident. If you are shown to be careless in hiring an unqualified worker or permitting a dangerous situation to exist, you could be held personally liable. An "umbrella" policy may protect you from these kinds of contingencies.

- *Automobile Insurance:* If the employee will be transporting the residents in a vehicle that you own, make sure your insurance is adequate and will cover this contingency. Most standard policies do not cover employment-related losses, so you would have to pay for a rider. Similarly, if the caregiver will be using his or her own car, make sure that any injuries or losses to residents would be covered and that the amount of insurance is adequate. If there is an extra premium for this coverage, the employer usually pays for it.

Perform Background Checks for All Employees

It is important to screen all prospective employees, even if you already know them. You should ask for references from former employers and also check their criminal background and driving records.

- *References:* You should ask for references from former employers and follow up. Some employers may be reluctant to give a candid assessment of a former employee for fear of liability. Still, it can be a valuable way to get information about a candidate.

- *Criminal Record:* Federal and state law enforcement agencies maintain criminal records that typically include police arrest reports, prosecution data, court determinations, and records from corrections departments (sentences served, parole, etc.). Many states require agencies to check the criminal backgrounds of employees who will be working with the elderly or individuals with disabilities. Private employers are not required to perform the checks, and it may be harder for them to obtain the information about a perspective employee. Nevertheless, most states allow individuals to obtain the information for good cause, such as hiring a caregiver for a vulnerable person. You would need the prospective employee's permission to do so.

- State criminal record checks indicate crimes that were proven and that took place within one state only. There is a national registry, but it is expensive and time intensive to obtain such records. They are also not as current as state records. There is a summary of the state laws on the website for the National Conference of State Legislatures: www.ncsl.org/documents/health/CBCstatesum.pdf.

- *Driving Record:* If an employee will be driving residents as part of the job, you must check his or her driving record. All states maintain a database of drivers whose licenses have been revoked or suspended, or who have been convicted of serious traffic offenses, such as driving while impaired by alcohol or drugs. Most states allow a prospective employer to obtain this record with the employee's consent. For information in your state, go to your state's department of motor vehicles.

    It can be harder to obtain information from states where the prospective employee is not currently living. The National Highway Traffic Safety Administration (NHTSA) maintains a National Driver Registry where you can check the person's record in other states. However, the driver must be licensed there, and the records only go back three years. For more information, go to the NHTSA's website: www.nhtsa.gov.

Interviewing and Hiring a Staff Person

If you are recruiting on your own, you should review applications and resumes to assess potential based on work history, volunteer involvements, educational background, and, most importantly, references. Unfortunately, most employers are bound by confidentiality laws and will often only provide limited information such as confirmation that someone worked there and the period of time of their employment. If at all possible, ask applicants for references with whom you might have informal contacts.

When you meet with potential applicants, you will want to provide a realistic idea of what you are expecting and to "share the story" about your family and the person with whom he or she will be working. Be sure to list five to seven situations they might encounter on the job. Be honest as well as positive, but make sure the person knows whether the job will involve physical care, medication administration, or possible medical emergencies.

Include information about your family and the role you expect to play. Detail a "typical" day and what it would look like.

The interview process should provide you with the information you need to make a good decision. Therefore, prepare your questions so that they yield this information. For example, ask about actual situations the person might encounter on the job. You might describe a behavioral incident or a "testing situation" such as the individual with disabilities wanting to do something that is not beneficial to her and find out whether the applicant would allow the behavior. Ask questions which get at how the person feels about human rights and independence. For example, if the person with disabilities expresses that she wants to wear the same clothes constantly, is it her right to do so? Would the applicant intervene, and if so, how?

A typical temptation for people inexperienced in interviewing is to talk too much during the interview and not give the applicant a chance to express who he or she is. Resist the temptation to speak first and "give away the right answer." Ask questions such as:

- Why do you think you would like this job?
- Where else have you worked that is similar to this job?
- Who was your favorite supervisor and why?
- What are your future goals in this field?
- Describe your favorite job, whether it was a volunteer or paid position.
- What makes you feel stressed and anxious?
- What do you like to do for fun? If you have a day to yourself, how do you spend it?
- What is the most difficult situation you ever encountered and how did you handle it?
- Describe a disagreement or conflict you had with a friend, employer, or co-worker. What did you do and how was it handled?
- If an individual wanted to learn how to cook but you felt he would be unsafe in the kitchen, how would you handle that?

Staff leave as much because employers don't make the right selection and match as for any other reasons. Therefore, your retention rate will be better if you trust your instincts, do your homework in preparing for the interview, and be honest about what you are looking for in the ideal candidate.

Once you have decided on the person you would like to hire, arrange for him or her and your child to spend time together engaged in an activity of their mutual choice. Sometimes transition visits are useful, but there are no definite answers as to whether they are useful in every situation. Your family can best determine whether your son or daughter benefits from long transition periods or whether transition periods simply create anxiety and confusion as to when a change might occur. We do recommend that the potential employee and your child spend sufficient time together, preferably with an activity, so that you can observe and ask both the applicant and your child questions about their experience together.

The Nuts and Bolts of Employing Staff Directly

If you decide to hire a staff person yourself, here are the minimum steps you will need to take to make sure you don't break any laws or leave yourself open to lawsuits.

Basic Requirements for All Employers in the U.S.
- Pay minimum wage and overtime
- Make the required tax withholdings
- Don't discriminate
- Buy workers' compensation insurance
- Verify that your employee can work legally in the United States

Going Beyond the Basics
- Have a written agreement
- Consider giving fringe benefits
- Develop an employee handbook

Protecting Yourself
- Have adequate insurance
  - Workers' compensation
  - Property insurance
  - Umbrella policy
  - Automobile coverage

- Perform background checks for employees
  - References
  - Criminal record
  - Driving record

Avoiding Conflicts with the Agency over Staff

Thus far in this chapter, we have discussed your responsibilities if you are employing staff directly. Sometimes a family can start out this way but then tire of the responsibility and hire an agency to take over. It can be a relief to have an agency assume the paperwork and cover the day-to-day running of the household.

Discuss Potential Problems in Advance

If you are going to switch to an agency, you should try to anticipate any problems that could come up. Have as many meetings with the agency as necessary to explain the situation in detail. If there is something that is important to you—like making sure a particular employee has a flexible schedule—let the agency know this in advance. Most agencies have uniform policies and procedures they apply to all their programs. You should find out how these policies will be applied to your situation. Don't assume the agency will manage the arrangement the same way you did.

Brenda had been employed for many years as a caregiver for Jane, who had suffered a head injury as an adult. Jane's sister employed Brenda for 30 hours a week and handled all the paperwork herself. Brenda and Jane developed a close relationship. Brenda brought Jane on personal errands (drug store, shopping, dry cleaners, etc.). Brenda often did her personal laundry at Jane's home. Some days Brenda left to pick up her daughter at school and brought her to Jane's apartment to watch television or do homework. Jane and Brenda were both satisfied with the arrangement.

Eventually Jane's sister tired of doing the paperwork and hired an agency to take over. The agency insisted that Brenda work a regular schedule—although the times could be mutually agreed upon by Brenda and Jane. Brenda could no longer do personal errands on work time or bring her daughter to Jane's apartment. Brenda and Jane resented the agency's insistence that Brenda be treated the same as their other employees. Their anger blindsided the agency, who thought they were just being hired to do the paperwork.

After a few months, Brenda resigned from her position because she did not want to live with the policies required by an agency that she felt restricted her ability to continue working well with Jane. The agency hired a new energetic caregiver, Claire, whom Jane likes very much. Jane and Brenda still keep in touch. Jane's sister is relieved that an agency is handling the paperwork and providing the coverage during Claire's scheduled absences.

Staff Terminations—See the Agency's Point of View

Staff terminations can be a source of conflict between the residents or their families and the agency. To many families, the staff function like surrogate parents who do everything the parents did before their children moved out. Families can overlook many deficiencies in a caregiver if he or she has a strong bond with their children.

The agency, however, has the responsibility to keep the residents safe and make the house run smoothly. If anything goes wrong, the agency bears the risk. Consequently, the agency has the right to decide all staff-related issues, including who is hired and who is fired.

Earlier in this chapter, we mentioned the example of Marie, the caregiver who was fired for spotty attendance at work. The problem of excessive or lengthy absences can be compounded when the employee is a house manager who has the responsibility to supervise other staff and keep the house running efficiently.

> Kathy had been the residential manager at a group home for three years. In the past year, she had taken sixteen weeks of leave on three separate occasions due to medical issues. Each time she used her vacation time, sick leave, and unpaid Family Leave and Medical Act time. After her last return from medical leave, Kathy planned a one-month vacation leave to visit her family in India. Before talking to her employer, she had already arranged for the flight, for her children to take time off from school, and to obtain coverage at work.
>
> When Kathy presented her request for a one-month leave, the agency who employed her denied it but it approved a two-week leave. Kathy rejected the shorter leave and was fired. The families wanted her to be reinstated. The agency refused, because, in their view, the house was suffering without a consistent manager. The agency was also concerned about future leaves and continuing disruptions to the house.
>
> The families chose to continue with the agency because they realized, after much discussion amongst themselves, that they valued what the agency had to offer, the consistency, and the progress their children had made. Even though they felt the rules should have been overlooked to keep this one staff person, they knew that it would have set a bad precedent for other staff who might enjoy similar long leaves and idiosyncratic application of policies that were established to protect the entire program.

It can be hard for residents and their families when a favorite caregiver departs involuntarily. When the agency fires the caregiver, families can be understandably upset and frustrated. The agency should provide the residents and families with a full explanation of what occurred, and why. Sometimes hearing the agency's point of view can clear the air and make the departure easier to accept.

Consider Separating Ownership from Residential Services

Ultimately, when it comes to decisions about staff, the power rests with the agency, not with the residents or their families. If you don't like the decision, your only option is to leave the agency, which could be difficult and disruptive for the resident. Moreover, you would likely encounter the same problem with another provider.

This is why some advocates for people with disabilities say that residents should own or rent the property where they live. According to these advocates, people with disabilities cannot have any real power as long as they live in housing the service provider owns. By separating housing from supports, they say, residents can gain more control over their lives. If you are interested in home ownership, Chapter 5 describes some options for individuals with disabilities and their families.

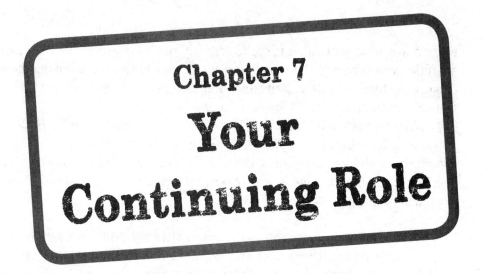

Chapter 7
Your Continuing Role

Helping Your Child Make the Move

At TILL (Dafna's agency), we are sometimes asked, "How long should the transition take?" There is no right or wrong answer to this question—it depends on your child. For some people, long transitions create anxiety, whereas others need time to process the idea of moving and become familiar with the new setting. Ask yourself: How has your child adjusted to new situations in the past? Is his sense of time and sequence of events realistic? Is asking him to wait a long time for an event useful or stressful for him? Once he is told that something will happen, does he obsess and become overly worried about it? The answers to these questions will let you know whether the transition should be short (a month or two) or long (several months to a year or more).

While there is no way to guarantee that the transition will go smoothly, there are some steps you can take to increase the chances of success. Depending on whether you are creating a new residence or your child is moving into a residence that is already up and running, the following strategies should work.

If you are creating a new residence, use the development time to create a true team bond among the future residents. Start a bowling, mini golf, or movie club that meets monthly or more frequently. This will help the group become unified and establish ties to one another. At some of these activities, a facilitator from the service provider could help the residents make household rules for their new home. (See the Appendix to Chapter 8 for examples of house rules.)

You can also use shopping trips to create bonds. The residents can go together to buy personal items for their rooms (sheets, comforter, curtains) and for the common areas (dishes, glassware, colorful artwork, etc.). Shopping can also help prepare individuals who are moving into an established residence. Buying items for your child's room can help make the move real. He can also choose items to bring from home (books, favorite stuffed animals, CD player, etc.). Pictures of family and friends—framed or placed in a photo book—can also help smooth the transition.

You should also help your child become familiar with the place and his new housemates. Arrange for him to visit the residence for a meal or an activity (music night, ice cream sundae party, etc.). In our experience, it is not necessary or helpful to visit overnight or for a weekend. Instead, it is the food, activities, and—most importantly—a welcoming attitude from others in the house that will create enthusiasm for the move. If your child can use the Internet safely or the telephone, he can exchange contact information with his future housemates.

Whether your child is moving into a new residence or one that is already established, you should have him participate in decisions to the extent he is able. Our experience has shown that children often make decisions based on different criteria than their parents use. Moreover, their instincts can serve them well, as this story about a new residence near Boston illustrates:

> A new five-bedroom house was being started for five women. In this house, there was one large sunny yellow bedroom that most of the mothers wanted their daughters to have. However, when the women visited the home with their new house manager, each of them picked a different bedroom without any argument. One chose her room because it was near the bathroom. Another made her selection because the room was in the back corner of the house where the sun would not wake her in the morning. Another wanted the room that was her favorite color—blue. Still another wanted the room with the large closet so she could "stuff everything into it before my Mom comes to inspect my room," which she was sure would happen.

Settling In: Where is "Home?"

After their child has moved in, some parents wonder whether they should visit or stay away for a period of time. Should their child come "home" for the weekend or stay at his new residence? How can they be most helpful to him? At TILL, we think it is usually best if the person does not return to his parents' home to sleep over for about a month. That way, he will not feel torn between his old home and his new home. You should decide whether a visit to your home for a few hours would be helpful or confusing to him. If he does visit during the first month—perhaps for a birthday party or holiday gathering—you should tell him what time he will be returning home and name the staff person who will be there to welcome him back.

Of course, during the transition period, you should visit your child at his new home. Bringing a treat or small gift for the entire house is a nice gesture and reinforces the message that you will still be a vital, yet different, part of his life than in the past. Taking your child to regular activities—religious services, family get-togethers, etc.—can also be reassuring. In the beginning, it is possible that your child will be upset when you leave his residence without him. You can reassure him by planning when you will see him again and what you will do.

After your child has settled in, how often should you see him? There is no right or wrong way to do things—every family is different. If your child lives independently close to your home, you might see him every day, or nearly so. Some adults with disabilities occasionally sleep at their parents' home overnight. Some families continue to attend religious services together and share their favorite recreation activities—bike riding, swimming, movies, eating out, etc. The emphasis should be on helping your child establish his own identity, which is not completely dependent on you. As time goes on, new patterns will develop as your child becomes involved in the routines and special events at his residence. Ideally, he will develop friendships with housemates and want to spend time with them on weekends and holidays. In this regard, adults with disabilities are no different than other young adults who have moved out.

If your child is in a shared living arrangement with another family, holidays can be tricky. One premise of shared living is that your child will become part of the new family and share their routines. The issues are similar to the ones encountered when any adult child gets married and wants to spend time with his or her spouse and children. Holidays may have to be negotiated. Sometimes both families celebrate together. One family's solution was for their daughter to celebrate Christmas twice—once with them and once with her new family.

Having a Formal Role

Besides spending time with their child after he moves out, another way that many parents stay involved is to have a formal role such as guardian, healthcare agent, or financial agent. If you haven't already taken on one of these important roles, you should consider doing so now. It will assure that you can obtain information about your child that would otherwise be considered private and confidential. Take medical information, for example. In the U.S., medical privacy laws dictate that when a person reaches adulthood (age 18 in most states), his personal medical information is considered to be private. No one—not even a parent—is supposed to be able to obtain it without the person's written consent.

Many people do not know that the concept of privacy also extends to residential agencies, employers, day habilitation programs, and others who deal with your child. Let's say you suspect there is a problem and try to intervene. Although most providers would probably voluntarily share information with you, some might refuse to do so, citing your child's (or his housemates') right to privacy. This can make it rather difficult to resolve the problem. Given that difficult situations *will* probably come up, we think it is best to be proactive by having legal documents in place that will assure your right to obtain confidential information. Some strategies to consider follow.

Guardianship

Most parents of children with disabilities know that they should consider guardianship when their child reaches the age of majority—18 in most states. Generally, this is something to think about if you have concerns about your child's abilities to responsibly and independently handle any of the rights that are ordinarily granted to adults. These rights include:

- directing (or refusing) their own medical care,
- deciding their education,
- handling their money and signing important legal documents such as credit card agreements, contracts, and car leases, and
- deciding to marry.

If you believe your child cannot reliably make these kinds of decisions on his own, you can ask the Court to appoint a guardian to make these decisions for him. Usually the parents are the initial guardians. If the parents develop health problems or become too old to serve, another relative— such as a sibling, niece, or cousin—can become the successor.

Note that each state has its own guardianship laws and procedures. For example, in some states, a person under guardianship can vote, while in other states, they lose this right. And in some states, a person under guardianship who obtains a credit card and

Common Questions about Guardianship

Can a person under guardianship vote? In most states, yes. Voting is a civil right, so in most states, a person under guardianship does not lose the ability to vote. Check with voting officials in your city or town to be sure. In states where guardianship blocks the person's ability to vote, the guardianship decree could be written to preserve that right.

Is a guardian financially responsible for the person? No. You are not required to spend your own resources to support the person. You are only responsible to use the person's income and assets to pay his or her bills. Similarly, your assets are not put at risk if the person harms someone, damages property, or makes ill-advised purchases.

Can a person under guardianship hire care providers? In most states, a person under guardianship loses the ability to sign legally binding documents, including care contracts. So any paperwork your child signs would not be enforceable. However, we don't necessarily see this as a problem because a guardian must respect the person's preferences when it comes to matters such as who will assist him in his home. If it is important to you that you child sign the paperwork himself, you can reserve that right in the guardianship decree.

Can a person who has a guardian own a house? Yes, in most states. The problem is that the person cannot sign legal documents related to the house such as a deed, mortgage, insurance contract, or application for a real estate tax abatement. It is almost always preferable to own real estate through a trust.

Is guardianship forever? No. If a person's functioning improves so that the guardianship is too restrictive, the guardian's power can be made less restrictive. For example, the guardian could only make medical decisions. A guardianship that is no longer needed can be vacated.

makes ill-advised purchases, or rashly signs a car or apartment lease, can have those transactions nullified by the guardian so there are no financial consequences. In other states, the person would have to return the property. If you opt for guardianship, be sure to work with a local attorney who is knowledgeable about the rules in your state.

Some parents are troubled by the need to have their child declared "incompetent" by a judge. After years of teaching their children to advocate for themselves, it can seem like a step backward. It is true that guardianship can be a rather blunt instrument. In some states, a person under guardianship cannot hire his own care providers or manage his own money. Fortunately, guardianship does not need to be an all or nothing proposition. Most states allow a guardianship to be tailored so that a person can still make his own choices about friends, lifestyle, and where he will live and work.

How do you know if your child needs a guardian? For some parents, the decision to seek guardianship is easy. In my case (Barbara is speaking), my son—who has autism and intellectual disability—cannot even understand that he has a choice in medical care, let alone decide the best treatment.

But if your child is more capable, the need for guardianship might not be so clear. In that case, you can obtain a *guardianship evaluation* from a professional (typically a psychologist, social worker, or developmental pediatrician). The examiner can gauge your child's ability to make important decisions by posing scenarios such as, "Your doctor wants you to take a certain medication. Should you do it?" Instead of giving a simple "yes" or "no" response (or turning helplessly to you), the examiner is looking for your child to ask questions about the purpose of the medication, its side effects, what would happen if he doesn't take it, etc. Other questions can gauge your child's understanding of money: "Someone calls and offers you a free magazine subscription. Would you accept it?" Or vulnerability to manipulation by others: "If a stranger asks you for ten dollars, would you give it to him?" These questions test your child's judgment, susceptibility to pressure, and ability to process novel scenarios.

Alternatives to Guardianship

In most states, before you can pursue guardianship, you must consider less restrictive alternatives. You must prove to the court's satisfaction that your child's interests cannot be protected by any less intrusive, voluntary arrangements. We list the most common alternatives below. Note that the alternatives require your child to be legally competent. This means that he must be able to understand the document he is being asked to sign, at least in a general way. If your child cannot comprehend the arrangement that is being proposed, guardianship is probably necessary.

Another important point is that except for representative payment of government benefits (discussed below), all the arrangements are voluntary and can be terminated at will by the person who agreed to them. Your child can withdraw consent at any time and nullify the arrangement. Your control may be illusory.

Documents for Medical Decision-making

The following are some documents that can help you manage your child's medical care.

- *Medical Release:* Your child can sign a medical release that will allow healthcare providers to communicate directly with you and give you any information they would give to your child. The physician's office probably has a form it uses. If staff from your child's residence take him to medical appointments, your child must sign a release form authorizing the agency and its employees to receive medical information. Your child will probably need to sign a separate release for each medical provider.

- *Permission to Share Forms:* These forms can be useful if you need to speak with medical insurance providers about benefits and coverage. Even if your child is covered under your policy, a provider might refuse to share information with you.

- *Health Care Directive:* Your child can sign a health care directive (also called a "health care proxy" or "health care power of attorney") that allows you or someone else to make medical decisions if he should become incapacitated due to illness or injury (stroke, seizure, accident, etc.). Every state has a law pertaining to health care directives. In most states, the document is *not* intended for routine communication, consent, and medical decision-making—in other words, it is not a substitute for guardianship. Moreover, even if a provider allows you to approve routine medical procedures, they would probably not let you consent to a risky procedure such as surgery unless you are your child's guardian. Except in the case of an emergency, medical providers insist that the patient—not the agent—must understand and personally consent to the risks. Before having your child sign a health care directive, be sure to check with an attorney who is knowledgeable about the laws in your state. You don't want to be lulled into a false sense of security.

Documents for Managing Finances

If your child needs help managing his finances, you could ask the court to make you his financial guardian or conservator. (Financial guardians and conservators manage a person's money through the court, but not the person's health care or personal decisions such as marriage or voting. The laws are different in every state.) A downside is that in most states, the ongoing court supervision process can be burdensome and expensive. You may be able to avoid court involvement by using one of these alternatives:

- *Representative Payee for Government Benefits:* If your child receives benefits from the Supplemental Security Income (SSI) program or Social Security Disability Insurance (SSDI) program, you could become his representative payee ("rep payee"). The checks can be deposited directly into a special bank account that you use to pay for items and services your child needs. You report annually to Social Security by completing a Representative Payee Report. (This can be done online.) Some local offices require rep payees to meet with them annually to share information about the recipient's income and assets.

- *Joint Bank Account:* You and your child can maintain a joint bank account. Your child can put paychecks, small gifts from family members, or other money into the account. You can help your child make purchases, pay bills, and manage the account. If your child receives SSI, make sure the bank balance (when added to your child's other resources) never exceeds $2,000. Even though the account may be joint with you, Social Security will count it as part of your child's resource limit.

- *General Durable Power of Attorney:* Your child can sign a general durable power of attorney (DPA) to appoint you (the "agent") to handle his finances and other important matters. The "durable" aspect of the DPA means the document will remain in effect if your child becomes seriously ill or incapacitated. Unlike with conservatorship, your child would not lose control of his money. He would merely appoint you to assist him in specific areas. Some financial powers that a young adult might delegate to an agent are:
  - Endorse and deposit checks payable to the person
  - Open a bank account
  - Sign checks to pay bills
  - Sign legal documents such as a lease or utility contact
  - Sign an agreement with a Personal Care Attendant
  - Get his mail at the post office, or change his mailing address
  - Manage assets through an investment account
  - Buy and sell property, including real estate

- *Limited Power of Attorney/Advocacy Agreement:* Perhaps your child needs help dealing with a temporary problem (a dispute with a service provider, employer, or state agency, etc.). He could sign a limited power of attorney authorizing you to assist him. The document could allow you to represent his interests and obtain information that would otherwise be considered private and confidential. The document could be limited in time and expire when it is no longer needed, such as after a year. Some agencies have their own forms that you would be required to use.

Having an Informal Role

Apart from having a formal role after their children move out, parents can be involved informally in their child's day-to-day life. At first it may be hard to find the right balance. But if you use your intuition and experience with your child as your guide, you will figure out what works best for your family. Some parents continue to take their children to medical appointments, buy their clothes, and take them for haircuts. Other parents are content to let the staff do this. Neither way is right or wrong. You have to take your cues from your child. Does he welcome your involvement, or resist it? If the latter, consider whether it is time to have staff take over these tasks.

If staff will be taking your child to medical and dental appointments, you must establish a system of communication. The staff person who makes the appointment should tell you in advance about the visit and then follow up to let you know what took place. Remember, if you are not your child's legal guardian, you should have a medical release, permission to share form, or other document that allows you to get this information.

Your idea of what is important may not be the same as the staff person's. One parent found out—after the fact and through her medical insurer—that a staff person had scheduled an expensive (and intrusive) sleep study for her son without her prior knowledge or consent. This should not have occurred. As her son's medical guardian, it was her role—not the staff person's—to approve or veto the procedure after weighing its risks, cost, and benefits.

For non-medical decisions, you have to determine whether or to what extent you want to stay in the loop. Your child's appearance is one example. If your adult child chooses his own clothes, or goes shopping with staff for clothes, the chances are he will dress differently than when you were buying his clothes. Without your input, your child may also acquire a new haircut, facial hair, a manicure, etc. If you aren't sure you like the change, should you intervene? We think it is best if you can be objective. Does your child look and dress like other people his age? Does he like his new look? Or is it a matter of personal taste—his style is different than what you would have chosen? If the latter, we think it is best not to intervene or you will risk alienating your child and the staff.

Of course, if you notice that your son or daughter looks dirty or disheveled, you must step in. This is true even if your child doesn't seem to notice or care. It can be stigmatizing to have a disability, and looking unkempt can only reinforce the most negative stereotypes. The staff who are responsible for your child should not let him appear in public unshowered, unshaved, with dirty hair or fingernails, or with torn or stained clothes. Sometimes you need to press the staff on this point. They should be encouraged to take the same care with the residents that they would exercise with their own children. If you take your case to the management, the agency will support you. They won't want lax grooming standards to create a negative impression of the agency.

> One day I visited Jack at his day program. He looked unkempt—
> unshaved, dirty hair, stained pants. I talked to the manager
> at his group home right away. He told me that everyone at
> the house bathed in the evening—no exceptions. There was no
> time for showering or shaving in the morning. After a year of
> negotiations—and tweaking the morning schedule—Jack began to
> shower in the morning. And by year two—more negotiations—a
> staff person helped him shave with a blade razor (not electric).
> Handsome son, proud mother— crisis resolved this time. . . .

What if your child is living independently or semi-independently without any live-in support and stops taking care of his appearance? You know he has the self-care skills to take a shower, brush his teeth, etc., but he is not doing it? Or what if he stops washing his clothes and using deodorant? Most experts would agree that someone who stops attending to his appearance is probably suffering from depression, anxiety, or overwhelming stress. If your child has a therapist or counselor, you should contact that person and let them know about your concerns. (If your child has not given you permission to speak with the clinician, you will need a signed release in order to share information. This is covered earlier in this chapter.) If your child is not seeing someone, encourage him to do so. A professional may be able to identify the cause of the symptoms and get your child back on track.

Spending Time at the Residence

Another common question is how often you should stop by the residence—and what you will do when you are there. Some residents like their parents to visit, while others want them to stay away. This is another area where you have to figure out how to be helpful without being intrusive. Take your cues from your child. One mother (Barbara) had the habit of going through her son's dresser drawers and throwing away his torn or stained clothes. She didn't understand why her son became agitated whenever she headed toward his room—until someone helpfully pointed out that she had never asked his permission to discard his clothes. Another mother had a regular "appointment" with her daughter to iron her clothes and organize her drawers and closet. She did it in a way that respected her daughter's preferences and was satisfying for both of them.

If you are going to visit, it is probably best to let your child know in advance. Few young adults like their parents to drop by unannounced. Why would your adult child with a disability be different? Some parents think there is an advantage to a surprise visit. They might find something amiss—staff yelling at residents or residents left unattended, etc. It's possible that you might uncover a problem, but it's also possible that your actions could alienate your child or make the staff uncomfortable. If you suspect there is a problem, it is probably better to tell the agency. A pop inspection from management usually yields more results than one from the family. Another option might be a joint visit with someone from the agency. You can explain your concerns and make sure the agency will investigate them.

Helping your Child Get Healthy and Stay Healthy

When our children are living at home, most of us work hard to keep them healthy by providing a balanced diet and encouraging them to exercise. But when they move out, we can lose control over what they eat. They can gain (or lose) an unhealthy amount of weight and develop diet-related medical problems such as hypertension or high cholesterol. This doesn't have to happen. Assuming there are no underlying medical problems, the basic formula for good health is fairly straightforward—proper diet and adequate exercise. Of course, eating right and getting enough exercise is easier said than done—otherwise everyone would be thin and healthy. Still, some families and agencies have managed to find strategies that work.

Staying Healthy with a Wholesome Diet

For some people who have recently moved out of the family home into their own place, the problem is too much choice. A young adult who is living on his own for the first time may celebrate his independence by eating whatever he wants, whenever he wants. He might subsist on junk food and gain an unhealthy amount of weight. Of course, weight gain is not something that just happens to people with disabilities—as any first-year college student who has succumbed to the Freshman Fifteen can attest.

A good starting point could be to make sure that your child understands the basics of healthy eating before he moves out. (In Chapter 3, we recommended that you obtain a residential assessment before your child moves out. This would let you know if he needs help to make healthy choices about food.) Don't just assume he knows which foods he should eat (fruits, vegetables, grains, low-fat dairy, etc.) and which ones to avoid (foods that are processed, high sodium, calorie dense, etc.). If he doesn't, a crash course that includes the food pyramid, reading labels, and portion control might be needed. Staff from the residential agency can often help, as this employee at an apartment program in Boston explains:

> I am a social worker at an agency that runs a supported independent living program. A lot of our folks are sedentary and overweight when they come to us. We teach them the basics about healthy eating. We have a picture of what a plate should look

like—about half fruits and vegetables, and the other half grains and protein like meat, chicken, or fish. We plan menus together and make a shopping list. We go food shopping together and read labels to make good choices for foods that are low sodium and low calorie. We help them make healthy substitutions, like veggie burgers and low-fat sausage, plus low-fat dairy products. Junk food like chips and sweets are not forbidden, but we ration them and they have to last until the next time we shop.

Even if you plan meals carefully, eating between meals can undo your plan—as any dieter knows. Some people with disabilities have a lot of unstructured time and can eat to fill up the time. Others just get hungry waiting for meals and make bad food choices. Here is how one mother of a 25-year-old woman solved the problem:

Alyssa's downfall has always been snacking. She gets hungry between meals, or maybe she is just bored, but she eats way too many calories between meals. When she lived with me, I was the Food Police. Now that she has her own apartment, I can't monitor her all the time. We made a list of foods that she can eat between meals and put it on the refrigerator. This month it was microwave popcorn (low fat, low salt), baked chips and salsa, fruit, raw veggies with low-fat dip, or a microwave potato (white or sweet with butter substitute). She checks off the snack she eats so we have a record and she doesn't "forget" what she ate. The 100-calorie snack packs are a lifesaver. So far, what we are doing seems to be working.

If your child lives in a group residence, you don't have the problem of unrestricted access to food. The selection of food and amounts are usually carefully controlled. Most agencies have a nutritionist on staff or someone they consult with. There are sample menus to make sure residents are eating the recommended amount of fruits and vegetables (five to eleven servings a day) and not getting excess sodium. The house manager usually makes the menus based on the residents' preferences. Staff who do the food shopping have guidelines to follow. Ideally, the food should be unprocessed, low salt, and low fat.

Families can encourage healthy eating by creating opportunities in which the residents can participate, as Barbara relates from her own experience:

The parents from my son's residence purchased a "farm share" as a holiday gift for the house. Every week from spring through fall, the guys go to a local farm to pick up a box of seasonal fruits and vegetables along with recipes for preparing them. It's an activity they can do together, and the menus have definitely become more interesting. It's a little challenging for the staff, who have had to learn to cook kale and tomatillos. But it was definitely an interesting experiment and everyone wants to do it again next year.

In our experience, most parents (usually mothers) have an opinion about the food their children are being served and would like to change some things if they could. We see this most often when their child is making the transition from the family home to a group residence. That can raise the question, to what extent, if any, should you intervene? Let's say you think a hot breakfast is important, but everyone at the group residence eats cold cereal in the morning. Or you want your daughter to eat brown rice instead of potatoes, or you want her to eat a salad every day. Or maybe you just don't like the menus in general.

This is another area where you have to take your cues from your child. Ask yourself: is my child reasonably satisfied with what he is eating, or am I imposing my preferences on him? If your child asks for specific foods, you can ask the house manager to incorporate them in the menu. Most house managers will accommodate you. Some parents bring dishes from home that can be frozen and reheated. Sometimes gifts of equipment (rice cooker, food processor) can make the staff's job easier. Perhaps your child likes a food that no one else wants to eat—tofu and sardines come to mind. He could take them for lunch. In these instances, you just have to be flexible and be aware of the staff's and other residents' concerns and preferences.

But if your child is having a food-related health problem that is causing him to gain or lose an unhealthy amount of weight, you must intervene. You could have your child's doctor write a letter explaining that it is medically necessary for your child to maintain a healthy weight. The doctor could make specific recommendations (calorie restrictions, low-fat diet, low-salt foods, etc.). The agency would make sure to follow the recommendations.

Some parents believe (or have been told) that it is not possible to follow a special diet when everyone eats together. This is not correct. If your son or daughter requires a special diet, the residence should be able to accommodate it. It just takes extra planning and vigilance. At one group home in Newton, Massachusetts, where four seniors live, three of the residents have special diets—gluten free/casein free, hypoglycemic, and low calorie. There are detailed lists of instructions, menus, and ingredients posted in the kitchen. While it can be challenging for the staff to manage, the residents are healthy and enjoy mealtimes together.

When you and the agency come up with a plan for healthy eating, everyone has to be on board. You don't want the staff to undermine your plan, as this mother relates:

> My daughter gained a lot of weight (over 20 pounds) really quickly when she moved into a staffed apartment program. The meals were reasonably healthy, but there was just way too much food and anyone who asked could have a second helping. The staff and residents go food shopping together once a week, and they let her buy her favorite Oreo cookies and other sweets. They said she was an adult, and if she wanted to eat Oreos, that was her "right." I appealed to the agency for help. Now she eats two cookies for dessert—if she has walked on the treadmill or has done some other kind of exercise for 20 minutes that day.

Staying Healthy through Exercise

Besides following a healthy diet, the other part of maintaining good health is getting enough exercise. Many people with disabilities are not motivated to exercise and do not get enough of it. In this regard, they are not different from much of the rest of the American population. But according to the American Heart Association, we only need about 30 minutes a day of physical activity in order to maintain good heart health. Almost anything that gets you up and moving can count. It could be walking (outdoors or indoors on a treadmill or at the mall), swimming, biking, or doing housework or yard work. According to the Heart Association's website, the activity can even be divided into 10- to 15-minute segments.

As with healthy eating, it is ideal if your child is exercising regularly while he is living at home. Almost every community has sports programs (soccer, basketball, softball, etc.) that can be adapted for people with disabilities. Other fitness activities such as walking, biking, hiking, swimming, and skiing can be done as a family.

When you are researching agencies, be sure to find out whether the agency has a commitment to keeping their residents fit. An agency should have a plan to make sure their residents are getting an adequate amount of exercise. For example, TILL has a winter bowling league that includes all the residences. The summer track program culminates in an agency-wide track meet that includes wheelchair races and features a staff-resident relay race.

In 2012, TILL challenged its residents and staff to an agency-wide Wellness Initiative in which participants earned points for exercise. Minutes of activity were traded for "miles" on a virtual trip across the country that began in Provincetown, MA, and ended in Long Beach, CA. There were weekly raffles and a final drawing of the top twenty participants' names. As a result of the challenge, many residents and staff had fun and got healthier together. See the box on the next page for more details about TWI—TILL Wellness Initiative.

If your child lives independently and would use exercise equipment, you could purchase an exercise bicycle, treadmill, Nordic ski track, or elliptical machine. Another option is a membership in a gym, health club, or YMCA. If you think your child would follow through, you could give a few sessions with a personal trainer as a gift.

Sometimes exercise is more appealing if you do it with other people. Your child could join a fitness club or walking group. Often you can find such groups at a local senior center, Arc, or community education group. Still another option is to join your child for a walk, bike ride, hike, or swim.

It can be challenging for residents in group living to get enough exercise if people are at different fitness levels. One person may be tired by a short walk, while another has the energy for a strenuous hike. Nevertheless, keeping in mind the American Heart Association's guidelines that only a half hour of exercise a day is needed for good heart health, there are many activities that residents can do alone or as a group to stay fit. Here are some things the residents do for exercise at the TILL residences:

- Walking
- Swimming at the local YMCA, fitness club, or high school pool
- Basketball (going to a gym or shooting baskets in the driveway)
- Badminton
- Mini-golf
- Beanbag toss
- Kicking a soccer ball
- Frisbee
- Croquet
- Wii
- Bowling
- Track

TILL's Wellness Initiative Wants You to TWI to GET MORE ACTIVE!

TILL's Wellness Initiative encourages everyone to focus on health and wellness in their everyday lives.

- Enjoy a healthy lifestyle
- Lose weight
- Reduce stress
- Increase physical strength & endurance
- Nutrition tips & low calorie recipes
- Free health screenings at Dedham office
- Win valuable prizes

TILL is proud to announce the kickoff of our Wellness Initiative, encouraging everyone to focus on health and wellness in their everyday lives, starting Sunday, August 5th with their first contest.

Take a Virtual Walk on Route 6—America's Longest Continuous Highway

Route 6 stretches from our very own Provincetown and ends 3652 miles away at the Long Beach Convention and Entertainment Center in Long Beach, CA. The time you spend engaged in any type of exercise will be tracked as virtual miles on Route 6.

Not only will you be improving your health, but your activity points will earn valuable TWIckets for our weekly raffles.

The rules are easy:

- Track the time you spend engaged in any type of exercise.
- Earn points each week by submitting your weekly activity tracking sheet.
- Each minute engaged in low intensity exercise earns one point and each minute engaged in high intensity exercise earns two points.
- For every 100 activity points you submit, your name will be entered on a raffle ticket for weekly prize drawings.
- The TOP 20 participants' names will be entered into the Final TWI Drawing at the TWI Health Screening Event.
- You could win great prizes like a Nexus Tablet or gift certificates!!

So get moving. You can be healthy, and win prizes too...if you just TWI.

- *Dance, Dance Revolution*
- Exercise videos
- Yoga
- Treadmill
- Exercise bicycle
- Elliptical machine
- Gardening
- Yard work—raking leaves or shoveling snow
- Housework—vacuuming, sweeping, dusting

Sometimes lack of staff can thwart your plans to keep your child fit. Staff shortages can be a chronic problem. But if you appeal to the agency, they may be willing to accommodate you. The state disability agency that funds the program would probably support you if you highlight the health and wellness angle. Here is how one mother persuaded her son's agency to get him the regular exercise he enjoys:

David loves to swim but was not getting the chance after he moved out. Even if there is a lifeguard, he needs a 1:1 in the locker room, and there weren't enough staff to supervise him. So I mentioned this at his annual service plan meeting with the state disability agency. It was decided to make swimming part of his fitness goal. I bought a membership at the local YMCA. On Sunday mornings when there is "open swim," the agency reassigns staff from another house so someone can take him. Sometimes they pick up a young man from another house who doesn't need as much help, so David has someone to swim with.

Chapter 8
On Their Own

The "traditional" group home as we know it is a fairly recent creation. As we explained in Chapter 3, residences for people with disabilities were developed several decades ago when institutions were being closed and community alternatives were needed. Yet most group homes were developed for people with disabilities—not by them. Most single adults without disabilities choose to live alone or with a roommate—not in a group of three to eight unrelated people.

Of course, there can be benefits to group living. We outlined some of them earlier in this book. One benefit is social. A group residence can provide a ready-made social setting for people who do not form friendships easily. We have seen housemates form bonds that last a lifetime. A group residence can be a "community within a community," as David Wizansky, the founder and president (with his wife Margot Wizansky) of Specialized Housing, Inc., eloquently explains:

"The adults we serve create communities for themselves at home, over time, that meet their most basic needs, needs we all have, needs we usually meet within our family or within a culture of our peers. They create a community at home where they can relax, be themselves, where they are not teased or made to feel uncomfortable, where they can do most things at their own pace, spend their time the way they choose, a community in which they are supported, cherished, validated, where they can be of help to another person and ask for help without being ashamed. We have even observed housemates acting as translator for housemates whose speech is hard to understand."*

In addition to these social benefits, there is an economic advantage to living with other people. The cost to live alone can be prohibitively expensive. But if several people share expenses and supports, it can become affordable. It can make the difference between staying home with your family and moving out.

---

* David Wizansky, *Identity, Self, and the World: Learning from Adults with Developmental Disabilities* (Brookline, MA: Specialized Housing, Inc., 2012), page 30.

Group living can have drawbacks too. Some group residences have a lot of rules—many of them made for the convenience of the agency and staff, rather than the residents. In some residences, mealtimes and even bedtimes are scheduled so that staff can complete a checklist before their shift ends. In homes where there is 24-hour support, staff come and go at all hours of the day and night. They enter the house without knocking. They aren't expected to, of course—it is their place of employment. Sometimes it can feel like the residents are living at the staff's job site, instead of staff helping the residents in their home.

Privacy

Lack of privacy can be a problem in group living. You have to share the kitchen, bathroom, and living room with others. Your only private space may be your bedroom—and even that may not be truly private. Staff may come into your room without knocking. Other residents may touch or even break your belongings. People from the agency or the state may go through your home from time to time to inspect it. Periodically you are jolted awake by a fire alarm and have to go outside in your pajamas.

But there are things that agencies and staff can to do enhance residents' privacy. They include:

1. Keep housemates out of a resident's room unless they are invited to enter. This can be a house rule and be reviewed at house meetings. Staff should set an example by knocking and asking permission to enter.
2. If someone will be going into the resident's room when the person is not there to make a repair, do an inspection, etc., the resident should be told in advance, except in case of an emergency.
3. Residents can help clean their rooms and arrange their things the way they like.
4. Nothing should be thrown away without asking the person's permission.
5. Residents should be permitted to put a sign on their door when they do not want to be disturbed.
6. If a resident wants to have privacy for a guest (such as in the living room), she should be allowed to do this.
7. All residents should have privacy in the bathroom unless they need staff assistance to use the toilet, shower, etc.

Over the years, I have belonged to several Human Rights Committees. One of the members' responsibilities is to visit the agency's group homes and talk to the residents. We are told to inspect the residents' rooms for health and safety problems like blocked exits, dirt, clutter, windows that don't open or close properly, etc. One agency told us to go into every resident's room—even if they were not home. But another agency instructed us to always ask permission to enter, and to never go into someone's room if they were not home. I quickly adopted the latter approach. It seemed more respectful of the person's privacy. It's true that the person might never know you had been in his or her room. But other residents could know and might assume that a stranger could intrude on their privacy at any time.

Individuality

When our children live at home, we try to make sure they enjoy their favorite activities outside the house. But when they are living with a group, doing activities alone outside the residence can be problematic. Instead, the staff try to find ways the residents can go out and have fun as a group. The challenge is that the residents may not have much in common besides living together and having a disability. Thus, choices may be made according to the lowest common denominator instead of individual preference. Most people can go bowling or for a van ride—but not everyone wants to. In homes like this, you usually have to go out with the group, even if you don't feel like it. Often there are not enough staff so that some people can go out and someone can stay home.

If your child is missing her favorite activities, you can begin by asking the agency for assistance. Although the agency doesn't have to accommodate your child's needs, most will try to do so. They may be able to redeploy staff in order to have more people working during certain shifts.

If the agency is not able to accommodate your child's individuality, you may be able to step in to help. Some families take their child to activities that she may be missing—religious services, swimming, shopping, etc. Another option is to hire one-to-one assistance privately. There is probably a direct care worker who already knows your son or daughter and would be willing to spend time with him or her on a paid basis.

In the long term, if the home cannot accommodate your child's preferences, you may have to consider a more individualized setting, such as shared living with a family. We offer some guidelines at the end of this chapter.

Conflicts with Housemates

Whenever people live together, conflicts are bound to arise. This is true in group homes as well. Someone might go into your son's or daughter's room without permission and take or break their things. Your child might turn her television or music up too loud and disturb a housemate. A housemate might be noisy, rude, or disruptive. Your child might even be injured by a housemate.

Housemates should be encouraged to resolve conflicts among themselves. One way they can do this is by having house rules that apply to everyone. The rules, which the residents develop together with assistance from the staff, cover things like privacy, quiet, mutual respect, and guests. House rules are covered later in this chapter, and the Appendix contains examples of house rules that were developed in some TILL residences.

Another way housemates can avoid problems is by having regular house meetings. In most residences, these meetings take place weekly. The meetings are a way to plan schedules, activities, menus, and chores. The residents can discuss any problems that come up with housemates and try to resolve them. House meetings are useful for residents regardless of their developmental level or ability to communicate. People who are nonverbal can participate by using pictures, calendars, or other visual means of communication. The important point is that there is a process for making decisions, and everyone is part of the process.

But sometimes problems come up that aren't resolved by discussion or peer pressure. If a housemate is habitually disruptive, the agency must step in. A behaviorist (usually a psychologist) can develop a behavior plan.

In its mildest form, a behavior plan involves giving a reward for good behavior. For instance, if a difficult resident habitually disturbs a housemate's room, the resident would be rewarded for staying out of the room. The reward would be something special the resident enjoys—going out with a favorite staff person to buy a magazine, spending one-to-one time with staff, etc.

If the behavior plan doesn't work to modify the person's behavior, the agency must try different strategies. But sometimes the strategies—while effective to curb the problem behavior—can create problems for the other residents, as this story from the father of a group home resident illustrates:

> Our daughter Judy liked her residence well enough, but she had a problem with a roommate who habitually went into her room and took small things like hair clips, lip gloss, and jewelry. The staff talked to her but it didn't help. So they put a lock on Judy's door. We complained that this violated Judy's human rights because she had to ask staff to let her into her room. So the staff put the key on a ribbon that Judy can wear around her neck when she is home. It's not perfect, but it's the best we can do, all things considered.

At another group home where a resident could not control his eating, the staff locked the food cabinets and refrigerator. The residents had to ask permission to eat. If staff were busy, they had to wait. Clearly the agency's solution violated the residents' human rights. But the residents, their families, and guardians had been consulted and had agreed (albeit reluctantly) to the plan. They reasoned that if staff were occupied guarding the food, their children would receive little, if any, attention.

If a resident is violent, the police might be called, although this is a rare occurrence in homes for people with developmental disabilities. Staff are usually instructed to only call the police if they cannot deescalate the situation and the safety of residents and staff is threatened.

If a resident is habitually disruptive or violent, the residents and their families might want the person removed for safety reasons. For families, these situations can be especially distressing because they highlight how little control we have once our children enter a residential setting. If you don't own the property, you can't decide who lives there. You can lobby the agency, but ultimately the composition of the house is their call. Moreover, some agencies must accept everyone the state refers to them—no matter how challenging the person's behavior may be. (In Chapter 2, we recommended that when you interview the residential provider, you ask if they can reject someone the state refers to them.) If the agency won't act, you can ask the state agency that is funding your child's placement to intervene. But if their efforts are not successful, your only option may be to leave the agency.

Sexuality and Relationships

"My daughter will get pregnant." We sometimes hear this from anxious parents who are reluctant to let their daughter move out. We know this can be a concern—but pregnancy is extremely unlikely. During the 32 years in which TILL has served over 10,000 individuals with disabilities, there has never been a pregnancy in one of our group residences. We don't think TILL is exceptional in this regard. In our experience, agencies are extremely protective of their residents and watch them closely. It would be highly unlikely that two residents could carry on a sexual relationship without staff being aware of it.

Sexuality Education

In addition to watching out for the residents, most agencies teach the residents how to protect themselves through training in sexuality and relationships. In many states, this training is required by the state office of disability services that oversees the agencies. Several award-winning trainings for people with developmental disabilities are offered by the James Stanfield Company (Stanfield.com). Two popular offerings are the *Circles* curriculum and *LifeSmart* curriculum. Planned Parenthood (www. plannedparenthood.org) has also developed widely used training materials.

During training, individuals receive different kinds of information according to their developmental level and ability to process information. Most residents receive basic information about gender differences and about their bodies. Depending on their interest in the topic and living situation (one gender or mixed gender household), some might also receive instruction about the reproductive process, birth control, and sexually transmitted diseases.

If you prefer that your son or daughter not have this kind of training, you should discuss this with the agency—preferably at the time you select the provider. This can avoid conflicts and misunderstandings later.

Self-governance and House Rules

Even though the residents are being taught about sexuality, this doesn't mean they are encouraged to act on their impulses. Many agencies segregate their residences by gender. And even in mixed gender homes, romance between residents is not encouraged. For the most part, this is for practical reasons. As in any group living situation, two people who are focused exclusively on each other can make their housemates uncomfortable. And if there is a break up, the former couple's animosity can ruin the harmony of the home, as demonstrated in this story from a house manager in Boston:

> Lou and Cindy, who both have developmental disabilities, lived
> in one of our eight-person group homes. They became an "item"
> and decided they were dating. They sat close to each other on
> the couch, held hands, and kissed when they thought no one was
> looking. This went on for a few weeks. Then Lou got interested
> in another housemate, Susan, and broke up with Cindy. It was
> just like high school—yelling, tears, and slamming doors. It made
> everyone in the house unhappy. We decided it would be best if
> Lou moved to a house with all men.

In some residences, Lou's and Cindy's conduct might not have been tolerated for so long, if at all. This is not to say that a resident can't openly express affection for someone she likes. She should be able to, assuming her feelings are reciprocated. But an excessive display of affection that makes housemates uncomfortable could affect everyone's quality of life. One way to resolve the situation might be to discuss the behavior at one of the regular house meetings. (We cover house meetings later in this chapter.) The residents could decide together what behavior makes them uncomfortable and what they can tolerate.

Intimacy

As part of sexuality training, residents can learn about what behavior is acceptable in public versus what they can do in private. This can be reinforced at the regular house meetings. Most agencies tell their staff to respect the residents' privacy when they are in their room alone with the door closed.

If a person in a group residence wanted to be intimate with a partner, this would probably become a topic of discussion at the agency level. The agency might seek input from both individuals' families. (This would depend on whether the person had a legal guardian. If the person was her own guardian, the agency could not share this kind of private information without the person's consent.) The individual might be encouraged to speak with someone in the family, a trusted friend, or a counselor that she has a good relationship with. There would be discussions with the person about their understanding of their bodies, the need for contraception, their values, their families' values, etc.

While most parents worry about their children being sexually active, a few want their children to be able to develop a mature relationship. If you are one of these parents, you should discuss this with the agency before your child moves in. Ask if any of the residents have been sexually active, and, if so, how it was handled.

Abuse Prevention

All parents worry that their child could be the victim of abuse. Agencies are extremely aware of this and know they must keep their residents safe. To prevent abuse by staff, they screen job applicants carefully, check references, and perform criminal background checks. In some agencies, male staff are not permitted to dress or bathe female residents. If you are worried about your daughter being abused, then at a minimum you should insist that she live in an all-female residence where the staff are also female.

Education can also help prevent abuse. Many people with disabilities can be susceptible to pressure, which can make them vulnerable. Training in this area focuses on basic safety skills, assertiveness, and respect for one's own body.

Last, some people with disabilities may be inappropriate with others. They might coerce susceptible individuals or take advantage of them. If this occurred, the agency would probably keep the residents separate. Extra staff might be needed to do this. The individual who behaved inappropriately would be educated about respecting other people's preferences and not pressuring them to do something they do not want to do. A behavioral psychologist might be brought in. As a last resort, the individual could be removed from the home.

Some people with disabilities are able to communicate that they have been mistreated. But what about people who are not so capable? Staff are trained to recognize signs of abuse, and families also need to be alert. Besides obvious visible signs such as bruises, scratches, burns, broken bones, or damage to clothing, some warning signs of abuse are:

- A change in eating habits, such as refusing food or overeating
- Reluctance to return to the residence after a visit with the family

- A change in behavior upon returning to the residence (for example, your child might avoid a certain person or go directly to her room instead of remaining in the common area if that has been her practice in the past)
- A change in the person's activity level compared to her normal activity level
- Reluctance to participate in group or 1:1 activities
- Expressing a bodily ache or pain that is not related to a physical ailment you can easily identify, such as a flu or infection, etc.
- Fear of being touched

Asking your child directly about possible mistreatment may not yield the desired information because she might be afraid to discuss it or not have the language to do so. It is also possible that your child might give you information that is inaccurate or unreliable in order to get attention or for some other reason.

If you suspect abuse, you should talk to a supervisor right away. While these may be difficult conversations to have, the agency will want to hear your concerns. In our experience, agencies take reports of abuse seriously. They do not want their residents to be harmed or their reputations to be damaged. They should document their investigation, share the results with you, and take any necessary action. Since any instance of abuse is also a human rights violation, the situation may be brought to the agency's human rights committee for investigation and corrective action.

If you are not satisfied with the way the agency handles the situation, you can contact the state department that oversees the agency. Depending on the state where your child lives, there may be an independent state body that protects persons with disabilities. For example, in Massachusetts, the Disabled Persons Protection Commission investigates and remediates instances of neglect and abuse of persons with a disability. However, keep in mind that an accusation of abuse—even one that turns out to be unfounded—can create ill will and damage the reputation of an agency or a staff person. Therefore, you should only involve others outside the agency as a last resort to protect your child or others served by the agency whom you believe may be at risk of harm.

House Meetings and House Rules

One way to encourage successful group living—even in a group as small as two people—is to have regular meetings. The residents can share information and discuss issues that come up, such as one resident eating another resident's food, going into someone else's room without permission, or making too much noise. Providing a regular outlet for such discussion even when there are no current issues ensures that tensions do not arise because people do not have a place to talk about things that bother them. The meetings can also be a forum for staff to teach the residents about their human rights. A staff person should facilitate the discussion in order to encourage open communication and fair solutions.

This can raise the question: how can people who are nonverbal or who have limited ability to express themselves participate in a meeting? This can be challenging, but we have seen it done. It is a gradual process—not something that happens suddenly when it is time to discuss "self-determination" or human rights.

It begins with the agency's "culture" that everyone's life has value, everyone has something to share, and everyone has opinions and preferences—even people who are completely dependent on others for their care. The family plays a role by educating the staff about their child's preferences for food, clothes, environment, ways of being touched and handled, etc. Staff can be trained to watch and listen for cues that the person is indicating a preference. Staff can also make their own observations as they get to know the person.

Many residents can be taught to express their preferences. For example, staff can provide them with choices throughout the day (what to eat, what to wear, whether to bathe before or after dinner, etc.). The goal is to progress to the point where residents can express their preferences, changes they do not like, or even signs of abuse.

A house meeting for such residents would be run differently than one for residents who can express themselves verbally. At one TILL residence, the staff made a bucket of materials that included a thermometer and bandages in order to help residents learn to talk about health care issues and reporting ailments. Another bucket contained soap, shampoo, and deodorant to represent good hygiene and personal care. The group focused on one topic a week until the association was made.

A by-product of these house meetings can be clearly defined *house rules* that apply equitably to everyone in the home. The rules, which are developed by the residents with assistance from support staff, can cover topics such as privacy, quiet times, guests, and mutual respect. The appendix contains examples of house rules that were developed in some of the TILL residences.

Moving On—When Is It Time for a Change?

Few adults live their entire lives in the same place, so why should people with disabilities be different? It's true that many adults with special needs thrive on familiarity and tend to resist change. Still, in our experience, people do move from one residential setting to another. Often the reason for the move is positive. Your child could:

- acquire new skills and want to live more independently;
- get married and move out to live with their spouse;
- become friends with someone and want to live with them;
- develop new interests and want to live with people who share her interests;
- become more mature and want to live with housemates who are more compatible.

There can also be troublesome reasons for the move:

- A housemate may be aggressive or mistreat your child. Perhaps you feel your child's physical safety is at risk, and the agency cannot or will not do anything about it.
- Your child's needs for assistance (such as mobility) could increase, and the residence cannot be adapted to meet her needs.
- Your child might have too much independence and could benefit from more structure in a family or small group setting.

In our experience, the need for change is not something that happens overnight. It develops over time. Pay attention to the signs and trust your instincts. You know more than you think. In Chapter 1, we described the tremendous amount of emotional effort it takes to let go of your child. Now all that is behind you and you can help your child move to the next stage of her life.

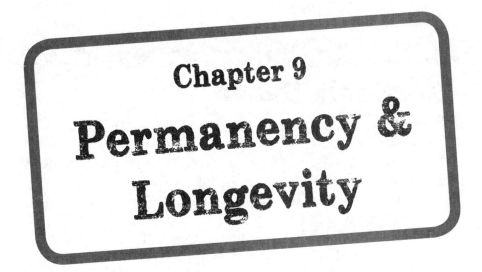

Chapter 9
Permanency & Longevity

Whether your residential arrangement is up and running or still in the planning stage, you will need to make sure there are sufficient funds to keep it going when you are no longer able to contribute—whether due to your retirement, disability, death, or financial reversals. You must also make sure that the funds you leave will be protected and properly managed for your family member.

Sound planning is not only important for your own family member—it benefits the entire project. Many residential projects are based on the premise that everyone must contribute his or her share. If someone stops paying, it can jeopardize the project's stability and risk everyone's well-being.

We recommend that you ask about the plans that others in the group have made for future funding of the project. This is a sound business practice.

This chapter covers the major aspects of future planning in this area. In general, you will need to:

- Plan to use your child's money in ways that maintain eligibility for public benefits.
- Plan to use your own funds to supplement costs that public benefits don't cover, or to pay the full cost if your child does not receive public benefits or you choose not to use them.
- Accumulate the necessary funds or maintain adequate life insurance (or both).
- Protect the funds from your creditors, including nursing homes, and minimize factors such as estate taxes that can deplete the funds.
- Assure that the funds will be properly managed after your death.

Planning with Your Child's Money: Maintaining Eligibility for Public Benefits

Government benefits—both federal and state—can play a crucial role in supporting a person with a disability. Some of these programs pay monthly cash benefits, and others provide housing, residential services, and one-to-one support. We described some of these programs in Chapter 4 and there is also information about them in the Appendix.

Even if your child does not need government benefits right now, it is important to position him to take advantage of them in the future. A good place to start is by making sure that your child only owns a minimal amount of assets—no more than $2,000—in his own name. Assets that you and other family members plan to leave your child for future support should be left to a trust. (In most cases, this will be a special needs trust.) Protecting assets in a special needs trust will assure that your child can participate in government benefit programs that have an asset cap. There is information about special needs trusts later in this chapter.

But what if your child participates in a public benefit program that does not have an asset cap? Should you restrict the amount of assets she can accumulate? Do you need to bother with a trust? It is true that not every program restricts the amount of assets a participant can own. The SSDI program (which pays a monthly stream of income), federal Section 8 (which pays for housing), and Medicare are cases in point. In many states, people under age 65 can receive community-based Medicaid benefits regardless of the amount of assets they own.

That can raise the question: If your child can own an unlimited amount of assets in his own name and still receive public benefits, why should you bother with a trust? Even if a trust is not needed for public benefits reasons, it might still make sense for sound management. Money that is held in a trust can be properly managed, invested, and distributed by a trustee that you choose. The money will be there when your child needs it. Moreover, government program requirements—including financial rules—can change. Even if a program does not have an asset test now, it might impose one in the future. Or your child might need to use a program at a later date—such as state-funded residential services—that imposes an asset cap. Either of these scenarios could leave your child scrambling to divest himself of asset he might need for his future support.

The following are some general strategies we recommend to maximize the chances that your child will be able to access public benefits when and if he needs them. Be sure to talk with an attorney or financial adviser to decide the best course of action for your family:

■ Do not set up savings or investments accounts in your child's name. These include custodial accounts under the Uniform Gifts to Minors Act (UGMA) or Uniform Trusts for Minors Act (UTMA), and college savings plans such as 529 plans. If you want to save money for your child, put it in an account in your own name and designate your child's trust to be the beneficiary of the account on your death. Most banks and investment companies allow you to designate an account as Transfer on Death (TOD) or Pay on Death (POD). Alternatively, you could create a trust and establish a savings account in the name of the trust.

■ If your child receives any monetary gifts from relatives, consider putting smaller amounts (say, under $10,000) in an account in your name. (See the discussion about saving your child's money in the previous bullet point.) Larger amounts could be put in a bank account in the name of a trust that you establish. There may be additional savings opportunities if the ABLE Act becomes law. The ABLE Act would allow people with disabilities and their families to save money for disability-related expenses. The money would not be counted as a resource for public benefit programs and could grow tax-free. (See the box on page 136.)

- Create an estate plan that includes a special needs or other kind of trust. On your death, some or all of your assets can flow into the trust. Assets owned by the trust—as opposed to assets owned directly by your child—will not interfere with eligibility for government programs that place limits on the amount of assets a person can own. We discuss special needs trusts later in this chapter.

- Discuss with your child's grandparents and any other relatives who might leave him an inheritance the importance of protecting eligibility for government benefits. Any gifts should be left to a trust for your child instead of directly to your child. Ideally, you have already created a special needs trust, and the relative can simply refer to the trust in his or her estate plan.

- Coordinate your life insurance policies, retirement accounts, and annuities with your overall estate plan. In most cases, your spouse will be the primary beneficiary, and your child's trust can be one of the alternate beneficiaries (or the sole alternate beneficiary).

- If you are separated or divorced and your child is receiving SSI (or will qualify for it in the future), consider asking for child support to be paid to a special needs trust for your child. Under the Social Security rules, child support is treated as your child's income and will reduce or eliminate SSI benefits. This reduction also applies to court-ordered support payments that are made for an adult (age 23 or older). However, support payments that are made directly to a properly drafted special needs trust are not counted as your child's income, and thus your child can receive SSI benefits.
    - Another strategy would be for the noncustodial parent to pay third parties who provide medical care, medical equipment, clothes, transportation, recreation, etc. Under the pertinent SSI rules, payments that are made directly to providers are not considered to be the child's income. Moreover, there is no dollar limit on the amount of funds that can be spent in this manner (although as we explain in Chapter 4, payments of food and housing will reduce the SSI benefit by up to $1/3$ each month).
    - Note that if your child receives SSDI benefits, you do not need to employ these strategies. Under the SSDI rules, a person's benefit will not be reduced no matter how much income or how many gifts he receives from outside sources. The SSDI program is covered in the Appendix to Chapter 4.

- If you or your child's other parent are receiving Social Security benefits due to retirement or disability, or if the parent has died, be sure to let Social Security know this. A disabled son or daughter may be able to receive Social Security Disability Insurance (SSDI) benefits based on the disabled or deceased parent's work record. The monthly

Disability Savings Accounts (ABLE Accounts)

The ABLE Act, which is pending in the U.S. Congress as of this writing, would allow individuals with disabilities and their families to save money for disability-related expenses.* Under the proposed law:

- A person with a disability, his relatives, or others could deposit money in a special savings account. The account would not be counted as a resource for government benefit programs, except that if the assets in the account reached $100,000, the person would lose SSI benefits (but not Medicaid.) If the account balance dropped back below $100,000, SSI benefits would resume.

- The money would grow tax-free.

- The funds would not be taxed when they are withdrawn as long as they are used for qualified disability-related expenses, including education, housing, transportation, employment support, medical needs, and assistive technology.

- The person with a disability could manage the account himself or appoint another person to manage it.

- If there are any funds left in the account when the person with a disability dies, they would be used to pay the person's Medicaid expenses that were incurred after the account was set up. Any funds that remain after the Medicaid agency has been paid would pass to other beneficiaries who were named when the account was set up.

These features could make an ABLE account an easy, low-cost way for a person with a disability to save for a home, car, or education without losing public benefits. The person could even manage the account himself.

But the Medicaid "payback" feature does not make these accounts especially attractive to families who want to leave an inheritance to a child with a disability. If you are like most parents, you want your money to go to other family members—not the government—when your child with a disability is gone. Your attorney will probably advise you to create a **third party special needs trust** for your child. (These trusts are discussed later in this chapter). Except in very limited instances, any funds that remain in a **third party special needs trust** when the beneficiary dies can go to family members or charities—not the state.

---

* The full name of the bill is the Achieving a Better Life Experience Act of 2011. The house bill is H.R.3423, and the Senate bill is S-1872.

SSDI benefit is often higher than the SSI benefit, and there is no asset limit for the SSDI program. In order to qualify for SSDI benefits, the child must have been continuously disabled since before age 22. There is information about the Disabled Adult Child program in the Appendix.

Planning with Your Own Money: Supplementing Public Benefits

The first step in planning with your own funds is to estimate how much money will be needed to support your child for the rest of his life. If he is already living outside the home, this is easier than if he is still at home and the residential arrangement is in the future. You already know the amount of money public benefits are contributing (or could potentially contribute). You can develop an annual budget and project it over your child's life expectancy. (To determine a person's life expectancy, you can use a table from the IRS or almost any company that sells life insurance. If the person has significant medical issues that might shorten his life expectancy or a disability such as Down syndrome that is associated with a shorter life span, you should factor this in.)

In addition to the residential costs that are already being paid, you should include funds to pay for the services of guardians, advocates, and trustees. You will also need to include items such as inflation and the need for additional services and supports as your child ages. A financial planner can assist you with this process. There is information about financial planners in the Resources section at the end of the book.

If your child is still living at home, the task is harder. It is difficult to develop a budget because there are so many unknowns. Even if you obtain the residential assessment that we recommend in Chapter 3, you may not have a very good idea of what services will be needed, what they will cost, and—most importantly—how much public benefit programs will contribute.

Faced with all these uncertainties, many families simply choose to leave a substantial portion—or all—of their assets to a trust for their child with a disability. They may also buy a life insurance policy that has a death benefit of $500,000, $1 million, or more. This may not be the most mathematically precise way to go about planning, but it makes a certain amount of sense. You can be certain that a substantial amount of assets will be available for your child. If his needs change while you are still living, you can change your plan.

Estate Planning: Is Equal Always Fair?

All this can raise the question: should you divide your assets equally among your children or leave more to your child with a disability? There is no right or wrong answer—every family is different.

In most families, the parents plan to leave their children equal inheritances. After all, they reason, you can't go wrong treating your children equally. If money equates with love, then your final statement to your children is that you love them all equally.

Also in most families, one of the children has been identified or has volunteered to take on the parent's role to care for their sibling with disabilities. While this doesn't necessarily mean this sibling will take her brother or sister into her home, she will have a formal role such as guardian, trustee, or advocate. There can be the expectation—sometimes self-imposed—that the sibling's well-being is her responsibility. We think it is easier for a caretaker child to assume this responsibility if the inheritance she receives is at least equal to her disabled sibling's—even if financial needs of the sibling with disabilities may be greater.

Other families do things differently. Some parents plan to leave more, or in some cases, everything, to the child with disabilities. The siblings expect it, accept it—and even welcome it, as this brother of a 55-year-old woman with cerebral palsy expresses:

> My sister has always lived with my parents, who are in their late 70s. My parents are going to leave their house and all their assets to a trust for my sister. I am fine with this. I even took them to the attorney who set it up. Even if my parents left money to me, I would probably end up saving it for my sister in case she needs anything. That's how I was raised. It is better this way, knowing that she will have enough money of her own.

Whatever you decide to do, we recommend that you discuss your plans with your adult children and perhaps involve them in the estate planning process. You should also involve your child with a disability in the planning process to the extent he is able to participate.

We know it is not always easy to talk about money (let alone disability and death). You might start by meeting with each family member individually to discuss your mutual expectations. If it turns out that your expectations are not reasonable, you can change your plans. Then you can hold a meeting, or series of meetings, with the entire family. You can't guarantee there will be harmony after you are gone. But you can probably minimize the chances that your plans will be undermined—and your disabled child's security jeopardized—by long-standing conflicts, misunderstanding, and resentment within the family.

Accumulating the Funds

Once you have a general idea of how much money will be needed, you might need a strategy to accumulate the funds. In many respects these strategies are not different from the ones you would employ to reach other goals such as saving for college, buying a house, or accumulating retirement funds. For most families, this is a two-pronged approach: reduce debt and increase savings.

Reduce Debt

There are some commonsense techniques that people use to reduce or eliminate debt. These strategies, which you can read about in *Money* magazine, *Kiplingers, Consumer Reports,* and other popular money-related publications, are no different than those families without a child with disabilities use.

You might be advised to "live below your means," which generally means you would buy a smaller house than you can afford, take modest vacations (or "staycations"), bring a brown bag lunch to work, and so forth. The publications typically recommend that you monitor your debt and pay off credit cards each month, but if you can't do that, transfer your credit card balances onto a single card that has a low interest rate.

Readers are also advised to create a budget and pay necessary items first (mortgage, utilities, health insurance, etc.) and discretionary items last (private school for your children, entertainment, and so forth). They also suggest tracking your spending so that you know how much is coming in and going out every month. You can use online software like Mint (free of charge at www.mint.com) or Quicken (Quicken.intuit.com), or do it the old fashioned way with a calculator.

Of course, we live in difficult economic times, with many families living paycheck to paycheck. You may be not be able to develop a workable budget, let alone save money. In this case, a nonprofit credit counseling organization could assist you to manage your money. They usually offer free workshops and materials and can work with you one-to-one to develop a personalized plan. If you are worried about debt collectors or may be facing bankruptcy, a debt management plan might make sense. You deposit money each month with a credit counseling organization that uses your deposits to pay your debts. Your creditors may accept lower interest rates and waive fees.

If you are considering credit counseling or a debt management plan, a good source of information is the Consumer Information section of the Federal Trade Commission website: http://www.consumer.ftc.gov/topics/money-credit.

Increase Savings

In addition to managing debt, you need a disciplined plan to save money. You probably have many other things to save for besides your child with a disability, such as college for your other children and your own retirement. Still, it helps to have a plan to get you where you want to be financially. Most experts recommend that you start saving early. Your savings can grow as interest compounds and dividends are reinvested. You should also diversify your investments in a mix of stocks, bonds, and real estate. According to *Consumer Reports* magazine, having a variety of investments correlates highly with net worth, regardless of one's income level.* You should also take advantage of any options offered by your employer. Many employers automatically enroll new employees in a 401(k) or other retirement savings plan. You can deposit money into your account and may receive matching contributions from your employer up to a specified amount.

You can work on a savings plan yourself or hire a financial adviser to assist you. The person could recommend specific investments or even take over investing your savings. Often a professional can spot opportunities you may have missed to increase earnings on your savings and decrease excessive fees.

You can also create an instant estate by buying life insurance. There are many different kinds of life insurance. Some policies are temporary. This is called "term insurance." You only pay for protection as long as you need it. When you no longer need the coverage—for example, your children have completed their educations and become independent—you can cancel the policy.

Term insurance probably doesn't make sense if you are buying it to fund a permanent residential arrangement. The premiums increase as you get older, and they can become unaffordable in the later years of the policy. Moreover, your health could change and pre-

---

* "15 Ways to Never Run Out of Money," *Consumer Reports* (February 2011).

vent you from renewing the insurance at the end of the term. A better solution is to consider permanent insurance. This kind of insurance is known by different names—whole life and universal are two examples. Permanent insurance is designed to last your entire lifetime. The premiums are usually higher than for term insurance. However, the premiums can be structured so that you will be done paying them at a future point in time. Then the policy will remain in effect until your death with no additional premiums due. When you die, the beneficiary you have named receives the amount that you insured your life for (the death benefit). In most states, the beneficiary does not pay income tax on the insurance he or she receives.

A popular way for couples to own life insurance is through a second-to-die policy. The policy covers both lives, but no benefits are paid until the second spouse dies. The premiums are usually less than if both members purchased separate policies. The policy would remain in effect as long as the premiums are paid, even if the couple gets divorced.

Whenever you buy a life insurance policy, you can name the person or persons who will receive the benefits on your death. This person is called the beneficiary. It is extremely important to name the proper beneficiary. In most cases, you should not name your child with a disability to be the direct beneficiary of the policy. You should create a trust for your child and name the trust to be the beneficiary. This could be a special needs trust or another kind of trust. If you have already named your child as the direct beneficiary of the policy, it is easy to change the beneficiary—you simply obtain a form from the insurance company, complete it, and return it.

Another option for life insurance is to set up an irrevocable life insurance trust (ILIT) to own the policy. Special needs trusts and ILITs are covered later in this chapter.

Protecting the Funds

Most families are understandably concerned about protecting their assets. They don't want to lose what they have accumulated due to unforeseen illness, accident, prolonged unemployment, or business reversals. Nursing home costs are another concern. Most of us have heard stories about someone whose assets have been depleted by the costs of long-term care. Protecting assets is especially important if you have made a financial commitment to fund a residential arrangement. You can't risk that the funds you have accumulated will be depleted or lost completely.

It is probably impossible to insure against every risk—so you need to prioritize. A middle-aged couple might focus on having adequate insurance to protect their home, savings, and retirement assets. An older person might focus more on reducing estate taxes and protecting against nursing home costs. Most asset protection strategies involve trade-offs. If you choose to buy long-term care insurance to cover potential nursing home expenses, the significant premiums may reduce your ability to accumulate savings. Similarly, if you place assets in an irrevocable trust—a strategy some people use to protect assets from nursing home costs—you could lose your ability to use the asset when you need it.

In this section, we cover some common concerns and discuss steps you can take to protect your assets. We recommend that you consult a qualified financial advisor or an attorney (or both) before attempting to implement any of the strategies we discuss. Every family's situation is different. You will need personal advice that is tailored to your particular situation.

Strategies to Protect Assets from Nursing Home Costs

Parents and other caregivers are understandably worried about becoming disabled and being unable to care for themselves. They may need expensive care at home or have to enter an assisted living facility or even a nursing home.

If you become disabled yourself, you may require help with everyday activities such as dressing, bathing, fixing meals, and using the bathroom. But since these kinds of services are considered to be personal rather than medical, it can be difficult to get a health insurance plan to pay for them. Some people have *employer-based medical insurance* that pays for care at home. There are usually limits on how long you can receive this insurance.

If you are a veteran and become disabled, you may qualify for assistance through the *Veterans Administration's Aid and Attendance Program.* Such income can be used to pay for home care, assisted living, or nursing home costs. The income can be combined with Social Security and pension benefits to provide veterans who served on active duty during World War II, the Korean War, or the Vietnam War with up to $2,054 of income per month to a married veteran (in 2013). Single veterans and surviving spouses of veterans can receive lesser amounts. Another source of funds to pay for home care is long-term care insurance, which is discussed later in this chapter.

The major public benefit program in the U.S. that pays for nursing home is the Medicaid program. The Medicaid rules that cover people who live in long-term care facilities are different than the rules for people who live in community settings such as group homes. (The Medicaid community rules are covered in Chapter 4 and in the Appendix to Chapter 4.) The rules in most states require nursing home residents to reduce their assets to $2,000 or less before the state will pay for care. Each state sets its own asset allowance for married couples when one spouse is healthy enough to remain in the community. For example, in Massachusetts, the spouse residing in the community may retain ownership of the home and up to about $110,000 of other resources.

The following are some general strategies that people use to pay for nursing home costs. Be aware that the Medicaid laws and practices change frequently. Each state's rules are different. Therefore, if you are considering any of the strategies we discuss, you should work closely with an attorney in your state who specializes in Medicaid planning.

■ *Long-term Care Insurance.* Long-term care insurance provides you with income to pay for care at home, in an assisted living facility (ALF), or in a nursing home. Most states regulate the sale of long-term care policies by specifying key factors such as the minimum amount of benefits and duration of benefits. You can obtain this information from your state's insurance commission. Some states offer long-term care partnership programs that promise consumers asset protection in exchange for buying long-term care insurance. For example, in Massachusetts, the state will not place a lien on your home if you have long-term care insurance and need to move into a nursing home. Timing can be important when it comes to buying long-term care insurance. It makes sense to buy a policy while you are young. The premiums increase as you age, and if you suffer a disability, you might not be able to obtain coverage.

■ *Asset Shifting.* Since Medicaid recipients can only retain $2,000 in resources, some people assume that they can give away their assets when they get sick in order to qualify for care. Congress has closed this loophole by imposing a five-year "look back" period during which the government can review your financial transactions. If you give away any amount of money during the look-back period, it triggers a penalty period that begins the day you apply for benefits. The length of the penalty period depends on the amount you gave away and the average daily cost of nursing home care in your state. Applicants can avoid the penalty by proving that the gift—for a granddaughter's wedding, grandson's bar mitzvah, annual donation to a favorite charity, etc.—was not made with the intent of impoverishing themselves to qualify for Medicaid.

- *Giving a Home or Funds to Someone with a Disability.* There are a couple of important exceptions that apply to people who are facing nursing home care and have a friend or relative with a total and permanent disability. You can give your home to your child or grandchild with a disability who is under age 65 or to a special needs trust for the person. You can also transfer money to a special needs trust for any person with a permanent and total disability who is under age 65. The trust must specify that when the beneficiary dies and the trust ends, the remaining funds will be used to pay the person's Medicaid bill with the state.

- *Irrevocable Trust.* Another technique that people use to preserve assets is to transfer them to an irrevocable trust. The assets must be transferred to the trust at least five years before you apply for nursing home benefits. Since each state has its own rules that govern irrevocable trusts, you need to proceed carefully. In Massachusetts, for example, you can retain the ability to receive income—but not principal—from the trust.

- *Irrevocable Life Insurance Trust.* The cash surrender value of a permanent life insurance policy is counted as part of the $2,000 resource limit for most government benefit programs, including nursing home-level Medicaid benefits. (The cash surrender value is the amount you would receive from the company if you cancelled the policy before your death. Most permanent life insurance policies have this option.) Thus, you might have to surrender your policy and use the cash to pay for your care. For example, if you owned a life insurance policy with a death benefit of $250,0000 and a cash value of $10,000, you would have to surrender the policy and spend the $10,000 on nursing home care before you could receive benefits. To avoid this result, you can own the policy through an irrevocable life insurance trust (ILIT). These trusts are discussed in more detail later in this chapter.

Strategies to Protect Assets from Creditors

Sometimes events can occur that are beyond a person's control. An accident, uninsured illness, property loss, or prolonged period of unemployment can erode or wipe out a family's savings. The funds that were accumulated for a son's or daughter's future care can be lost. The following are some common ways to protect against these kinds of losses:

- *Medical Insurance.* About half of all families filing for bankruptcy do so in the aftermath of a serious medical problem.* The comprehensive federal health care law that was passed in 2010 is supposed to prevent such hardships. Parts of the new law,

---

* Elizabeth Warren and Leo Gottlieb, "Medical Bankruptcy: Middle Class Families at Risk" (testimony before House Judiciary Committee, Washington, DC, July 17, 2007).

including the requirement that family coverage must be extended to children until they reach age 26, has already taken effect. However, other parts of the law, such as discrimination based on a pre-existing medical condition, will not take effect in every state until 2014. It is critical to maintain adequate family medical insurance that covers all contingencies. Government medical insurance coverage is available for family members with disabilities. Recipients of Social Security Disability Insurance (SSDI) get Medicare automatically after they have received SSDI for 24 months, and in most states, SSI recipients get Medicaid automatically. (Medicare and Medicaid are covered in Chapter 4.) These programs can provide stand-alone coverage or supplement a private medical insurance plan.

- *Property Insurance.* Make sure that you have adequate homeowner's coverage to protect against loss. Some key factors to look for in a policy are replacement coverage (which pays the full cost to repair or replace your damaged home or possessions as opposed to paying the decreased value of the items at the time of the loss) and inflation protection (which adjusts your homeowner's policy annually to include the increase in building costs). Review your auto insurance coverage and make sure it is adequate. Also consider purchasing an umbrella policy, either as part of your homeowner's policy or separately. These policies can provide coverage above and beyond the standard limits of your primary policies. They can also cover claims that are excluded from traditional policies such as personal injury lawsuits that are unrelated to your residence. See Chapter 6 for information on umbrella policies.

- *Disability Insurance.* According to analysts at the Life and Health Insurance Foundation for Education, Americans have a one in five chance of being out of work for at least a year before the age of 65. Disability insurance will replace income if you are unable to work due to a mental or physical disability. Coverage can be short- or long-term. Many people who are employed have this kind of coverage as part of their benefit package. Some employer plans allow you to buy additional coverage through the same group plan at low cost. Self-employed people can purchase a private policy through an organization, club, or professional association that offers that kind of coverage.

- *Homestead Protection.* An important source of protection for the equity in a home can be a Homestead exemption. This protects the equity in your home from being seized by creditors. Some states have automatic protection so that if you file for bankruptcy or are sued, you can keep a specified amount of equity. Most states permit homeowners to obtain additional protection by filing a "declaration of homestead" or similar document at their local registry of deeds.

- *Asset Shifting.* In some states, simply owning your residence jointly with your spouse will convey protections from creditors. For example, in Massachusetts, couples who own their home as "tenants by the entirety" can prevent a creditor from forcing a sale of the home while both spouses are living and occupying the home. People in high risk professions such as physicians, as well as self-employed individuals, are sometimes advised to have their spouse be the sole owner or divest themselves of their assets completely by placing them in an irrevocable asset protection trust.

Strategies to Protect Assets from Estate Taxes

Estate taxes—both federal and state—can reduce the amount of assets your survivors will receive. Your taxable estate will comprise everything you own when you die. This can include your personal residence and other real estate, retirement accounts, savings, investments, life insurance policies, and personal effects such as automobiles, jewelry, and artwork. Under the federal estate tax rules and those of most states as well, you can pass everything to your spouse free of estate tax. Thus, you can postpone the tax by leaving everything directly to your spouse. The problem can be that when your surviving spouse dies, all the property he or she received—together with your spouse's own assets—can trigger an estate tax.

At the time of this writing, an individual can pass up to $5.25 million to his or her heirs without incurring a federal estate tax. However, 15 states and the District of Columbia impose their own estate taxes. For example, the exemption amounts (the amount that is not taxed) are $1 million in Massachusetts and $2 million in Connecticut. If you are within the range that is subject to the federal or state estate tax, you should discuss strategies to reduce estate taxes with your financial advisor, accountant, or estate planning attorney. Proper planning in this area can increase the funds that will be available to support your child with a disability when you are gone.

Using Trusts to Reduce Estate Taxes

Two kinds of trust—the bypass trust and the irrevocable life insurance trust—are common ways to reduce estate taxes.

- *Bypass Trust.* A bypass trust (also called a credit shelter trust or family trust) allows you to leave selected assets for your spouse and children (including your child with a disability). The trust "bypasses" your spouse's estate, so no taxes are owed upon your death or your spouse's death. This is true even if the assets in the trust appreciate significantly after your death. Typically the surviving spouse can receive the income and specified amounts of principal from the trust. When the surviving spouse is gone, the remaining funds are distributed to the children. The share for the child with a disability can remain in the trust for his or her lifetime use or be distributed to a special needs trust.

- *Irrevocable Life Insurance Trust (ILIT).* Some people who are concerned about estate taxes buy life insurance to cover the tax. But life insurance proceeds can add value to your estate, so the more life insurance you buy, the larger the tax. You can avoid this problem by owning life insurance through an ILIT.

  An ILIT is a trust that is both the owner and beneficiary of a life insurance policy. To pay the premiums, you give money directly to the trustee. An ILIT can be rather restrictive:
  - There must be an independent trustee or co-trustee. Under the IRS rules, the trustee cannot be, among others, the grantor (creator) of the trust or the grantor's spouse, parent, sibling, child, or grandchild.
  - The trust must be irrevocable. That means that once you set up the trust, you cannot change the terms, including the beneficiaries.
  - You cannot borrow against the life insurance policy or have any access to its cash value.

If you can live with these restrictions, an ILIT can be an effective way to own life insurance. Since the ILIT is a separate trust with an independent trustee, the policy is protected from your creditors, including nursing homes, if you should need long-term care.

Managing the Assets after You Are Gone

Money that is earmarked for the future care of a person with a disability should be left to a trust. In most cases, this will be a special needs trust. (In some states, a special needs trust is called a supplemental needs trust. We use those terms interchangeably.) Using a trust will maximize the chances that the funds will be properly managed when you are gone. A trust can also assure that the person can receive government assistance despite having the trust. Under many government programs (for example, SSI and, in most states, Medicaid), a person can only own a limited amount of assets. Funds held in a properly drafted special needs trust will not be counted toward the asset limit for government benefit programs.

How a Trust Operates

A special needs trust is managed by one or more trustees. Trustees usually have sole discretion to spend—or not spend—the trust funds according to instructions in the trust document. The trust funds can be used to pay for items the beneficiary needs that are not covered by public benefits. When the beneficiary dies and the trust ends, any funds that are left in the trust can pass to one or more remainder beneficiaries who were named when the trust was established.

Some people are reluctant to use a special needs trust due to the impression that when the beneficiary dies, the funds must pass to the state. This is not the case with every special needs trust. If the trust contains funds that belonged to the beneficiary's parents or other third parties (such as grandparents) before they were put in the trust, the remaining funds can pass to family members or charities who were named to be the remainder beneficiaries. (This is called a *third party special needs trust*.)

By contrast, if the funds belonged to the beneficiary before they were put in the trust—this would be the case if the source of the funds was an inheritance or accident settlement—the funds must be used to pay back the beneficiary's lifetime Medicaid expenses. (This kind of trust is called by different names—*first party special needs trust*, *payback trust*, or *(d)(4)(A) trust*.) There is another instance when repayment to the state is required. That is when a parent or other relative puts money into a special needs trust as a way to obtain immediate Medicaid nursing-home-level benefits for themselves. We described this kind of trust earlier in this chapter.

For a thorough discussion of special needs trusts, including so-called payback trusts, see *Managing a Special Needs Trust: A Guide for Trustees*, by Barbara D. Jackins, Richard S. Blank, Ken W. Shulman, and Harriet H. Onello (DisABILITIESBOOKS, 2012).

Selecting Trustees

You will need to select one or more trustees to manage the trust. Usually parents are the initial trustees. The trustee's job is to manage the trust by investing the funds, paying the taxes, and using the trust funds for the beneficiary's needs. Managing a special needs trust can be rather challenging. You need to make sure that you do not inadvertently disrupt the beneficiary's public benefits. Most trustees work closely with an attorney who is knowledgeable about public benefits and special needs trusts.

Choosing Successor Trustees

Selecting successor trustees who will take over when the parents are gone can be difficult. You can probably identify qualified people in your own generation, such as your siblings, close friends, or professionals. But statistically, your child with a disability will probably outlive your contemporaries, and so you will have to tap people in your child's generation, and maybe even people younger than he is.

If you have a child who does not have a disability, that child could be the successor trustee—assuming he or she is reliable and is interested in the job. But if your other child is still young, it may be too early to determine whether he or she is willing and able to act as the successor trustee. A strategy some attorneys recommend is to allow any trustee who is resigning to name his or her successor. So you could name your sister to manage your child's trust after your death, and if she has to resign, she can name someone to take over (such as her child). The child can name someone else (such as his spouse), and so on. But if you follow this to its logical conclusion, your disabled child's money could end up in the hands of someone you have never met, or who has not even been born yet.

But let's say that you decide to name your child without a disability to be your successor. You might meet with resistance from your attorney. Some attorneys do not think it is a good idea to name a child without a disability to be a successor trustee. They warn that it can create a conflict of interest: a trustee sibling who will be receiving the remaining money in the trust when the sibling with disabilities dies might not be motivated to spend it as generously as needed. Most parents are aware of this potential conflict of interest and choose to ignore it. They believe that their child's love and affection for their sibling will prevail. Moreover, they believe the sibling knows his or her brother or sister better than people outside the family do and can make sound choices. Most importantly, they know the sibling will be around for the long term, unlike others who will come and go in their child' life.

Yet another question that can come up is if it is all right to name the same person to be the legal guardian and the trustee. This is common in small families where there are not enough qualified people to fill both roles. If the same sibling is the guardian as well as the trustee of her trust, there is a potential conflict of interest because the trustee may be paying herself to provide guardianship services. In this situation, some attorneys recommend having some built-in checks and balances such as an independent person (someone in the family, an attorney, or the court) who reviews the trustee's financial accounts to make sure the fees are reasonable. But this kind of oversight can be expensive, and in our experience, most families opt to not impose this cost burden on the trust.

If conflicts of interest are a concern, however, or if you are struggling with issues of longevity, you could use one of the following strategies:

- Set up a co-trustee arrangement in which a family member (such as your sibling, child, niece, etc.) and a professional (such as a bank or trust company) are co-trustees. The professional trustee will invest the money and handle the tax reporting. The family member will keep in close touch with the beneficiary and tell the professional how to spend the money on items the beneficiary needs. The family member can remove the professional trustee and replace it with another bank or trust company.

- Have two trustees who will serve as co-trustees. If one resigns, he or she selects a successor. In that way, there will always be at least two trustees who are accountable to one another and to the beneficiary. For extra protection, you can specify that the trustees will provide regular financial accounts to another family member or a neutral third party, such as an attorney, accountant, or other professional.

- Select a pooled trust or master trust to manage the funds. There are nonprofit agencies in most states that assist people with disabilities who cannot manage their own funds. These groups can be a valuable resource for families who have no one to manage the trust in future generations. The trusts invest the funds so they earn a reasonable rate of return. They charge an annual fee (typically 2% or 3% of the trust principal) and deduct it from the funds they are managing for your family member.

When to Fund the Trust

Another issue that can come up is when to put funds in the special needs trust—while you are living or at death. There is no right or wrong answer. Each family's situation is unique. Depending on your circumstances, there can be significant personal, financial, tax, and public benefits considerations to each approach. It can be worthwhile to discuss these with your attorney and/or financial advisor. The following summarizes the benefits and drawbacks of each method.

Funding the Trust at Death

Most families—especially when they are young—plan to fund the trust at death. This means that while they are living, they will continue to own their assets in their own names. They have a will that directs some or all of their assets into the special needs trust for their son or daughter with a disability. They might also name the special needs trust to be a beneficiary of some or all of their life insurance policies and retirement accounts. The advantages to this kind of arrangement are:

- The trust can be flexible. You can retain the ability to change its terms or revoke it altogether if your circumstances should change. (By contrast, a trust that contains assets before your death should be irrevocable.)
- You retain full access to your funds. You can use them to pay your routine expenses and any unforeseen items that come up.

There can be some drawbacks to keeping the funds in your own name:

- Your assets are exposed to your creditors, including nursing home costs, if you or your spouse need long-term care.
- You might have to pay estate taxes on the funds, thereby reducing the amount that is available to your child with a disability.

Funding the Trust While You Are Living

Another approach is to put funds in the special needs trust while you are living. The advantages to funding the trust while you are living are:

- You have the comfort of knowing that funds have been earmarked for the person with a disability. You don't have to worry that every dollar you spend might reduce the funds that are available to pay for his care.
- The funds can be protected from your creditors. The availability of creditor protection would depend on the trust language and the state where you reside.
- The funds can be protected from your or your spouse's nursing home costs.
- Grandparents and other relatives could give cash, life insurance, or a portion of their estates to the trust.
- You can spend some of the funds on your child's behalf while you are still alive and therefore make sure he is getting items and services he needs. If you have named your child without a disability or another relative to be the successor trustee, that person can learn how the trust operates while you are still alive.

The drawbacks to this approach are:

- Flexibility is reduced because, in most cases, you can't change the terms of the trust if your family circumstances change.
- Taxes are more complicated. The trust should have its own employer identification number (EIN) and file its own income tax return. Depending on the amount of income the trust earns, taxes might be higher than if you had reported the income on your personal return. You will also have to pay someone to prepare the annual returns.

Transitioning to Future Caretakers

Another part of planning involves arranging for others to assist your child when you are no longer able to do so. Ask yourself the question: what would not get done if I were not here to do it? A good starting point might be to list the things you do for your child. The list might look something like this:

- Attend service plan meetings
- Visit your child and/or take him to your home from time to time
- Monitor your child's health and address any medical issues
- Go to medical appointments and/or review medical records
- Manage public benefits by completing paperwork for applications, reviews, and re-certifications
- Speak with staff on a regular basis and review log books or other records at the residence
- Do fun things together like walking, biking, swimming, amusement parks, restaurants, and vacations
- See that your child stays in touch with other family members
- Make sure your child's grooming and hygiene are adequate (shower, shave, haircut, nails, clean clothes, etc.)
- Attend agency events to support your child and meet other families and staff
- Periodically take inventory of clothes and personal possessions and replace any worn or broken items
- Make sure your child has enough money to meet his needs

- Use your child's money to pay his bills
- Research promising new therapies or treatments to see if your child might benefit from them
- Make sure your child has something meaningful to do during the day, such as a job, volunteer position, or day program
- Celebrate birthdays, holidays, and other special occasions with your child, his friends, other family members, or staff

Now think about how much you can reasonably expect others to do on your child's behalf. The list will probably be a lot shorter. You might decide to prioritize some items (medical care and money) and discard others (taking your child home for visits and attending agency events). Then think about who is available to help your child. The list might look like this:

- ***Siblings, Other Relatives, and Friends.*** Sometimes a sibling will come forward and say she wants to take over responsibility for her brother or sister with disabilities when you are gone. This is ideal—you can show her what is involved in being a guardian. She can come to service plan meetings with you, attend social events, and meet the people who are important in your child's life—whether they are friends he lives with, key staff, or decision makers at the residential agency or state level. If you don't have a child to take over, you can tap family and friends to assist your child. They might be willing to take him to lunch, shopping, or church; attend doctor visits; or help him solve problems or make important decisions.

- ***Circle of Support.*** Sometimes the family and friends form a "Circle of Friends" or "Circle of Support." The group could be expanded to include coworkers, neighbors, service providers, and others who take an interest in the person. These individuals would meet on a regular basis to help your child accomplish certain goals that he cannot meet on his own, such as finding a job or locating an apartment. There is information about Circles of Support in the Resources section.

- ***Private Case Manager.*** A private case manager is someone you hire privately instead of going through an agency. Private case managers usually have a background in social work, mental health, or direct care of people with disabilities. Their services are not covered by insurance, so you have to pay them privately. He or she can teach practical skills, as well as oversee your child's general well-being. They can do things such as:
  - Help with routine paperwork such as applications, public benefit reviews, leases, vouchers, etc.
  - Teach the person how to use public transportation
  - Help the person manage his finances, including setting up automatic deposits, paying bills, and balancing the checkbook
  - Assist with meal planning, shopping, and buying personal items
  - Set up medical appointments, take the person to the appointment, or make sure he attends them
  - Coordinate the person's medical care among different providers
  - Help the person do laundry, organize his home, and make sure the home is reasonably neat and clean
  - Help the person obtain his medications and see that he takes them

- Help locate, interview, and hire Personal Care Attendants and others who can help the person on a daily basis
- If the person has a trust, coordinate with the trustee to make sure the funds are being used to meet the person's needs

- *Social Worker, Therapist.* A social worker can perform some of the same functions as a private case manager. A therapist can assist the person with interpersonal issues such as getting along with roommates, family, coworkers, etc. Unlike with a private case manager, a social worker's or therapist's services may be covered by insurance, although there may be limits on how often your child can see him or her.

- *One-to-One Paid Staff.* A common concern of parents whose children live in group homes is that their child will be bored. When the parents are gone, there may not be anyone who can take him to his favorite activities. It is true that in most group homes, one-to-one time with staff is quite limited. The residents tend to do things as a group. However, it is possible to pay someone to spend one-to-one time with your child. These people are usually direct care workers (former or current) who want to supplement their income. The agency that serves your child can probably locate someone.

- *Service Coordinator.* Service coordinators (called case managers in some states) work for the state agency that provides funding for direct care services, job training, and other services for qualified adults with disabilities. Their job is to make sure the agencies are actually delivering the services they are being paid to provide. The service coordinator can attend planning meetings and advocate on the person's behalf for things like additional funds, a change of residence, different work or day program, etc.

- *Provider Agency.* An agency can be a surrogate family. They provide a ready-made social group; make sure the person has someone to celebrate holidays with; and arrange for friends and staff to visit if the person is sick in the hospital. A good agency can also be attuned to the resident's needs by offering new therapies that might become available or a different residence if the person's needs have changed. A good agency will also advocate on the person's behalf with the service coordinator, or assist the family to do so.

Tools the Future Caretaker Will Need

Whether you are choosing a family member or a professional (or both) to be your successor, it is important to leave enough money for them to do their job. Most professional caregivers charge a fee for their services. A relative who does not have the time to assist your child according to your standards can hire a private case manager. Money to pay the guardian's and case manager's fees can be left to a special needs trust.

In addition to providing funds for the caretakers, you must make sure they have the necessary legal authority to do their job. A person cannot oversee an adult's medical care, manage his money, or advocate for him, without proper legal authority.

- *Legal Guardian.* If you are your child's legal guardian, you can ask the court to appoint a co-guardian to serve with you. If you have to resign due to poor health, or if you die, the person will become the sole guardian. Alternatively, you can name a successor guardian in your will. Be advised, however, that in most states, the person you nominate will have to apply and be approved by the court. There is more information about guardianship in Chapter 7.

- ***Representative Payment.*** If you are managing your child's Social Security benefits as the representative payee ("rep payee"), you can resign and ask Social Security to appoint another family member to be the rep payee. If no one in the family will accept this role, you can have the agency that serves your child become the rep payee. This is discussed in Chapter 4, "Finances."

- ***Agent.*** An adult who is not under legal guardianship can appoint one or more agents to assist him. An attorney can help you draw up the paperwork. A health care agent can review records and help the person make important medical decisions. An agent under a durable power of attorney can handle tasks such as managing your child's money, reviewing personal records, and dealing with insurance benefits. Your child can nominate you to be his agent, and he can also nominate one or more successor agents to serve in the future if and when you can no longer assist him. Unlike guardianship, which can only be revoked by a court, agency arrangements are voluntary. The person who appointed the agent can revoke the appointment by tearing up the document or stating that he no longer wants assistance. Thus, your child could nullify the arrangement at any time, for any reason (or for no reason). If your child is not under guardianship and does not seek out information about agents, powers of attorney, etc. on his own initiative, it is up to you to educate him about these options.

- ***Trustee.*** You should review your child's special needs trust and make sure the people you have named to be the successor trustees are qualified and are interested in the role. If they are not, you should nominate different people to be the successor trustees.

Training Future Caretakers

Ideally, there should be a transition period when you can supervise the person and show him or her what is involved. You can also make sure your child likes the caretaker and that the caretaker treats him with respect. You can gradually withdraw your participation as the caretaker becomes familiar with the new responsibilities.

Stepping into a parent's shoes can be daunting, even for a sibling who knows your child well. You should encourage the new caretaker to see the role not just as a burden, but as something that can be quite positive. There are steps you can take to help future caretakers understand their responsibilities and become comfortable with the role.

Write a Letter of Instructions (Letter of Intent)

A Letter of Instructions explains your wishes for your child's care when you are no longer here. You can include anything you want future caregivers to know about your son or daughter. Here are some kinds of information you may want to consider:

- Basic factual information: your son's or daughter's date and place of birth, Social Security number, religion, place of residence, and place of work
- Likes and dislikes, including food, recreation, hobbies, interests, and kinds of environments

- Important people, including names and addresses of siblings, special relatives, people your son or daughter especially likes, guardians, trustees, advocates, representative payee, and people with power of attorney (if any)
- Medical information, including diagnoses, level of functioning, vision, hearing, speech, mobility, medication, allergies, operations, and recent testing
- Names, addresses, and telephone numbers of regular physicians, dentists, therapists, and specialists
- A particular church, synagogue, mosque, or other religious establishment that your son or daughter prefers to attend
- What works well for your son or daughter, including current and past school programs, living arrangements, work, education strategies, and approaches to learning
- Your perspective on your son's or daughter's capabilities in terms of education, employment, and social relationships
- Information about how your child typically communicates his wants and needs if non-family members have difficulty understanding him
- An overview of your child's life and your vision for his or her future
- Anything else you want future caregivers to know about your son or daughter
- Final arrangements for your son or daughter, including your preference for cremation or burial, location of the plot, any pre-paid arrangements, and specific instructions

After you have written your letter of intent, sign and date it. Then give a copy to your son's or daughter's future caregivers. Don't forget to periodically update the letter of intent, perhaps annually, to reflect any changes in your son's or daughter's circumstances.

Since a letter of intent is a personal document, you do not have to follow any particular format. We like the Special Letter of Intent kit that is included with *The Special Needs Planning Guide* (listed in the Resources section). Another resource is the Footprints for the Future document, which is available as a free download from the Arc of East Middlesex in Reading, Massachusetts (http://www.theemarc.org).

Attend Service Plan Meetings

You should invite the future caretaker to your child's service plan meetings, which usually take place annually. You can introduce him or her to the service coordinator, the representative from the provider agency, nurses, occupational therapists, and others who provide services to your child. (Service plan meetings are covered in Chapter 1.) It is important to attend these meetings because your presence shows your commitment. And if any problems come up, the people you have formed alliances with will be more likely to support your position.

Visit Your Child and Spend Time with Him

If the future caretaker doesn't know your child very well, make sure they get to know each other. Invite the person to your child's home for celebrations and other special occasions. It can be a good way to meet staff and other families. For some caretakers, the key is finding something they can enjoy together. It could be going to lunch, shopping, or just spending time together at the person's home.

Involving Your Child

Thus far this chapter has focused on all the people who will be helping your child after you are gone. But while you are still in the planning process, there is one person you should not to forget to include: your child. You don't necessarily need to talk about your own death, if this would be upsetting to him. But it is important for him to understand that you may not always be there and that others will be helping him with things you are doing now.

Depending on your child's cognitive ability, you might make sure he understands his financial situation. He also needs to be comfortable with prospective guardians, agents, trustees, and others who will be assisting him. A bad match can be stressful and difficult for your child as well as those you have chosen to help him. Moreover, it can be potentially expensive for your child if he opposes the arrangements you have made or tries to undo them through legal channels. Therefore, you should seek his opinions on things that matter to him, and, to the extent possible, take them into account.

Books, Articles, and Other Publications

The Autism Transition Guide: Planning the Journey from School to Adult Life, Carolyn T. Bruey and Beth Urban (Woodbine House, 2009).

> This transition resource provides ideas and strategies to prepare students with autism for life beyond high school.

"Creating a Circle of Support," Kim Davis (Available from the Indiana Institute on Disability and Community at *www.iidc.indiana.edu*).

> An article on creating a circle of friends from the perspective of a woman with a significant disability.

The Down Syndrome Transition Handbook: Charting Your Child's Course to Adulthood, Jo Ann Simons (Woodbine House, 2010).

> Advice for families on transition planning, postsecondary options, legal and financial issues, finding and keeping a job, and other essential issues related to preparing a teen or adult with Down syndrome for independent adult life.

Housing Options for Adults with Autism Spectrum Disorder, Diana T. Myers and Associates (Housing Options Committee of the Pennsylvania Department of Public Welfare's Bureau of Autism Services).

> Describes housing choices available to adults with autism in Pennsylvania. Available at: www.dpw.state.pa.us/ucmprd/groups/webcontent/documents/report/p_012904.pdf.

Identity, Self, and the World: Learning from Adults with Developmental Disabilities, David Wizansky (Specialized Housing, Inc., 2012).

> The author's observations about the inner lives of people with disabilities. Order from www.specializedhousing.org.

"The Impact of Special Needs Trusts on Eligibility for Subsidized Housing," Emily S. Starr (*The Voice,* March 2011, volume 5, issue 4).

> This article contains useful information for trustees who are managing a special needs trust for someone who has a housing subsidy. Obtain from www.specialneedsalliance.org.

It's My Choice, William T. Allen (Minnesota Governor's Council on Developmental Disabilities, n.d.).

A self-guided workbook on person-centered planning; includes a housing checklist. Obtain from www.mnddc.org/extra/publications/choice/Its_My_Choice.pdf.

Legal Planning for Special Needs in Massachusetts: A Family Guide to SSI, Guardianship, and Estate Planning, Barbara D. Jackins (Authorhouse, 2010).

Although this book is targeted to Massachusetts audiences, the sections on SSI and estate planning are useful in any state. Order from www.disabilitiesbooks.com.

Managing a Special Needs Trust: A Guide for Trustees, Barbara D. Jackins, Richard S. Blank, Ken W. Shulman, and Harriet H. Onello (DisABILITIES Books, 2012).

A reference guide for trustees who are managing a special needs trust for a person with a disability. 2012. Order from www.disabilitiesbooks.com.

"Medicare and You."

The official government booklet provides a summary of Medicare benefits, coverage decisions, rights, protections, and answers to the most frequently asked questions about Medicare. Available from the Medicare website (www.Medicare.gov).

Passport to Independence: A Manual for Families (Specialized Housing, 2002).

Contains information on financial planning, supported housing, and social and vocational issues. Order from www.specializedhousing.org.

Priced Out in 2010: The Housing Crisis for People with Disabilities (Technical Assistance Collaborative in collaboration with the Consortium for Citizens with Disabilities Housing Task Force, 2010).

The publication is available at www.tacinc.org/media/21969/PricedOut2010.pdf.

Red Book on Employment (Publication 64-030 of the Social Security Administration).

The Red Book contains information on the employment-related provisions of the Social Security Disability Insurance (SSDI) and Supplemental Security Income (SSI) Programs. Obtain from the SSA website (www.ssa.gov) or by telephone at 800-772-1213.

"Section 8 Made Simple" (Technical Assistance Collaborative, 2003).

Reader-friendly guide to the Section 8 program. Available on the TAC website (www.tacinc.org).

Special Needs Planning Guide, John W. Nadworny and Cynthia R. Haddad (Brookes Publishing, 2007).

Financial planning for individuals with disabilities of every age.

Special Needs Trusts: Protecting your Child's Financial Future, Stephen Elias (Nolo Books, 2011)

Information on how to prepare and manage a special needs trust for a person with a disability.

State of the States in Developmental Disabilities, 2011, David Braddock, Richard Hemp, Mary C. Rizzolo, Laura Haffer, Emily Shea Tanis, and Jiang Wu. Department of Psychiatry and Coleman Institute for Cognitive Disabilities (University of Colorado, 2011).

Contains state-by-state revenue, spending, and programmatic data for years 1997-2011. Order from www.stateofthestates.org.

"Supplemental Security Income" (Publication 05-11000 of the Social Security Administration).

This booklet contains information on the SSI program. Obtain from www.ssa.gov or by telephone at 800-772-1213.

Organizations, Agencies, and Websites

Disabilities (General Information)

National Association of Councils on Developmental Disabilities (NACDD)
202-506-5813
www.nacdd.org

NACDD serves as the national voice of state and territorial Councils on developmental disabilities, supporting councils in implementing the Developmental Disabilities Assistance and Bill of Rights Act promoting the interest and rights of people with developmental disabilities and their families.

National Dissemination Center for Children with Disabilities
202-884-8200; 800-695-0285
www.nichcy.org
www.nichcy.org/espanol

A central source of information on disabilities in children and young adults. Easy-to-read information on IDEA, specific disabilities, special education, as well as contact information for disability agencies and organizations in each state.

Parent Center Network
www.parentcenternetwork.org

Parent Centers provide training, information, and assistance to families of children with all disabilities ages birth to 26 years and the professionals who work with them.

Disabilities (Specific)

American Society for Deaf Children
800-942-2732
www.deafchildren.org

ASDC is a national nonprofit organization dedicated to the belief that deaf or hard-of-hearing children are entitled to full communication access in their home, school, and community.

The Arc of the United States
202-534-3700; 800-433-5255

www.thearc.org

A national organization that advocates for and serves people with intellectual and developmental disabilities and their families.

Attention Deficit Disorder Association
www.add.org

An organization whose mission is to provide information, resources, and networking opportunities to help adults with AD/HD lead better lives.

Autism Link
412-364-1886

www.autismlink.com

Autism Link's mission is to provide opportunities for inclusion, information, and support; disseminate news and information; and help individuals with autism and their families find services.

Autism Speaks
888-288-4762; 888-772-9050 (español)

www.autismspeaks.org

An autism science and advocacy organization, dedicated to funding research into the causes, prevention, treatments, and cure for autism; increasing awareness of autism spectrum disorders; and advocating for the needs of individuals with autism and their families. The website includes a resource guide by state.

CHADD
800-233-4050

www.chadd.org

Children and Adults with Attention-Deficit/Hyperactivity Disorder is a nonprofit organization that offers support and information for individuals, parents, teachers, professionals, and others.

Epilepsy Foundation of America
800-332-1000

www.epilepsyfoundation.org

A national voluntary agency dedicated to education, advocacy, and research on behalf of the almost 3 million people with epilepsy in the U.S. and their families.

National Alliance on Mental Illness
703-524-7600; 800-950-6264

www.nami.org

A grassroots mental health organization dedicated to building better lives for Americans affected by mental illness. NAMI advocates for access to services, treatment, supports, and research, and works to raise awareness and build a community of hope for all of those in need.

National Association for Parents of Children with Visual Impairments
617-972-7441; 800-562-6265
www.spedex.com/napvi
A nonprofit organization of, by, and for parents committed to providing support to the parents of children who have visual impairments.

National Down Syndrome Congress
770-604-9500; 800-232-6372
www.ndsccenter.org
The country's oldest national organization for people with Down syndrome, the NDSC provides information, support, and advocacy for people with Down syndrome, their families, and the professionals who work with them.

National Down Syndrome Society
800-221-4602
www.ndss.org
A nonprofit organization that advocates for the value, acceptance, and inclusion of people with Down syndrome, supports research into Down syndrome, and disseminates information.

National Fragile X Foundation
800-688-8765
www.fragilex.org
National site devoted to the dissemination of information and increasing awareness of Fragile X-associated Disorders (FXD).

Online Asperger Syndrome Information and Support (OASIS)
www.aspergersyndrome.org
A website that provides information and news about Asperger syndrome and other autism spectrum disorders, as well as links to local sources of support.

Prader-Willi Syndrome Association
941-312-0400; 800-926-4797
www.pwsausa.org
An organization of families and professionals working together to raise awareness, offer support, provide education and advocacy, and promote and fund research to enhance the quality of life of those affected by Prader-Willi syndrome.

United Cerebral Palsy
202-776-0406; 800-872-5827
www.ucp.org
United Cerebral Palsy (UCP) educates, advocates for, and provides support services to ensure a life without limits for people with cerebral palsy and other disabilities.

Williams Syndrome Association
800-806-1871
www.williams-syndrome.org
The Williams Syndrome Association provides resources, support, and medical information for individuals with Williams syndrome and their families.

Legal and Financial Planning

Academy of Special Needs Planners
866-296-5509
www.specialneedsplanners.com

A national organization of special needs planners that provides information to consumers through this website and a monthly e-mail newsletter.

Americans with Disabilities Act (ADA)
800-514-0301
www.ada.gov

Information and Technical Assistance on the Americans with Disabilities Act.

Certified Financial Planner Board of Standards
800-487-1497
www.cfp.net

The professional regulatory organization in the United States that fosters professional standards in personal financial planning so that the public has access to, and benefits from, competent and ethical financial planning.

National Academy of Elder Law Attorneys
www.naela.org

A national organization of attorneys who specialize in elder and disability law. The website can help you locate an attorney in your area.

Special Needs Alliance
520-546-1005; 877-572-8472
www.specialneedsalliance.org

A national organization that provides information to attorneys and families on special needs planning and entitlement. The website can help you locate an attorney in your area.

Special Needs Planning
781-756-1804
www.specialneedsplanning.com

A private financial planning firm located in Winchester, MA, that provides financial planning for families with a member with a disability. The website has many useful articles and links.

Housing Resources

Agricultural Communities for Adults with Autism
www.ac-aa.org

Agricultural Communities for Adults with Autism (ACAA) is a consortium of existing and information organizations focused on sharing best practices and advocating for holistic, agricultural based employment and housing models for adults with autism.

Bazelon Center for Mental Health Law

202-467-5730

www.bazelon.org

This organization protects and advances the interests of adults and children who have mental disabilities, including access to housing.

INDEX

www.disabilityinfo.org

INDEX addresses the information needs of people with disabilities. They collect and maintain information on a wide variety of programs, agencies, and individual providers in Massachusetts who have something to offer people with disabilities. Much of the information is local, but there are a number of national and state resources as well.

Quality Mall

www.qualitymall.org

A website maintained by the Research and Training Center on Community Living that provides many articles and resources related to supported living for adults with disabilities.

Technical Assistance Collaborative

617-266-5657

www.tacinc.org

National organization that provides a wealth of information on housing for people with disabilities. Offers many useful manuals and guides and a searchable database of vouchers targeted to people with disabilities.

Transition Resources

Individuals with Disabilities Education Act (IDEA)

idea.ed.gov [note: there is no www in this URL]

The Individuals with Disabilities Education Act (IDEA) governs how states and public agencies provide special education and related services to children with disabilities in the U.S., including transition services and supports for teens and young adults.

Pacer Center

952-838-9000

www.pacer.org

The Parent Advocacy Coalition for Educational Rights Center provides resources with the aim of expanding opportunities and enhancing the quality of life of children and young adults with disabilities and their families; based on the concept of parents helping parents.

Youthhood.org

www.youthhood.org

A website developed by the National Center on Secondary Education and Transition for young people with disabilities to use in exploring transition issues.

U.S. Government Programs

Center for Medicare Advocacy, Inc.
860-456-7790

www.medicareadvocacy.org

An advocacy organization for Medicare recipients. It provides helpful information about the Medicare drug benefit.

Low Income Home Energy Assistance Program (LIHEAP)
202-401-9351

www.acf.hhs.gov/programs/ocs/programs/liheap

This federal government program assists low-income individuals with heating and cooling costs.

Medicaid Reference Desk
800-433-5255

www.thedesk.info

This site, a project of the Arc, allows people with intellectual and developmental disabilities to link to the Medicaid program in their state. It also contains a person-centered planning toolkit.

Medicare
1-800-Medicare (633-4227)

www.medicare.gov

The official government site for information on Medicare, including who qualifies, what is covered, where to find participating providers, and making claims and appeals. The toll-free number is staffed 24 hours a day, including weekends and holidays.

Social Security Administration
800-772-1213

www.ssa.gov

The agency to contact for information about SSI, SSDI, and Social Security retirement benefits. The toll-free number is staffed 24 hours a day, including weekends and holidays.

Supplemental Nutrition Assistance Program (SNAP)
703-305-2022

www.fns.usda.gov/snap

SNAP offers financial assistance to help eligible low-income individuals and families buy food.

U.S. Department of Agriculture Rural Development
800-670-6553

www.rurdev.usda.gov/rhs

The website for this office contains information about grants and loans to assist with financing housing in rural areas and provides links to RD offices in each state.

U.S. Department of Housing and Urban Development
www.hud.gov
  The website for this agency contains information on affordable housing, grants, and loans, including the Community Development Block Grant (CDBG) Program and the Home Investment Partnerships (HOME) Program. There are links to community development offices in each state.

Direct Support Professionals: Training Materials and Resources

Crisis Prevention Institute
888-426-2184
www.crisisprevention.com
  CPI is an international training organization committed to best practices and safe behavior management methods that focus on prevention. They offer courses throughout the U.S. and Canada on prevention and management of aggressive behavior, positive behavior supports, nonviolent crisis intervention, etc., and also produce training DVDs.

James Stanfield Company
www.stanfield.com
  The James Stanfield Company produces materials to promote social competence and transition readiness in students with disabilities, including the *Circles* and *Life Horizon* programs.

"The Importance of Competency-Based Training for Direct Support Professionals," Traci LaLiberte and Amy Hewitt (*Impact,* fall/winter 2007/08).
  Article can be downloaded at ici.umn.edu/products/impact/202/over7.html.

"15 NADSP Competency Standards" (National Association of Direct Support Professionals).
  A list of 15 areas with corresponding skill statements approved by NADSP, describing the knowledge and skills direct support professionals must have to demonstrate competency in each area. Available at: www.nadsp.org/images/NADSP_Competency_Areas.pdf

"Find, Choose, and Keep Great DSPs: A Toolkit for Families Looking for Quality, Caring, and Committed Direct Support Professionals," Amy Hewitt, Katie Keiling, John Sauer, Nancy McCulloh, and Marijo McBride (Institute on Community Integration, 2006).
  Available at: www.state.il.us/agency/icdd/communicating/pdf/toolkitforfamilies[1].pdf.

National Association of Direct Support Professionals
518-449-7551
www.nadsp.org
  A national organization that sets competency standards and administers a credentialing program for direct support professionals. There are links to state chapters of the NADSP on the website. (Several states have their own DSP associations; for example, Tennessee.)

Appendices

APPENDIX 1-1   **Individual Profile Form**   Date reviewed _____

(Reviewed when there are life changes or new personnel, and at the annual ISP)

Name:	Date of Birth:

Diagnosis (age and time of onset):

Life History and Family History

History of Residential Living:

History of Education:

Family History (Contact frequency and preferences/relevant birthday information):
Parents' names—
Siblings' names—
Guardians' names—

Safety— Equipment, Supervision, Safety plans— prompting needs for fire drills

Health History

General health concerns (See health care plan categories)

Current medications and reason for medication and dosage (See health record)

Surgeries—

Allergies—

Current Doctors, surgeons, specialists (Name/Place of practice):

Positioning and physical handling— In Wheelchair, In Bed, Alternative Positions, Frequency of Position Change, Positioning Equipment, Splints, Other

(Appendix 1-1 continued...)

(Appendix 1-1 continued...)

Transfers and lifting— Techniques Required, Other

Mobility— Staff Assistance, Equipment, Stairs and Uneven Surfaces, Other
Footwear— hand splints — Shoes/Shoe Inserts, Foot & Ankle Splint (AFO's), Hand Splints
Range of motion—Extremities Involved, Frequency, Description of Exercise
Skin care— Preventive Treatments, Incontinent Care, Pressure Points, Other

Habits/Routines/likes and dislikes

AM Routine: What time does he/she get up? Describe morning routine; things needed for work.
PM Routine: Describe, in detail, afternoon routine starting at 3 pm.
Weekend Routine: Focus on morning activity, afternoon activity, evening activity
Overnight Routine: Sleep patterns, checks, and interventions
Activities— What does he/she like? What has he/she done?
Eating— Food Textures, Fluid Consistency, Assistance Pacing, Equipment, Positioning, Other
Safety (Positioning and physical handling needs)

(Appendix 1-1 continued...)

(Appendix 1-1 continued...)

Behavior plan or guidelines

Target behaviors to increase: Target behaviors to decrease:
Reinforcement utilized, with frequency
Behavior interventions:
Data collection system:
Current ISP Goals (Long term)/Objectives (yearly) 1. 2. 3.
Implementation strategies (materials needed, location of training, task analysis):
Data collection and summary systems:
List skills person has and level of assistance needed: Dressing— Showering— Laundry— Hair care— Shaving— Tooth brushing— Chores—
Best ways to develop a relationship with this person:

APPENDIX 2-1

Photos of Community Living and Connections

The photos in this appendix illustrate a variety of living arrangements that may be appropriate for adults with disabilities. They were taken predominately in New England and represent housing that was constructed specifically for people with disabilities as well as homes that were converted from existing structures. Ideally, residents living in the community enjoy that community and their connections to people and places. We have therefore included a few examples of what a full life of activities can look like.

Group residence for five men in urban Boston.

Homey dining room in four-person group residence.

Renovated home converted to eight condominiums.

TILL's six-unit apartment building with live-in support.

(Appendix 2-1 continued...)

(Appendix 2-1 continued...)

Lobby of the apartment building.

Fully accessible kitchen.

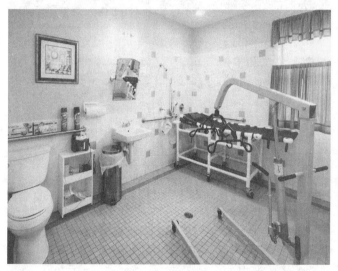

Fully accessible bathroom for medically involved individuals.

Fully accessible group residence with 24-hour supports.

Open floor plan in the group residence.

Working together.

(Appendix 2-1 continued...)

(Appendix 2-1 continued...)

Being part of a team.

Challenging oneself.

Accessible container gardening.

Celebrating with family...

...and friends.

Home Alone Guidelines

The following guidelines have been developed to provide agencies with a list of core competencies that should be assessed before applying to DDS for a home alone waiver for an individual. The primary area of evaluation concerning the removal of supervision should be at the individual's level of comfort with being home unsupervised. Application for the removal of staffing from a program must be driven by the individual's needs and abilities and should only be pursued with the full support and encouragement of the individual.

All responses should allow for the use of accommodations, if needed, for an individual to demonstrate necessary safety skills to be home without staff for periods of time. It is important to keep in mind that individuals should be provided with the supports and assistive technology (whenever possible) to encourage growth and independence. It is the Department's intent to support and work closely with individuals and agencies to help develop more opportunities to provide creative supports. If accommodations are utilized, those accommodations should be clearly identified in the report.

This tool should not be viewed as an "all or nothing" test. It should be used as an opportunity to review the skills and abilities of individuals, point out areas that are in need of further development and provide a forum for creative problem solving around skill development. Often times, a new support, adaptation, or option will allow for the same level of safety. Responses to questions should include demonstration as well as verbal responses.

The core competencies questions to be asked are outlined in each topic area. Overall, these guidelines will establish the basic skills that an individual needs to have in order to be unsupervised at home. The length of time the individual is unsupervised needs to be discussed with the individual and take into consideration the comfort level of the individual as well as what the individual can safely do while unsupervised. For example, it is recommended that an individual who is unsupervised for over 4 hours be able to safely prepare food. Other activities and skills need to be specifically identified. Activities that are not safely completed without supervision should not be attempted during the unsupervised time periods.

In residential settings where more than one individual is interested in applying for the home alone waiver, complementary skills and abilities should be considered. It is not necessary for each individual to possess all skills at 100% if the group can and will work together. Natural supports can include roommates. However, the reduction of staff supervision cannot be replaced by peer supervision. It is essential that individuals in the home are requesting the removal of staff supervision to allow them more freedom and independence. This process is not meant to be used as a means to address staffing concerns or issues.

Finally, it is recommended that individuals returning to a home without supervision or leaving the home after staff have left must be able to demonstrate additional skills. If the skills are not demonstrated, accommodations should be made to teach them while allowing for some time unsupervised.

(Appendix 3-1 continued...)

(Appendix 3-1 continued...)

Home Alone Assessment

Fire Safety Questions

Core Competencies—Fire Safety

1. Does the individual evacuate the building within 2½ minutes when an alarm is sounded?
2. Can the individual independently evacuate the residence by two (2) different routes within 2½ minutes?

Fire Safety Questions

These areas should be considered only if the individual participates in these activities while unsupervised. (If the individual does not engage in these activities, he or she does not need to demonstrate these competencies.) These skills can be taught to extend what individuals do while unsupervised, but are not prerequisites to getting the waiver.

1. Does the individual demonstrate proper precautions when smoking (if applicable)?
2. Does the individual demonstrate appropriate fire safety skills when cooking?
3. Does the individual know what to do if the alarm goes off when taking a shower?

First Aid Skills

Core Competencies—First Aid Skills

1. Is the first aid kit accessible and does the individual know where it is located?
2. Is the individual able to dial emergency numbers and describe the problem or use a prerecorded emergency message (or other such accommodation developed) to summon help?
3. Is the individual self-medicating or will not require medication during unsupervised times?
4. Does the individual wear a medical identification bracelet if necessary?
5. Does the individual recognize the need for caution when using items marked poison?
6. Is the individual able to distinguish between minor problems and those that require further medical attention?
7. Is the individual able to recognize and understand various medications in the first aid kit and not abuse them?
8. Can the individual show, tell, and demonstrate the appropriate measures to be taken, including calling for assistance per established procedures (either by calling 911 or other emergency numbers established for home), if he or she:

   - had a bad burn
   - had a cut that would not stop bleeding
   - had a bad headache
   - had a pain in the chest
   - had a bad fall and injured an arm/leg
   - began to vomit

Core Competencies—Household Safety

1. Can the individual identify the smell of gas (if gas is in the home)?
2. Can the individual lock/unlock the doors appropriately?
3. Can the individual respond to unexpected emergencies by obtaining help using a prearranged system in the event of any of the following:

   - Power failure
   - Telephone failure
   - Gas leak
   - No heat
   - Leaking pipes
   - Broken window

(Appendix 3-1 continued...)

(Appendix 3-1 continued...)

Household Safety Skills

These questions should only be evaluated if the individual participates in this activity during unsupervised periods. (If the individual does not engage in these activities, he or she does not need to demonstrate competencies in these areas.)

1. Does the individual exercise appropriate care when using electrical appliances?
2. Does the individual demonstrate the skills to safely:
   - Do the laundry.
   - Do household cleaning.
   - Use kitchen appliances.
   - Use other household appliances.

Core Competencies—Individual Safety

1. Does the individual respond appropriately when someone comes to the door and it is a stranger? A familiar person?
2. Can the individual show/tell or provide identification card or other adaption for his or her full name, address, and telephone number appropriately as needed?
3. Does the individual know what to do if someone were trying to break into the house?
4. Does the individual know what to do if an unfamiliar person is hanging around the house?
5. Does the individual know what to do if expected staff does not show up?

Core Competencies—Telephone Safety

1. Can the individual use the phone (with accommodations if needed)?
2. Does the individual know where the other emergency numbers are posted in the house?
3. Is the individual able to contact appropriate assistance?
4. Is the individual able to call the emergency number and provide information?
5. Can the individual demonstrate how to use the emergency call system (if one is used)?
6. Can the individual demonstrate appropriate precautions when asked to give out information over the phone?
7. Is the individual able to use a backup system if calling for staff and he/she reaches an answering machine?

Coming Home/Leaving the House Unsupervised (If Applicable)

1. Can the individual reliably keep a key to the house (if no, can accommodations be made)?
2. In the event the key is lost, can the individual find a solution?
3. Can the individual recognize the signs that there has been an intruder/break-in and respond appropriately?
4. Can the individual request assistance from the public at-large if lost using augmentative communication systems, cards or other accommodations developed, if needed?

APPENDIX 3-2

Routine Essential Needs

Activity	I Need Assistance (Describe type needed)	I Am Independent with this Activity
Cooking/meal planning		
Shopping		
Laundry		
House cleaning		
Making my bed		
Organizing my clothes		
Budgeting my money		
Organizing my mail		
Organizing my bills		
Paying my bills		
Shaving		
Dental care		
Showering		
Hair grooming		
Toileting		
Menstrual care		
Getting to sleep		
Taking my medication(s) if any		
Traveling to/from work		
Getting to stores/shopping		

Learning Style Assessment Tool

Name: _____ **Date:** _____

This tool has been developed to assist in determining an optimal, individualized learning style. Please fill in the blanks and check yes or no to all statements.

I. General Information

	YES	NO
Individual wants to learn new skills.		
Individual will ask for assistance when needed.		
Individual accepts correction.		
Individual is able to maintain skills over long periods of non-practice.		
Individual has a desire to succeed.		
Individual responds impulsively.		
Individual rushes through tasks.		
Individual likes to be told reasons for things.		
Individual's performance will suffer if subjected to a large amount of new information/material at once.		
Individual's behavior sometimes interferes with work/skill development.		
Individual's behavior often interferes with work/skill development.		
Medical/physical problems affect performance.		
Individual has short-term memory deficits.		

Individual is easily frustrated by/when _____

_____

_____

Individual is easily distracted by _____

_____

_____

(Appendix 3-3 continued...)

(Appendix 3-3 continued...)

II. Teaching Techniques

	YES	NO
Individual works best in the morning.		
Individual works best in the afternoon.		
Individual works best in the evening.		
Individual needs only verbal instruction to learn a new skill.		
Individual requires physical assistance to learn a new skill.		
Individual requires highly structured training to learn a new skill.		
Individual acquires new skills by observation and/or imitation.		
Individual learns by role playing.		
Individual learns with counseling.		
Individual learns through rote practice.		
Individual learns well with 1:1 instruction.		
Individual learns well with small group instruction.		
Individual requires the use of adaptive equipment.		
Individual learns best when only limited amounts of materials are presented.		
Individual responds well when new tasks are gradually added.		
Individual learns best through back chaining.		
Individual learns best through forward chaining.		
Individual learns best when tasks are broken down.		
Individual works best when given a variety of tasks.		
Individual requires a quiet area with few visual distractions.		
Individual is usually unaffected by visual/auditory distractions.		
Individual learns best in frequent sessions (5X/week) of short duration (less than 10 minutes).		

(Appendix 3-3 continued...)

(Appendix 3-3 continued...)

	YES	NO
Individual learns best in long sessions (10 minutes or more).		
Frequency of instruction does not appear to affect learning.		
Individual responds well to verbal contracts.		
Individual responds well to written contracts.		
Individual requires concrete reinforcers.		
Individual learns best through auditory modality.		
Individual learns best through visual modality.		
Individual learns best through tactile modality.		
Individual prefers to self-monitor (e.g., keep own chart)		
Individual prefers to work with familiar staff.		
Individual prefers to work with male staff.		
Individual prefers to work with female staff.		
Individual works best on functional tasks (e.g., doing banking at the bank).		

Other:_____

_____

_____

_____

_____

(Appendix 3-3 continued...)

(Appendix 3-3 continued...)

III. Reinforcement

	YES	NO
Individual responds well to peer pressure/praise.		
Individual responds well to staff praise.		
Individual requires immediate reinforcement.		
Individual is not reinforced by money.		
Individual is highly reinforced by money.		
Individual is intrinsically motivated.		
Individual will work for a token or on a check system.		
Individual responds to 1:1 special time.		
Individual responds to community activities.		

Individual can delay tangible reinforcement (e.g., special events) for up to_____

_____

Individual works to go out with peers/staff to_____

_____

The most successful reinforcement schedule for this individual is_____

_____

IV. Preferred Activities

	YES	NO
Individual enjoys community activities.		
Individual enjoys group activities.		
Individual enjoys solitary activities.		
Individual enjoys movies. Favorites are:		
Individual enjoys spectator sports. Favorites are:		

(Appendix 3-3 continued...)

(Appendix 3-3 continued...)

Individual's favorite food is_____

_____

Individual's favorite leisure activities are_____

_____

Individual's favorite topics of conversation are_____

_____

V. Dislikes/Ineffective Procedures

	YES	NO
Written contracts		
Verbal contracts		
Group Instruction		
Role playing		
Demonstration		
Token reinforcement		
Infrequent instruction (less than once a week)		
Hand over hand instruction		
Delayed reinforcement		
Money is ineffective		

Other:_____

_____

_____

_____

_____

_____

(Appendix 3-3 continued...)

Community Strengths and Training Needs

This is an opportunity to talk about the things that you like to do or can do and to think about the things that will help you be more independent in the community.

Here are some examples of places where people go in the community:

Grocery store	Department store	Shopping mall
Laundromat	Repair shop	Convenience store
Fast food restaurant	Sit-down restaurant	Ice cream parlor
Doctor's office	Dentist's office	Beauty shop
Barber shop	Health club	YMCA/YWCA
Track	Concert	Swimming pool
Recreational park	Sporting event	Bowling alley
Skating rink	Pool hall	Tennis court
Video store	Library	Movie theater
Club	Ball park	Basketball court

Where do you go and what do you do there?

Place:
Example: Grocery store

Activities:
Example(s): Shop from a list, uses pointer to select item, wait in line

_____

_____

Where and what would you like to learn to do in the community?
Example: Get a haircut at the barber shop.

_____

_____

What gets in the way?
Example: I don't know how to take the bus.

_____

_____

Comments:

_____

_____

_____

(Appendix 3-3 continued...)

(Appendix 3-3 continued...)

Recreation and Leisure Strengths and Training Needs

Here are some examples of things that people do for fun:

Frisbee	skateboard	swimming	aerobics	TV
board games	music	sewing	visiting friends	bike riding
ball games	exercise bike	computer games	cards	movies/videos
assembling models	dancing	skating	video games	jogging
coins	books	knitting	radio	

What do you do for fun?
Activity:
Example: Listen to music

Where do you do it?
Place:
Example: Library

_____

_____

_____

What would you like to learn to do for fun?
Example: Go to the mall.

_____

_____

What gets in the way?
Example: Transportation

_____

_____

Comments:

_____

_____

_____

(Appendix 3-3 continued...)

(Appendix 3-3 continued...)

Home Chore Strengths and Training Needs

Here are some examples of things that people do at home:

hand wash dishes	dry dishes	operate dishwasher	cook packaged foods
cook frozen foods	empty garbage	clean counters	empty trash
use microwave oven	make sandwiches	set table	strip bed
operate washer	operate dryer	put laundry away	fold laundry
care for pets	iron	use a blender	vacuum
clean sink	clean bathtub	clean toilet	dust
water lawn	pull weeds	mow grass	sweep sidewalk

What chores do you do at home?
Activity:
Example: Make my own bed.

_____

_____

What would you like to learn to do or do better at home?
Example: Make my own lunch.

_____

_____

What gets in the way?
Example: I can't follow a recipe.

_____

_____

(Appendix 3-3 continued...)

(Appendix 3-3 continued...)

Home Interview Neighborhood Inventory

This "map" of the neighborhood will help develop a picture of where people live, work, and play. It should be filled out first.

Streets:

What are the streets in your neighborhood that you use a lot? How do you use them?

Street Name	Walk/Car/Bus?	If you walk, are there Signals/Crosswalks?
	W C B	S C
	W C B	S C
	W C B	S C

Family and Friends

Where are the homes of family and friends that you visit? How do you get there? How often do you visit?

Who?	How far away?	Walk/Car/Bus?	How often?			
	1-5 blocks 5+ blocks	W C B	Daily	Weekly	Monthly	Other
	1-5 blocks 5+ blocks	W C B	Daily	Weekly	Monthly	Other
	1-5 blocks 5+ blocks	W C B	Daily	Weekly	Monthly	Other
	1-5 blocks 5+ blocks	W C B	Daily	Weekly	Monthly	Other
	1-5 blocks 5+ blocks	W C B	Daily	Weekly	Monthly	Other

Community

Where do you go in the community? How do you get there? When? How often? (For example, stores, outings, library, movie, doctor, dentist, etc.) Place a (/) next to those places you go to alone.

Place/City?	Walk/Car/Bus?	When?	How often?			
	W C B	Weekday Weekend	Daily	Weekly	Monthly	Other
	W C B	Weekday Weekend	Daily	Weekly	Monthly	Other
	W C B	Weekday Weekend	Daily	Weekly	Monthly	Other
	W C B	Weekday Weekend	Daily	Weekly	Monthly	Other
	W C B	Weekday Weekend	Daily	Weekly	Monthly	Other

(Appendix 3-3 continued...)

(Appendix 3-3 continued...)

Utilizing Resources to Make Connections within Community

Do you have connections with other citizens who have an understanding of disabilities (employers, landlords, staff, friends, staff and family, relatives)?

Check off those things utilized

	Restaurants / Stores/ Library	**Community Resources**
	Laundromat / Bank / Grocery	
	Polling place	
	Planned Parenthood / Men's group / Women's group	**Activities utilizing outside agencies**
	YMCA/ health club	
	Adult education	
	Wt. watchers or other diet group	**Self—Improvement**
	Walking clubs/ Aerobics	
	Knights of Columbus	**Civic Clubs and/or organizations**
	Explores clubs	
	Garden club/Lions / Jaycees	
	Parks departments	**Volunteer within community**
	Nursing homes	
	Public library	
	Food banks	
	Usher/Greeter	**Members of local place of worship**
	Choir	
	Attends religious services	

APPENDIX 3-4

Home Safety Checklist

Name: _____ **Date:** _____

Record if the individual is able to use the following appliances:

Appliance	Does Not Use	Uses Safely with Supervision	Uses Safely without Supervision	Unsafe Use
Stove				
Oven				
Microwave				
Toaster				
Toaster Oven				
Electric Grill/ Fry Pan				
Blender				
Coffee Maker				
BBQ Grill				
Dishwasher				
Washing Machine				
Dryer				
Scissors				
Cleaning Supplies				
Bathtub/Shower				
Hair Dryer				
Curling Iron				
Electric Razor				
Disposable Razor				
Computer				

APPENDIX 3-5

Program Maintenance Agreement with Management Company (Sample)

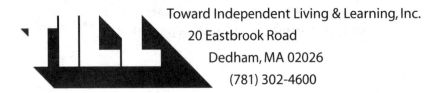

Toward Independent Living & Learning, Inc.
20 Eastbrook Road
Dedham, MA 02026
(781) 302-4600

When a house is owned by one or a group of families, the following procedure will be followed.

Capital Improvements include the following items and must be addressed by the participating families to determine how these issues will be addressed. These items are not included in routine upkeep provided by the Management Company, TILL, Inc.

All operating systems in the home:

Heating	Air Conditioning
Electrical	Water and Sewer
Roof	Structural Issues
Windows	Exteriors—siding, porches, stairs, fencing
Masonry	

Routine Maintenance Responsibilities of the Management Company – TILL, Inc.

- All routine facility needs in the home that are associated with the usual wear and tear of daily life shall be handled by TILL, Inc. As a rule, all repairs and maintenance costing under $250.00 to complete will be considered routine upkeep.

- TILL will be responsible for handling routine landscaping and snowplowing.

- All identified maintenance needs will be written on the "Facilities List" posted on the bulletin board in the kitchen. One person will be the parent liaison to communicate specific issues or concerns about repairs or upkeep that will be included on the facilities list and coordinated directly with facilities.

- All maintenance will be completed within one month. If a repair cannot be completed within this time, you will be informed of the reason why it has not been completed.

- Maintenance of equipment such as appliances—refrigerator, stove, microwave, trash compactor, washer, and dryer—will be evaluated to determine whether they can be fixed or need to be replaced. If replacement is needed, this will be the responsibility of the parent group. If it can be fixed, TILL's property manager will fix it. Any replacement parts costing more than $250.00 will fall under capital expenses and will be approved by the parent liaison.

(Appendix 3-5 continued...)

(Appendix 3-5 continued...)

- Any listed requests costing more than $250.00 that our facilities staff determines they are unable to complete and that require hiring an outside company to do the job will be communicated as soon as possible to the staff contact, who will then communicate this to the parent liaison for them to decide how to proceed.

Repairs and Maintenance over $250.00

- Any repairs or maintenance issues costing more than $250.00 to complete will be referred to the parent liaison to review with all families to decide how to handle it. If it is decided to complete the repair, the request will be reviewed by TILL, Inc. upper management to determine the responsibility for getting it done.

- Please note that TILL will be responsible for all repairs and maintenance as identified; however, if the costs for all repairs exceed the annual budget allocation, we will inform the parent liaison to discuss how additional repairs will be handled.

Renovations and Upgrades

- Any renovation of the living space or upgrades in furnishings in the common areas of the house will be the responsibility of the families. Any upgrades or purchases for individual bedrooms will be the responsibility of the family or individual occupying that bedroom.

Sample Staff Schedule

Name: _____   **Date:** _____

Name	SUN	MON	TUES	WED	THURS	FRI	SAT
Manager			12n–8p	10a–6p	9a–5p	12n–8p	8a–5p
Staff	9a–11p	3p–11p	3p–11p	1p–11p			
Staff				1p–11p	3p–11p	3p–11p	9a–11p
Staff	9a–8p	3p–8p	3p–8p	1p–4p	3p–9p		
Staff	-9a 11p-	-9a 11p-	-9a			11p-	-9a 11p-
Staff			11p-	-9a 11p-	-9a 11p-	-9a	

APPENDIX 4-2

Resident's Personal Expense Worksheet

Name: _____ **Date:** _____

Item	Monthly Budget	Actual Expense
Clothing and accessories		
Recreation/Entertainment		
Medical		
Insurance premiums		
Uninsured costs		
Vitamins and supplements		
Special therapies		
Food		
Special dietary items		
Personal care (haircut, manicure, etc.)		
Gifts		
Vacations/travel		
Toiletries		
Spending money		
Educational/vocational/skill building		
Transportation		
Subtotal		

Projected Totals		

APPENDIX 4-3

APPENDIX 4-3

Budget Template

PROJECTED EXPENSES   **PROJECTED TOTALS**

Staff

Manager/Supervision	
Direct Support Staff	
Relief staff (to cover vacancies, terminations, vacations, holidays)	
Overtime expenses if they occur for staff coverage of over 40 hours per week	
Fringe benefits	
Health Care and Dental Benefits—employer share	
Retirement, extra care benefits—offered by employer	
Taxes	
Medicare tax	
Social security payroll tax (FICA)	
Federal Unemployment Tax	
State Unemployment Tax	
Worker's compensation (required by most states)	
Subtotal:	

Consultation

Stipends (if offered to live in staff and life share companions)	
(Benefits are not offered to consultants)	
Subtotal:	

Occupancy

Rent or mortgage (interest only portion is the norm)	
Insurance	
Utiliities	
Heat	
Electricity	
Gas/Oil	
Water	
Cable	
Telephone	
Internet	

(Appendix 4-3 continued...)

(Appendix 4-3 continued...)

Maintenance and repairs	
Minor repairs (under $500 or whatever figure you set)	
Landscaping	
Snow removal	
Furniture and appliance replacement	
Exterminator (depending on location)	
Subtotal:	

Administration

Advertising/ recruitment	
Financial Reporting	
Bookkeeping and Payrolll	
Insurance—liability, professional, commercial *(both required & recommended coverages)*	
Management Fees	
Training—required by regulating body if any, as well as by provider agency	
The administrative costs can be handled either by individual expense items as noted above or can be set as an agreed upon management fee between the individual/group/family or operating entity	
Subtotal:	

Travel

Vehicle Lease	
Vehicle Insurance	
Travel Reimbursement for Staff	
Gas, oil, minor maintenance, and repairs for vehicle	
Subtotal:	

Daily Living

Food (depends on the size of the group, the ages, medical limitations on diet, religious dietary restrictions)	
Recreational expenses (a budget item set aside for activities agreed upon by the group if one is in a group living situation)	
Subtotal:	

Reserves/Replacement:

Vehicle Replacement Reserve	
Capital Expenses (one time purchases to set up home)	
Reserve account (can be set based on the age of the site and the rental/ownership arrangement)	
Subtotal:	
Projected Total:	

Public Benefits

Supplemental Security Income (SSI)

The Supplemental Security Income (SSI) program is a poverty program for low-income people in the U.S. who are elderly or have disabilities. The program is run by the Social Security Administration.

Who Can Get Benefits

In order to receive benefits, a person must meet certain disability and financial criteria.

- A person must have a severe medical or mental condition that has lasted, or can be expected to last, for a continuous period of 12 months. The condition must affect the person's ability to support himself through work. If a person cannot earn more than $1,040 or more per month in competitive employment (in 2013), the government would determine that the person is entitled to benefits.
- A person cannot have more than $2,000 in liquid resources. A person's home, car, and personal possessions are not included in the $2,000 resource limit.

Benefit Amounts

As of 2013, the basic monthly benefit for adults is $710. Nine states and the District of Columbia supplement the benefit. Those states are California, Hawaii, Massachusetts, Nevada, New Jersey, New York, Pennsylvania, Rhode Island, and Vermont. In most states, SSI recipients receive Medicaid insurance free of charge. (The Medicaid program is covered on pages 200-202.)

Income and SSI

The program treats income differently depending on whether the source is earnings, cash, food, or housing items.

- *Earnings:* If an SSI recipient has earnings from employment or self-employment, the monthly benefit will be reduced if the earnings exceed a certain amount. The formula to compute the reduction is rather complicated. Social Security disregards the first $65 of earned income (or $85 if the person has no other income), plus one-half of the remaining income. The resulting sum ("countable income") is subtracted from the regular SSI benefit to arrive at the reduced benefit.

  For example, Jennifer receives monthly SSI benefits of $710. Then she begins to work and earns $500 per month. Social Security will disregard the first $85 of earnings plus one-half of the remaining earnings. This leaves $312.50 of countable income. ($710 - $85 = $625 ÷ 2 = $312.50.) Jen will receive a reduced SSI benefit of $397.50 per month. ($710 - $312.50= $397.50.) She will also have her income of $500, for a total of $897.50. ($397.50 + $500 = $897.50.)

- *Cash Gifts:* If a person receives more than $20 in cash in any month, the SSI benefit will be reduced on a dollar for dollar basis.

  For example, Calvin's grandfather gives him $100 every month to assist with living expenses. Each month, Calvin's SSI benefit will be reduced by $80. (Social Security disregards the first $20 of income.) To avoid reducing SSI, Calvin's grandfather could pay his cable bill, telephone, or cell phone bill, or buy his clothes instead of giving him cash. This is explained in more detail on the next page.

(Appendix 4-4 continued...)

(Appendix 4-4 continued...)

- Food and Housing Items: If a person receives more than $20 in food or housing items in any month, the SSI benefit will be reduced. The program considers the following items to be housing expenses that will reduce the SSI benefit:
  - mortgage (principal and interest)
  - rent
  - real estate taxes
  - gas
  - electricity
  - water and sewer
  - garbage removal
  - homeowner's insurance (if required by the lender)
  - condominium charges that include any of these items

If a person receives financial assistance with any of these items, the program uses a rather complicated formula to figure the amount of the reduction. The SSI benefit will be reduced by the cost of the item or one-third of the SSI benefit, whichever is larger. Fortunately, Social Security caps the reduction at $256 per month (in 2013).

- Peter's father pays his electric bill of $150. That month, Peter's SSI benefit will be reduced by $130. (The first $20 of income is disregarded.)
- Rachael's mother pays her landlord $500. That month, Rachael's SSI benefit will be reduced by $256. (The monthly benefit will be not be reduced by more than $256.)

Social Security will reduce the benefit regardless of the source of the payment. Some people receive assistance with their housing costs from a special needs trust instead or from a family member. The SSI benefit will still be reduced regardless of who made the contribution.

- Sam receives assistance from a special needs trust that was set up by his mother. The trustee pays Sam's rent and utility bills that average $750 per month. Sam's monthly SSI benefit is reduced by $256.

Where to Get More Information

The Social Security Administration has a lot of useful information in its publications and on its website (www.ssa.gov). The explanations are easy to follow. Another source of information is *Managing a Special Needs Trust: A Guide for Trustees,* by Barbara D. Jackins, et al. (See the Resources Section.)

Social Security Disability Insurance (SSDI)

The Social Security Disability Insurance (SSDI) program is part of the Social Security program and is run by the federal government.

Who Can Get Benefits?

There are three ways to get SSDI benefits:

- A worker who becomes medically disabled can collect benefits based on his or her own work record. To qualify, a person must not be working (or, if working, earn less than $1,040 per month in 2013). A person must also have worked a sufficient number of quarters of "covered" employment before becoming disabled. In general, that means the worker must have accrued 20 quarters of employment in the last 10 years ending with the year the disability began.

(Appendix 4-4 continued...)

(Appendix 4-4 continued...)

- A minor (under age 18) dependent of a disabled, retired, or deceased worker can collect benefits through age 18, or through age 19 if enrolled in school.
- The disabled son or daughter of a disabled, retired, or deceased worker can get benefits for life. To qualify, the son's or daughter's disability must have started before age 22 and remained continuous through the time he or she is claiming benefits.
    - Jonathan, who is age 25 and has developmental disabilities, can collect SSDI benefits based on his father's work record when his father begins to draw benefits.
    - Melissa, who becomes disabled at age 25 due to a car accident, cannot get SSDI based on her parent's work record because she has not been continuously disabled since before age 22.

There is no asset limit for the SSDI program, so recipients can own unlimited amounts of resources and still qualify.

Benefit Amounts

A disabled dependent's SSDI award is based on his parent's benefit. That benefit amount is set according to the parent's earnings record. In most cases, a disabled dependent receives 50 percent of the parent's benefit while the parent is living and 75 percent of the benefit after the parent has died.

These amounts are subject to a "Family Maximum Benefit" that Social Security establishes for the insured worker. Under this formula, if a disabled, retired, or deceased worker has dependent family members, the total benefits payable to both the worker and the family members may not exceed a Family Maximum Benefit established by Social Security. The worker is paid first, and the worker's benefit is not reduced by any dependent's benefits that may be paid on his or her record.

SSDI recipients can get Medicare after they have qualified for SSDI for 24 months. Note that SSDI recipients—unlike SSI recipients in some states—do not automatically qualify for Medicaid benefits.

The Section 8 Program

The Section 8 program is funded by the federal government and run by the Department of Housing and Urban Development (HUD). The formal name of the program is the Housing Choice Voucher Program, or HCVP. The program is managed at the state level by Public Housing Authorities (PHAs). Some nonprofit organizations are also awarded vouchers to manage for their consumers.

The program uses a voucher process. The PHAs issue vouchers to individuals who qualify. An individual pays about 30 percent of his or her income as rent. The housing authority pays the balance of the rent directly to the owner.

Most of the vouchers that HUD issues are portable. This means that if the person moves, he can use the voucher for the new unit. Some Section 8 vouchers are site-based. A group home could receive a site-based voucher. A person who moved into the group home would be covered by the voucher. (The person must have low income according to the program rules—see below.) If the person moved, he could not take the voucher—it would stay with the program and cover the new participant.

(Appendix 4-4 continued...)

(Appendix 4-4 continued...)

When the PHA issues a voucher, the tenant has six months to find a landlord who will accept the voucher. The amount of time can be extended for good cause.

The Importance of "Income"

In the Section 8 program, a person's income is important for two reasons:

- A person must have low income to qualify for the program.
- After the person qualifies, he or she will pay about 30 percent of his monthly income as rent.

In order to participate in the Section 8 program, a person must have "low income." There is no limit on the amount of assets a person can own. The definition of "low income" is quite generous—it is 50 percent of the median income for the area. For example, in 2013, a single individual who lives in Boston and has income of $46,300 would be considered to have low income and could qualify for Section 8. The low income figures, which are adjusted annually, are published on the HUD website, www.huduser.org.

To determine a person's income, the housing authority counts all amounts the person receives annually or can reasonably expect to receive in the coming year. This includes items such as:

- public benefits such as SSI and SSDI
- earnings from employment and self-employment
- regular gifts and contributions from family members
- amounts that are distributed from the person's trust on a regular basis
- earnings that are generated by the person's assets, such as savings or investment accounts. (This does not apply to earnings that are generated by a person's special needs trust.)

The PHA does not count as income items such as:

- sums the person receives on a one-time basis, such as an inheritance, personal injury award, or accident settlement
- occasional gifts
- any amounts that are earmarked for (or given as reimbursement for) medical expenses
- earnings generated by the participant's special needs trust

How Much the Tenant Will Pay

A tenant who qualifies for Section 8 pays about 30 percent of his or her income to the landlord as rent. The housing authority pays the balance of the rent directly to the landlord.

- Sean, who has a Section 8 subsidy, has income of $1,200 per month from SSDI benefits and employment. His apartment costs $900 per month. Sean will pay about $360 in rent and the housing authority will pay the balance of the rent.

How Much the Program Will Contribute for Housing

The maximum amount that Section 8 will pay for housing depends on two factors:

- the size of the unit (the number of bedrooms it contains) and
- the geographic location.

Using Section 8 Payment for Conventional Housing

If you are going to rent conventional housing such as an apartment or condominium, the process is relatively straightforward.

(Appendix 4-4 continued...)

(Appendix 4-4 continued...)

The PHA will approve a studio or one-bedroom unit for a single person. Two people with disabilities who are going to live together could rent a two-bedroom unit. A single person who requires a live-in aide could also be approved for a two-bedroom unit.

As for the geographic area, you don't have to live in the city and town where you are applying for a voucher. Moreover, you don't have to use the voucher in the city of town that awards it. For example, Sam, who lives in Boston, obtains a voucher from the Cambridge Housing Authority and uses it to rent an apartment in Concord, Massachusetts.

Once you know the size of the unit and the area where you want to live, the PHA can tell you the maximum amount of rent it will approve. The technical term for the maximum amount of rent is a "payment standard." The payment standards are based on "fair market rents" that HUD sets for all housing markets in the country. The fair market rents, which are adjusted annually, are based on the number of bedrooms in the rental unit (studio, one-bedroom, two-bedroom, etc.) and reflect modestly priced housing units in the geographic area. The fair market rents for every housing area in the country, which change annually, are posted on the HUD website: www.huduser.org/portal/datasets.

Under a temporary policy that will remain in effect until March 31, 2014, the PHA may approve rents for units leased by people with disabilities of up to 120 percent of fair market rents. This temporary policy is important for tenants with disabilities because fully accessible units and rental units with other special features, such as access to public transportation, sometimes have rents that are higher than units without these features.

So let's say that a single person wants to rent an apartment in San Diego. Since the person is single, the PHA would approve a one-bedroom apartment. (If the person needed a live-in aide, he could rent a two-bedroom apartment.) The HUD website shows that in 2013, the fair market rent for a one-bedroom apartment in San Diego is $1,054 per month, and the fair market rent for a two-bedroom unit is $1,382 per month. Since the local PHA can adjust this amount by 20 percent, it could approve a rent that is from $1,054 to $1,264 for the one-bedroom unit, and $1,382 to $1,658 for a two-bedroom unit.

Section 8 and Creative Living Options

Not every person with a disability can live independently in an apartment. Fortunately, Section 8 vouchers can be used for the different kinds of residential models that we discuss in this book. (HUD calls these "special housing types.") In our experience, many PHAs have not had experience with the different models and do not have any procedures to assist them in setting the rent. However, under federal law, the PHA must make a reasonable accommodation for a person with a disability. HUD considers four special housing types:

1. Single Room Occupancy Unit: A single room occupancy (SRO) is a room that is occupied by one person. The SRO does not have a kitchen or bathroom, although it may have a shared kitchen and bath. A room in our group living model would be considered an SRO. The payment standard for an SRO is 75 percent of the payment standard for a studio (zero bedroom) apartment.

2. Group Home: A group home is a residence for up to twelve individuals (not including any live-in aides) who are elderly or have disabilities. To qualify, the group home must be "licensed, certified, or otherwise approved by the state as a facility for the elderly or persons with

(Appendix 4-4 continued...)

(Appendix 4-4 continued...)

disabilities." The voucher can be given to the entire group home, or each resident can have his or her own voucher. If a voucher is given to the individual, the PHA will divide the total rent for the group home (including an allowance for any utilities the tenants pay) by the number of residents. Then the PHA can set the payment standard as the lesser of 1) the PHA's payment standard for a zero or one bedroom unit, or 2) the prorated portion of the rent.

3. Congregate Housing: Congregate housing is an arrangement in which people with disabilities and/or elderly people share housing. Unlike group homes, congregate housing does not have to be licensed by the state. For purposes of Section 8, an unlicensed group home would be considered congregate housing. If the tenant resides in one room, the PHA uses the zero bedroom payment standard. If the unit consists of more than one room (not including the kitchen or bathroom), the one bedroom payment standard is used.

4. Shared Housing: The HUD rules also permit a voucher to be used in shared housing. This can include a person with a voucher who has a live-in aide, or a roommate who has a separate voucher, or a roommate who has no voucher. The PHA divides the rent (including any utilities the tenants pay) by the number of tenants (not including any live-in aides) to arrive at the tenant's pro rata share.

Renting to Family Members

Sometimes families want to rent housing they own to a relative with a disability. This could be an in-law type apartment in their home or separate unit in a building they own. In most cases, families are not permitted to rent to a close family member (parent, child, grandparent, grandchild, sister, or brother). However, there is an exception for people with disabilities who require this kind of arrangement as a "reasonable accommodation." A typical example would be parents who want to rent an apartment in their home to an adult child with a disability. The child needs close supervision, and the parents would be nearby to provide that supervision. The housing authority should approve the arrangement as a reasonable accommodation. If the housing authority refuses, the decision can be appealed.

If you are considering renting to a relative with a disability, we recommend that you meet with the housing authority in your city or town to find out if they will approve the arrangement. That way, when the person is ready to move in, there will not be any surprises.

Section 8 Mortgage Assistance

In addition to paying rent, the Section 8 program can contribute to the monthly homeownership expenses for the property. These expenses include:

- mortgage principal and interest
- mortgage insurance premium (if required by the lender)
- real estate taxes
- homeowner insurance
- PHA utility allowance
- PHA allowance for routine maintenance costs
- PHA allowance for major repairs or replacements
- principal and interest on debt to finance costs to make the home accessible for a family member with a disability if the PHA determines that it is needed as a reasonable accommodation

(Appendix 4-4 continued...)

(Appendix 4-4 continued...)

The PHAs are not required to offer the homeownership program. However, HUD does require a PHA to make this kind of assistance available if the person requires it as a reasonable accommodation. For example, let's say that a person with autism needs 24-hour care and supervision, and that kind of care is available in a cooperative congregate living situation. The cooperative requires the occupants to buy shares—rental is not an option. In this case, the PHA should permit the person to use his Section 8 assistance for homeownership costs in the cooperative.

The property must pass inspection by HUD and by an independent home inspector. The Section 8 participant must:

- Meet the general requirements for the Section 8 program (have low income, as defined by HUD, etc.)
- Have participated in the Section 8 rental program for at least twelve months
- Have minimum annual income that is equal to the monthly federal SSI benefit for a single person living alone multiplied by twelve ($8,520 in 2013)
- Participate in a homebuyer counseling program that covers items such as home maintenance, budget and money management, credit counseling, locating a home, and negotiating the contract
- Make a down payment that is not less than 3 percent of the purchase price, of which 1 percent must come from the homeowner's own resources

Strategies to Obtain a Voucher

It can take a long time to obtain a Section 8 voucher—several years in some states. The local PHAs are given leeway in running their waiting lists. Some close their lists and do not accept new applications. Others accept applications and hold a lottery when a certificate becomes available. Other PHAs have preferences for certain categories of applicants, such as local residents or homeless families. The following are some strategies that might help you shorten the waiting time:

- Apply well before the time your family member will need the certificate.
- Apply in several communities.
- Find out if your state has a central registration. This will allow you to file one application in a central location. You will be considered when a voucher becomes available anywhere in the state. Remember that you do not have to use the voucher in the municipality that awards it.
- Consider applying for a state housing subsidy. Most states run their own programs using state funds. The income guidelines, rent formula, and other rules may be different than for a Section 8 voucher.

Medicaid

Many people with disabilities receive assistance from the federal Medicaid health insurance program. Medicaid is funded jointly by the federal government and the states. Most states give their Medicaid programs a special name, such as MassHealth (in Massachusetts) and MediCal (in California). There are certain Medicaid services that states must provide. These mandatory services include:

- Inpatient hospital services
- Outpatient services
- Physician services
- Medical procedures and surgical supplies
- Nursing home coverage for persons age 21 and older
- Home healthcare for persons eligible for nursing home services
- Laboratory and x-ray services

(Appendix 4-4 continued...)

(Appendix 4-4 continued...)

Who Can Get Benefits

In many states and in the District of Columbia, SSI recipients automatically qualify for Medicaid. The states that confer automatic eligibility are: Alabama, Arizona, Arkansas, California, Colorado, Delaware, Florida, Georgia, Iowa, Kentucky, Louisiana, Maine, Maryland, Massachusetts, Michigan, Mississippi, Montana, New Jersey, New Mexico, New York, North Carolina, Pennsylvania, Rhode Island, South Carolina, South Dakota, Tennessee, Texas, Vermont, Washington, West Virginia, Wisconsin, and Wyoming.

In seven states, SSI recipients must apply separately for Medicaid; however, the eligibility rules are the same for both programs. The states are: Alaska, Idaho, Kansas, Nebraska, Nevada, Oregon, and Utah.

Eleven states use their own eligibility rules for Medicaid, which are different from the Social Security Administration's rules for SSI. SSI recipients in these states must file a separate application in order to receive Medicaid. These states are: Connecticut, Hawaii, Illinois, Indiana, Minnesota, Missouri, New Hampshire, North Dakota, Ohio, Oklahoma, and Virginia. You can obtain information on how to apply for Medicaid benefits by calling the state's Medicaid office or going to its website.

Medicaid Waiver Services

All states have their own version of "optional" and "waiver" programs. When the Medicaid program was originally set up, a person with disabilities had to live in an institution in order to receive Medicaid services. The government has "waived" this requirement so that people who live in the community can receive services. You may hear these programs referred to by specific numbers, such as 1915(b), 1915(c), or 1115 waivers. The numbers themselves are not important because they only refer to specific sections of the Medicaid law. What is important is that these waiver programs can allow people with disabilities to live in the community instead of in institutions.

It is important to note that the Medicaid waiver programs do not pay for residential housing. However, they do pay for services and supports for people that allow people to live independently. These services can include:

- Case management
- Personal care attendant services (PCA)
- Day programs
- Supported employment
- Homemaker/home health aide services
- Transportation

Medicaid Recovery

In some cases, when a person who has received Medicaid dies, the state Medicaid agency must be reimbursed for the benefits it provided to the person. This can occur if the person:

- was age 55 or older;
- was a permanent resident in a nursing home or other medical setting; or
- had a special needs trust that provided for such reimbursement.

In most states, the Medicaid agency can only recoup the funds it is owed if the person had money or property in his name at the time of death (probate property). (An exception is if the person had a special needs trust that instructed the trustee to make reimbursement from the remaining trust funds.) In a common scenario, the person's family or heirs file for probate in order to access the person's assets, so they can use the money to pay his bills and distribute the remaining money among the people who

(Appendix 4-4 continued...)

(Appendix 4-4 continued...)

are entitled to receive it. The Medicaid agency receives notice of the filing and places a lien on the estate for the value of services it provided. In most states, the lien has priority over all other expenditures except for the person's funeral, medical bills, and the cost of administering his estate. If the Medicaid lien, when added to these items, amounts to more than the value of the estate, the heirs will not receive anything.

In some cases, proper advance planning can avoid this scenario. Medicaid recipients are sometimes advised to own assets through a trust. When the person dies, the trust assets pass directly to the remainder beneficiaries who were named to receive them when the trust was created. Another strategy is to own assets such as joint accounts, life insurance policies, and annuities that pass directly to the co-owner or the named beneficiaries on the owner's death. Similarly, an individual can transfer real estate to family members but retain the right to live there for life ("life estate"). Since none of these assets are part of the probate estate of the person with disabilities—and thus no probate proceedings are filed—the Medicaid agency will not have any way to recover its costs.

This strategy will not work in every state. Some states have passed laws that allow them to recover their costs from any asset in which the Medicaid recipient had a legal interest at the time of his death—including joint accounts, life insurance policies, annuities, life interests in real estate, and trusts. An attorney who specializes in disability planning can explain the laws in your state.

Food Stamps

The Supplemental Nutrition Assistance Program (SNAP) helps low-income people buy food. People who qualify are given an EBT (Electronic Benefit Transfer) card they can swipe at a participating store. The card is loaded at the beginning of each month with the month's allotment.

To qualify, a person must have low income (about 100 percent of the federal poverty level, which is $903 per month for a single person) and limited assets (no more than $2,000 in countable resources). People who live in group settings can qualify, although their benefit may be reduced.

To get more information about your state's program and to find out how to apply, go to the federal SNAP website, www.fns.usda.gov/snap.

Utility and Fuel Assistance

All states assist low-income residents in paying their utility and fuel bills. The source of federal funds is the Low Income Home Energy Assistance Program (LIHEAP). Each state has its own eligibility rules. Most states also have their own programs that are funded with state money. In addition to having low income, as defined by the state, a person would probably need to rent or own their home. The assistance would not be available to someone living in another person's home or in a group residence. You can search on the Internet for the programs in your state.

APPENDIX 4-5

Sources of Funds to Acquire and/or Operate a Residence

Community Development Block Grant Program

Program Basics

The Community Development Block Grant (CDBG) is a federally funded program that provides communities with resources to address a broad range of community needs, including housing for low-income people. The program is managed at the federal level by the U.S. Department of Housing and Urban Development (HUD). The funds are allocated to local and state governments who then decide how to use them within guidelines established by HUD.

How the Funds Are Awarded

Each state has different policies for distributing its CDBG funds. The policies are outlined in the state's Consolidated Plan (ConPlan). (The ConPlan is described in the materials in the HOME Program section of the Appendix.)

The local communities that receive the funds can award them to non-profit agencies, nonprofit and for-profit housing developers, individuals, and others.

What the Funds Can Be Used For

At least 70 percent of CDBG funds must be used to benefit low- and moderate-income people by providing adequate housing and improving economic opportunities. The uses can include:

- Rental Housing. CDBG funds can be used to acquire land and build or renovate rental housing that can include single occupancy units and group homes. Funding for new construction is only available to non-profit groups.
- Homeownership. The program can provide funds for a down payment or closing costs or for a subsidized mortgage.
- Home Repair. Funds can assist homeowners to make their homes accessible, improve energy efficiency, or correct problems that threaten the occupants' health and safety.
- Accessibility Modifications. Funds are available to both landlords and homeowners to make their properties accessible.

Where to Find More Information

There is information about the CDBG program on the HUD website (http://hud.gov/offices.cpd). This site allows you to search for funding in your state.

Home Investments Partnership Program

Program Basics

The purpose of the Home Investments Partnership Program (HOME) is to create affordable housing for low-income households. The program is funded by the federal government and managed at the federal level by the U.S. Department of Housing and Urban Development (HUD). About $2 billion is distributed annually among all 50 states and hundreds of localities across the country (called

(Appendix 4-5 continued...)

(Appendix 4-5 continued...)

"participating jurisdictions"). The states and localities have discretion to use the funds within guidelines established by Congress.

How the Funds Are Awarded

All communities that want to receive HOME funds must prepare and submit a Consolidated Plan (ConPlan) to HUD. The ConPlan is a long-range master plan that is developed by local and state governments with input from citizens and community groups. The ConPlan describes the local housing needs and priorities and shows how the federal funds will be used to meet those needs. If a community is approved for funds, residents can apply for funds at the local office where the housing will be located. (See "Where to Get More Information.")

What the Funds Can be Used For

HOME funds can be used for:

- Rental Housing: Funds are available to nonprofit agencies and to for-profit developers who agree to commit a certain number of units for affordable housing. The housing can range in size from a single group home to a multi-unit apartment complex.
- Home Ownership: Funds are available to provide a down payment or underwrite a mortgage for individuals who own one- to four-family residences, condominiums, or shares in a cooperative.
- Home Repair: The funds can be used to help individuals repair, renovate, or rehabilitate a home, including replacing a roof or furnace, adding a wheelchair ramp, or modifying a bathroom or kitchen.
- Rental assistance: The HOME program has a tenant-based rental component that provides a rental assistance program for a two-year period. The assistance can be renewed if program funds are available. The rental assistance is similar to the Section 8 voucher program that is described in this book. The tenant locates a rental unit in the community at a pre-approved rent from a participating landlord. The tenant pays a portion of his monthly income (usually 30 percent) as rent, and HOME funds pay the balance of the rent directly to the landlord.

The funds can be provided in the form of:

- Conventional loans at a low interest rate that must be repaid
- Grants that do not have to be repaid
- "Forgivable" loans that do not have to be repaid as long as the property is committed to a specific purpose (such as providing housing to low-income people with disabilities) and is not sold within a specified period of time

Where to Get More Information

For information about the HOME program in your state, go to the Office of Community Planning and Development on the HUD website (www.hud.gov/offices/cpd) and locate your state. The website includes all local consolidated plans and contact information.

(Appendix 4-5 continued...)

(Appendix 4-5 continued...)

Rural Housing Programs for Owner-Occupied Homes and Multi-Family Rental Properties (Including Group Residences)

Program Basics

The Rural Housing Programs are administered by the U.S. Department of Agriculture (USDA) and make federal money available to increase both the amount and quality of housing in rural areas. Within the USDA, these programs are administered by the office of Rural Development. Most states have Rural Development offices, although some states have merged their offices with other states' to create multi-state jurisdictions. Every office has a Director who helps decide funding priorities. A list of local offices is available online at www.rurdev.usda.gov/recd_map.html.

Programs for Owner-Occupied Homes

There are two programs for owner-occupied family houses (including condominiums).

- The Section 502 Direct Loan Program finances the purchase, construction, and rehabilitation of owner-occupied single family homes. The homes must be modest in cost, size, and design. The standard loan term is 33 years, although loans can be made for a shorter or longer (up to 38 years) period of time.

- Applicants must demonstrate that they can afford to repay the loan. Their income cannot exceed the low-income limit for the respective household size and area in which the property is located. Applicants can file their applications with the office that covers the area in which the property they plan to buy, build, or repair is located.

- The Section 504 Loan Program offers loans and grants to elderly or disabled homeowners. The funds can be used for emergency repairs, to make the property accessible for household members with disabilities, or to correct health and safety hazards. Grants may have to be repaid if the property is sold within three years. Borrowers must demonstrate that they cannot borrow the funds from any other source.

Programs for Multi-Family Rental Properties

There are three programs for multi-family rental properties, which can include cooperatives, condominiums, and group homes for persons with disabilities.

- The Section 515 Rural Rental Housing Program provides low-interest loans to finance affordable multi-family housing, including congregate living facilities and group homes. The funds can be used to buy, build, or rehabilitate housing. The standard loan term is 30 years, although loans can be made for a shorter period of time. The Office of Rural Development lends the funds directly to housing developers.

- The Section 521 Rural Rental Housing Program is a project-based subsidy. Tenants pay about 30 percent of their income as rent, and the rural housing office pays the balance directly to the landlord. Section 521 funds are often used in Section 515 housing projects.

- The Section 538 Guaranteed Rural Rental Housing Loan Program provides loans to acquire, construct, or rehabilitate rural multi-family properties (including congregate living facilities and group homes) for low-income occupants. All projects must include at least five rental units. Loans are made through private lenders and are guaranteed by the USDA. There is no tenant subsidy available for this program, and Section 521 funds may not be used for these projects.

(Appendix 4-5continued...)

(Appendix 4-5 continued...)

Who Can Qualify

Individuals, nonprofit organizations, for-profit developers, and state and local agencies can receive the funds, which are awarded competitively by Rural Development. A Notice of Funding Availability (NOFA) is published annually in the Federal Register. The NOFA explains the loan terms and the application process. The NOFAs are located on the website for the Federal Register, which is www.gpoaccess.gov/fr/index.html.

Where to Find More Information

There is information about all the Rural Development programs on the office's website, www.rurdev.usda.gov.

Section 811 Supportive Housing for Persons with Disabilities

Program Basics

The Section 811 Supportive Housing for Persons with Disabilities Program provides federal funds to construct or repair buildings, operate the property, and subsidize the rents. The program is run by the U.S. Department of Housing and Urban Development (HUD).

What the Funds Can Be Used For

The housing that can be created through the Section 811 program includes multi-family complexes, condominiums, cooperatives, and group homes. The program has three parts:

- Capital Advance: The funds can be used to acquire the land, build (or renovate) the structure, and pay for the so-called soft costs for the project such as architects, attorneys, building permits, and insurance. The program will also reimburse recipients for their pre-development costs, including a housing consultant, to evaluate the project, develop a budget, and apply for the funds. The funds are awarded in the form of a grant that does not have to be repaid as long as the property is used for very low-income people with disabilities for 40 years.
- Operating Subsidy: The program includes an operating subsidy that pays for ongoing costs, including the mortgage, real estate taxes, insurance, and maintenance. The program also funds a reserve account for major repairs that may be needed (new roof, furnace, cooling system, etc.). The amount of the operating subsidy is the difference between the tenants' contribution for rent and the HUD-approved cost to operate the project (see below). The subsidy initially lasts for five years and can be renewed if funds are available.
- Tenant-based Rental Assistance: The program also includes tenant-based rental assistance through the Section 8 program. In most cases, the tenants pay 30 percent of their income as rent and the Section 8 program pays the balance of the rent directly to the landlord.

How the Funds Are Awarded

HUD distributes the funds annually among different regions of the country. When the funds become available, a notice is published in the federal register. Based on this NOFA (notice of funding availability), nonprofits can apply for the funds.

Section 811 funds are limited, and the application process is extremely complicated and competitive. If you formed a nonprofit group, you would be competing against established agencies with a track record of developing nonprofit housing. Moreover, it usually takes five to seven years from the time of application to project completion. You would probably need to hire a housing consultant

(Appendix 4-5 continued...)

(Appendix 4-5 continued...)

to help you decide if it is worthwhile to apply. You might also incur fees for an architect or attorney before you apply. These fees would only be reimbursed if your application is accepted and the project is completed. Your chances of success would be improved if you partnered with a nonprofit agency that has a track record of accessing these kinds of funds.

Where to Get More Information

There is information about the Section 811 program on the HUD website (www.hud.gov). The website explains the application process and has links to the notices of funding availability.

Live-In Expectations/Tenancy Agreement

Name: _____ **Date:** _____

The following agreement is between _____ and TILL, Inc. This lease agreement will begin on _____ and will continue for the period of time that is mutually agreed upon by the tenant/live-in and in conjunction with TILL, Inc.'s contract for services with families.

1. You are expected to sleep at the residence 5 nights per week. If you are not going to be at the home you must notify the Director of the Program to ensure there is proper coverage. During the overnight hours, you are expected to be available to the tenants for emergencies. You will be available Sunday through Thursday from 10 pm – 8 am, as well as at other times as outlined in this agreement.

2. You are required to attend weekly house meetings held each week as scheduled.

3. You are expected to be an integral part of the home. This includes making yourself available to the tenants to ensure they are comfortable with you as a resource and an emergency contact. You will be expected to participate in at least one house recreational activity and eat dinner with the group at least one time per week, to help build a trusting relationship with the individuals. Initiation of new ideas for assisting the cooperative spirit of the building is a part of living in this home.

4. You are expected to do weekly facility checks with each tenant to see that everything is going smoothly. These checks should include making sure facility is maintained in a clean and orderly manner. You should address any issues that arise, such as excessive noise, difficulties between tenants, etc.

5. You are responsible for making sure the trash is taken out each week. Although we encourage the tenants to assist in completing this task, it is the live-in's responsibility to ensure that the systems for trash removal work. Whenever possible, empty trash cans should be brought in prior to leaving the home in the morning.

6. You are responsible for ensuring that the outside of the building is free of trash and garbage. Again, we encourage you to solicit the assistance of the tenants in the building, but it is your responsibility.

7. You are responsible for ensuring that the common areas inside the building are maintained in a clean, orderly manner. This includes making sure laundry facilities are maintained and lint traps are emptied. You should also make sure that the front entryway is clean and free of papers and other trash. You should also attempt to have the tenants involved in these tasks, but this is your responsibility. The front foyer should be inviting, clean, and aesthetically pleasing at all times. Light fixtures need to be working properly.

(Appendix 6-1 continued...)

(Appendix 6-1 continued...)

8. During the winter months, you are expected to shovel the snow and ice from all egresses of the building, as well as the sidewalks around the building. This is the responsibility of the live-in; however, we encourage you to get the tenants to assist in completing this task.

9. You are entitled to 2 weeks of vacation from the live-in position. You are required to give a minimum of 3 weeks advanced notice of your planned vacation. During your time away, we will provide relief to cover your live-in responsibilities.

10. You are expected to maintain your living space in a clean and orderly manner.

11. During the hours of 6 am – 8 am, you will be expected to remain downstairs to make sure all individuals have eaten a healthy breakfast and that the kitchen area has been cleaned. Based on the approved menus you may need to assist individuals in preparing their meal as assigned by the program coordinator.

12. You will ensure that when needed, individuals have taken medications and treatments as required and documentation is completed.

13. You will monitor all individuals to ensure they are prepared for their day, including having lunch, and are properly dressed and groomed appropriately for work and the weather.

14. In exchange for performing these duties, you will receive compensation in the form of free room and utilities (heat, hot water, electric). You will be responsible for obtaining your telephone service and any additional expenses associated with additional cable and Internet for your personal use.

Thank you for your time and effort in making this a safe, comfortable place for everyone to live. If you have any questions, please don't hesitate to contact me. I look forward to a long relationship in this situation.

I agree to the expectations established in this agreement/lease for living at:

Live-In Staff Signature: _____ **Date:** _____

Director Signature: _____ **Date:** _____

APPENDIX 6-2

JOB DESCRIPTION: RESIDENTIAL SUPPORT PROFESSIONAL

The Residential Support Professional is an integral part of the residential service. He/She is responsible for working as a team member of the household. The specific duties of the Support Professional will be those defined by the Residence Manager. He/She is directly accountable to the Residence Manager, and is thereby equally responsible, along with, and under the direction of, the Residence Manager.

ESSENTIAL JOB FUNCTIONS:

1. To develop a warm, home-like, cooperative atmosphere in the residence in which both individuals and staff share.
2. To safeguard the privacy and confidentiality of the residents and staff.
3. To develop and implement the teaching plans.
4. To perform duties that ensure the health and safety of the individuals and staff.
5. To work with the Residence Manager on the development, updating, and implementation of the residents' individual support plans.
6. To maintain appropriate progress notes and pertinent records corresponding to individual ISP and other pertinent record keeping requirements.
7. To work with the Residence Manager on the location and/or development of recreational activities for the individuals.
8. To assist the Residence Manager on the follow through of all individual medical and mental health treatment plans and medical orders; to assist in the development of new medical service procedures as needed.
9. To assist in the training of all individuals in self-preservation skills and the development of fire and emergency procedures, which may require going up and down stairs.
10. To follow the regulations as outlined by the agencies responsible for licensing and approving the residence.
11. To train individuals in ADL's and self-help and socialization skills. These essential teaching plans may require physical assistance, including lifting the individuals, passive restraints, and hand-over-hand implementation.
12. To drive individuals to and from work when necessary.
13. To drive and participate in recreational events and individuals' doctor's appointments when necessary.

OTHER RESPONSIBILITIES INCLUDE:

1. To cover the residence when necessary on an emergency basis.
2. To attend orientation, in-service and required trainings, and regular residence staff meetings as outlined by the Residence Manager.
3. To represent TILL's residential services to the public.

QUALIFICATIONS:

Must be 18 years of age or older. A valid driver's license is required. Must possess good written and verbal skills to effectively communicate individual needs and objectives. Must be able to pass the Medication Certification Training in English. CPR and First Aid training are a condition of employment. This position includes providing direct care for the individuals, including lifting individuals, passive restraint, and hand-over-hand assistance.

JOB DESCRIPTION: INDIVIDUAL SUPPORT MANAGER

The Individual Support Services Manager is responsible for implementing Individual Support Services. The coordination, integration of resources, and access to the community is crucial to this service. This position is accountable to the Director of Residential Alternatives. Responsibilities may require varied day, evening, and weekend hours, depending upon the client base at any particular time.

ESSENTIAL JOB FUNCTIONS:

1. Locate and identify existing agencies and resources available to families and individuals needing support services in the area.
2. Based on the number of hours assigned to the individual, the ISM will supervise direct support staff in implementing specified goals for certain individuals. Assigning a direct support staff to the case will also depend on the specific needs of the individual. In most cases, the Individual Support Manager will be the direct support staff.
3. Responsible for assessing the initial and ongoing needs of the individuals to determine the need to continue providing services. This may include completing initial residential and support need evaluations.
4. Responsible for completing all required paperwork, including assessments, teaching plans, and monthly progress notes, based on the public or private funding source for the assigned services.
5. Responsible for documenting the number of hours of service provided to the individual on a weekly and monthly basis.
6. Submit accurate records of hours of service provided for the purpose of billing for those services on a monthly basis. The billing information will be submitted according to identified timelines.
7. Assist individuals in finding new living arrangements or assist in obtaining housing subsidies and other benefits to which they may be entitled.
8. Maintain ongoing contact with families and state agencies necessary to meet the needs of the individuals.
9. Responsible for coordinating services to meet the needs of the individuals. This may include, but is not limited to, travel training, apartment hunting, scheduling medical appointments, and meeting with school or vocational services personnel.
10. Responsible for properly accounting for the finances of specific individuals and program funds. Financial records must be submitted according to agency policy.
11. Responsible for making ongoing clinical decisions when out in the field to ensure the individuals' needs are being met.
12. Assist the Director of Residential Alternatives with the development of new services for individuals living in the community.
13. Be available by telephone to provide assistance or support when crises arise.
14. Participate in emergency beeper rotation.
15. Make suggestions and recommendations as to the hiring, firing, advancement, promotion, or any other change of status of other employees.

(Appendix 6-3 continued...)

(Appendix 6-3 continued...)

QUALIFICATIONS:

A BA/BS in human services, psychology, sociology, special education, or related field. Three to five years of experience will be considered in lieu of a BA/BS. A minimum of two years experience working directly with individuals who have developmental disabilities. Supervision skills and experience strongly preferred. A valid driver's license and vehicle is required. Good written and verbal skills are essential. This position includes direct care in essential programs for the individuals. These essential programs may include lifting individuals, passive restraints, and hand-over-hand assistance. Must be able to work independently and be highly motivated. CPR and First Aid are a condition of employment.

APPENDIX 7-1

Furnishings List for Setting Up a Home

Kitchen

- ❑ Table
- ❑ Pots/Pans/Skillets
- ❑ Toaster
- ❑ Pasta maker
- ❑ Glasses
- ❑ Napkin rings
- ❑ Cutting board
- ❑ Cooking knives
- ❑ Measuring cups
- ❑ Wastebasket
- ❑ Serving trays
- ❑ Wall clock
- ❑ Recipe holder
- ❑ Coffee thermos

- ❑ Chairs
- ❑ Microwave
- ❑ Toaster oven
- ❑ Blender
- ❑ Mugs
- ❑ Serving dishes
- ❑ Colander
- ❑ Steak knives
- ❑ Pitchers
- ❑ Coffee maker
- ❑ Can opener
- ❑ Pot holders/Mitts
- ❑ Towel holder

- ❑ Stools for Counter
- ❑ Refrigerator
- ❑ Food processor
- ❑ Steamer basket
- ❑ Flatware
- ❑ Bread baskets
- ❑ Vegetable peeler
- ❑ Serving utensils
- ❑ Serving platters
- ❑ Salad bowl
- ❑ Vegetable bins
- ❑ Dishtowels
- ❑ Trivets

- ❑ Curtains and Blinds
- ❑ Freezer
- ❑ Popcorn popper
- ❑ Dishes
- ❑ Place mats/Table cloth
- ❑ Casserole dishes
- ❑ Paring knife
- ❑ Slotted spoons
- ❑ Measuring spoons
- ❑ Mixing bowls
- ❑ Fruit bowl
- ❑ Cookbook holder
- ❑ Dish rack/drainer

Misc. Appliances, etc.

- ❑ Fire extinguisher ABC
- ❑ Drying rack
- ❑ Answering machine
- ❑ Message board (wipe off)
- ❑ Telephone
- ❑ Tool box
- ❑ Sewing box (filled)
- ❑ Broom
- ❑ Pail
- ❑ Dustbuster/Bissel
- ❑ Dehumidifier

- ❑ Ironing board & Iron
- ❑ Laundry basket
- ❑ Intercom
- ❑ Misc. cookbooks
- ❑ Hammer
- ❑ Divided box for nails
- ❑ Photo albums
- ❑ Mop
- ❑ Retractable tape measure
- ❑ Portable wet vac
- ❑ Air conditioner

- ❑ Washer/Dryer
- ❑ Rolling cart
- ❑ Bulletin board
- ❑ Medicine box (locked)
- ❑ Screwdriver set
- ❑ Starter nails, etc.
- ❑ Vacuum cleaner
- ❑ Dust pan
- ❑ Yardstick
- ❑ Fans

Dining Room

- ❑ Table
- ❑ Hutch

- ❑ Chairs
- ❑ Tablecloths

- ❑ Centerpiece
- ❑ Chandelier

- ❑ Sideboard
- ❑ Folding serving tables

(Appendix 7-1 continued...)

(Appendix 7-1 continued...)

Bathroom

- ❏ Wastebasket
- ❏ Shower curtain
- ❏ First aid kit
- ❏ Folding shower chair
- ❏ Toothbrush
- ❏ Cosmetic holders

- ❏ Toothbrush holder
- ❏ Shower liner
- ❏ Bath mat
- ❏ Towels
- ❏ Electric toothbrush
- ❏ Tub mat or decals

- ❏ Cup
- ❏ Window curtain
- ❏ Decorative pictures
- ❏ Wash cloths
- ❏ Shaver (Electric)

Bedrooms

- ❏ Comforter
- ❏ Pillow cases
- ❏ Clock radio
- ❏ Decorative dresser items
- ❏ Dresser
- ❏ Closet organizers
- ❏ Floor lamp

- ❏ Sheets
- ❏ Blankets
- ❏ Area rug
- ❏ Bed
- ❏ Night table
- ❏ Curtains
- ❏ Tie rack

- ❏ Pillows
- ❏ Laundry hamper
- ❏ Scatter rug
- ❏ Mattress
- ❏ Mattress cover
- ❏ Blinds
- ❏ Hangers

- ❏ Pillow covers/shams
- ❏ Alarm clock
- ❏ Bulletin board or strip
- ❏ Box spring
- ❏ Jewelry box
- ❏ Table lamp
- ❏ Misc. boxes, crates, storage

Living Room

- ❏ Couch
- ❏ Table lamps
- ❏ End table
- ❏ TV/wall mount

- ❏ Arm chairs
- ❏ Floor lamps
- ❏ Decorative pictures
- ❏ VCR/DVD

- ❏ Rugs
- ❏ Magazine rack
- ❏ Curtains
- ❏ CD player

- ❏ Rocking chairs
- ❏ Coffee table
- ❏ Blinds
- ❏ TV stand

Outdoor Area

- ❏ Picnic table
- ❏ Food cooler
- ❏ Outside games
- ❏ Rakes
- ❏ Hoses
- ❏ Work gloves
- ❏ House numbers

- ❏ Picnic chairs
- ❏ Volleyball set
- ❏ Lawn mower
- ❏ Shovels
- ❏ Hose roller
- ❏ Shelves for storage
- ❏ Mailbox

- ❏ Umbrella
- ❏ Swing chair
- ❏ Snow blower
- ❏ Trash barrels
- ❏ Hand trowel
- ❏ Door/welcome mats
- ❏ Welcome sign

- ❏ Gas grill
- ❏ Freestanding hammock
- ❏ Wheelbarrow
- ❏ Sand container
- ❏ Sprinklers
- ❏ Chimes

Basement/Recreation

- ❏ Pool table
- ❏ Beanbag chairs

- ❏ Ping pong table

- ❏ Folding chairs

- ❏ Air hockey set

(Appendix 7-1 continued...)

(Appendix 7-1 continued...)

Office

- ❏ Desk
- ❏ Misc. chairs
- ❏ Cash box
- ❏ Calculator
- ❏ File box/file cabinet
- ❏ Medicine box (locked)

- ❏ Desk chair
- ❏ Bulletin board
- ❏ Stapler
- ❏ Desk trays
- ❏ Computer

- ❏ Telephone
- ❏ Clip boards
- ❏ Hole punch
- ❏ Mail holders
- ❏ Copy/fax/scan/printer

- ❏ Bookcase
- ❏ Pencil sharpener
- ❏ Staple remover
- ❏ Rulers
- ❏ Computer desk

APPENDIX 8-1

Sample House Rules

One way to encourage cooperative living is to have house rules that apply to everyone. The rules, which residents develop with assistance from staff, cover things like privacy, quiet times, mutual respect, and guests. The appendix contains examples of house rules that were developed in the TILL residences. Each program might choose to use some or all of them, or add some of their own.

Another way to minimize disputes and to have housemates take an active role in the group residence is to have regular house meetings. In most residences, these meetings take place weekly. The residents can discuss any problems that come up with housemates or staff and can set new rules. The meetings are also a forum for planning schedules, activities, menus, and chores. Even if people are nonverbal, it is a good opportunity to establish a structure and routine for residents to be a part of the planning and to offer as much or as little participation as they can to the week's plans.

Examples of House Rules

- Knock before entering a housemate's bedroom.
- When the bathroom door is closed, you must knock before entering.
- Close the bathroom door when you are using it.
- Talk respectfully to one another.
- Wear a robe or clothing whenever you are in any public place in the house.
- Wait until your housemate is finished speaking before you start to speak.
- Do not boss your housemates around. You don't like to be bossed around, and others don't either.
- Do not interrupt when others are speaking or expressing themselves and their opinions. Some people need more time than others to explain themselves.
- When you are feeling frustrated, use some of these ideas to help you calm down:
    - listen to music,
    - meditate,
    - use a punching bag,
    - hit a pillow,
    - squeeze a stress ball,
    - ask a staff person to go for a walk with you, or if you typically go out by yourself, then go alone, but be sure to tell someone where you are going and when you will return.
- If you need help, please ask a staff person or your support person. Don't wait until you get frustrated. Ask for help when you feel you need it.
- Be honest at all times.
- There is no physical abuse allowed in the house.
- If you are living with another housemate but no staff, then let your housemate know if you will be out longer than usual in the evening and when you plan to return. Housemates worry about one another and want to be sure you are safe.
- When answering the phone, be polite and take a message. If you cannot write down the message, then ask the person to call back later. Try to remember to tell the person who was getting the call about who called.
- ___ p.m. is quiet time in the house. This is time to chill out and do quiet activities.
- Do not enter the office or go through people's personal belongings.
- Do not take anything that does not belong to you.

(Appendix 8-1 continued...)

(Appendix 8-1 continued...)

- If you have any issues in the bathroom or kitchen, tell someone immediately. Be sure you are not clogging the toilet or leaving the water running because it can cause damage in the house.
- Movies that you watch in the house should be rated PG-13 or lower unless you have discussed this with staff or support people. If a subject in a movie bothers you, just take a break from it and leave the room.
- Don't take up more than your time if you are using the shared house phone or computer.
- When people are watching TV or a DVD, don't interrupt and don't change the channel or movie. You can ask when it will be over if you want to watch something else.
- Never yell, swear, or argue with someone after they have asked you to stop.
- Do not eat anywhere other than in the kitchen or dining room to avoid bugs and a mess.
- Clean up after yourself. Leave the rooms in the house as neat and clean as you found them.
- Do your chores so that others do not have to do them for you or get angry at you because they have to do your work.

Index

About the Authors

Dafna Krouk-Gordon is the founder and President of Toward Independent Living and Learning (TILL), a not for profit human service agency based in Dedham, Massachusetts. The agency was established in 1980 in response to the need for developing community-based services for people who were mandated to leave the large public institutions as a result of parent-led class action lawsuits and resulting consent decrees. TILL has been a leader in developing a community-based service system of innovative residential, vocational, and support services. She has served on the Governor's Commission on Mental Retardation and is active on a statewide level in fiscal planning, policy development, advocacy, and legislative issues affecting individuals with disabilities. She has worked with hundreds of families in creating unique housing and vocational services in the Commonwealth of Massachusetts and other state systems. She presents extensively at conferences and professional groups on developing and operating residential services.

TILL operates a diverse and extensive range of community-based services that support several thousand people each year with varied diagnoses of developmental disabilities, including autism spectrum disorders, intellectual disabilities, and mental health, physical, and medical needs. The mission of the agency is to develop services that are fully integrated in the community and maximize peoples' abilities and interests. The agency is credited with developing residential models that are both privately and publicly funded and incorporate the talents and energies of families and public agencies in creating integrated, full lives for people with special needs.

Barbara Jackins is an attorney in Framingham, MA, where she practices in areas of the law that affect people with disabilities and their families: special needs planning, public benefits, guardianship, and trust management. She has served on the Governor's Commission on Mental Retardation: Task Force on Public-Private Partnerships. She currently serves on several Boards of Directors and committees of nonprofit agencies that support people with disabilities and their families. Barbara is a member of the National Academy of Elder Law Attorneys and a 1978 graduate of Suffolk Law School. She often speaks to parent groups, professionals, and others interested in issues related to disability, planning, and finances.

In addition to *Moving Out,* Barbara has written three books: *The Special Needs Trust Administration Manual: A Guide for Trustees* (coauthor); *Managing a Special Needs Trust: A Guide for Trustees* (coauthor, 2012); and *Legal Planning for Special Needs in Massachusetts: A Family Guide to SSI, Guardianship, and Estate* Planning (2010). Barbara is the parent of a young adult with autism and developmental disabilities.